IN SEARCH OF WISDOM

A Daily Devotional Book

6-14-20

Bro. John,
May the Lord continue to fill you with Wisdom as you serve Him faithfully.
Jean

Jean Robert Lainé, Ph. D.

ABOUT THIS PUBLICATION

First Edition

Copyright © 2018 Jean R. Lainé
All rights reserved.

Published in 2018 by Jean R. Lainé
Oklahoma City, Oklahoma

No part of this book may be reproduced without the permission of the publisher.
For permission to use material from this text, contact us at **Laineed2017@gmail.com**.

Scripture quotations are taken from the Holy Bible, New International Version (NIV). Copyright © 1973, 1978, 1984, 2011, Biblica, Inc. ™ Used by permission. All rights reserved worldwide.

Title: In Search of Wisdom: A Daily Devotional Book
All rights reserved.
ISBN: 978-1718123755

TABLE OF CONTENTS

Acknowledgements	1
January	2
February	34
March	63
April	96
May	127
June	160
July	190
August	221
September	352
October	382
November	314
December	345
About the Author	381
Personal Notes	382

INTRODUCTION

In Search of Wisdom is a daily devotional book based on 366 key verses from the New International Version of the Holy Bible. It is written to help you keep your mind on God daily. If you start and finish your year with an optimistic spin on life, you will most likely experience more success on your journey through life.

Each daily devotion is written to give you the opportunity to meditate on the Holy Scripture. This is truly an uplifting devotional book.

Since the New International Version of the Holy Bible does not utilize capital letters for pronouns referring to divinity, I followed the same pattern for all direct biblical quotes. However, when it is not a direct quote, capital letters are used to refer to divinity. Sometimes, Lord is written in all caps when it refers to the Godhead. In this connection, LORD is synonymous to Yahweh, the true God.

As you take a few minutes each day from your hectic schedule to read this devotional book, I pray that the Lord will grant you wisdom as you meditate on His words. Jesus loves you!

DEDICATION

This daily devotional book is dedicated to Jesus Christ, the Son of God. It is also dedicated to all who put their trust in Jesus Christ as their Lord and Savior.

ACKNOWLEDGMENTS

I thank my brother, Dr. Emmanuel Lainé, for making sure that the devotional book is theologically sound. I also thank Cheryl, my wife, for spending countless hours reading the devotions to ensure that everything sounds grammatically correct.

JANUARY 1

"The fear of the Lord is the beginning of knowledge, but fools despise wisdom and instruction." – Proverbs 1:7 NIV

The Hebrew noun for fear is *Yirah (yi-aw')* which means awe, fear, love, and respect.

In this verse, the word fear is used to denote awe, love, and respect for Yahweh, the true God. When you decide to love and respect the LORD, you then begin to acquire knowledge.

Since Yahweh is omniscient, knowledge begins with Him. From a natural perspective, the world is full of impressive knowledge in multiple fields or disciplines. However, when natural knowledge is viewed from supernatural lens, suddenly, it becomes inadequate because it is confined to the four known dimensions of the universe.

Your knowledge of astronomy and quantum physics and/or mechanics may help you have a deeper understanding of the universe, but you don't have the ability to know it all. The more you know, the more you will discover your cognitive limitations. You will always have a desire to know more about the universe.

While it is important for you to work hard so that you can experience professional success in life, you should also spend quality time with your Heavenly Father. Whether you know it or not, you need God in your life. When the dust has settled, the only thing that will remain is your faith in the Almighty. As you begin the New Year, ask God to grant you wisdom from above so that you will be able to deal with this year's challenges victoriously.

JANUARY 2

"For the Lord gives wisdom; from his mouth come knowledge and understanding." – Proverbs 2:6 NIV

*T*oday's exponential growth of technology has put knowledge within your reach. You can learn almost anything you want if you have access to the Internet. You only need to go to school if you need a degree or specialized knowledge in a specific field or discipline. That means knowledge is no longer a rarity. What is rare, however, is wisdom from God, which cannot be obtained from natural knowledge and experience.

Divine wisdom enables you to use knowledge in accordance with God's will. Have you ever wondered why smart people do foolish things? Perhaps they have knowledge and experience, but they may be lacking in divine wisdom.

True wisdom is from Yahweh, our true God. If you really want to be wise, you must ask God to impart wisdom to you. Don't be wise in your own eyes. A wise person is one who has been acquainted with his or her Maker. Being aware of whose you are can change your perspective about life. If you know your Heavenly Father is the King of kings, you are not likely to behave like a pauper.

As you pursue your dreams this year, continue to ask the Heavenly Father to endow you with knowledge, understanding, and wisdom from above. In this connection, you will have a sense of balance and purpose as you deal with others, and you will gain scriptural insights into life in general.

JANUARY 3

"Trust in the Lord with all your heart and lean not on your own understanding; in all your ways submit to him, and he will make your paths straight." – Proverbs 3:5 and 6 NIV

When you see yourself through the lens of what Jesus did on the cross for you, you will have a different picture of your self-worth. This passage does not say you should not be thinking for yourself or get involved in short-term or long-term planning for your future on earth. You should know that it is important to include God in your plans because He knows everything about your future.

The fact that you belong to God should tremendously shape your opinion of yourself. If God is your Father, you can then say that you belong to the King of kings. If you belong to the King of kings, you can then conclude that you are a prince or a princess.

Being armed with such powerful truth about your spiritual identity, you now have unlimited resources at your disposal. Your perspective about life should be rather optimistic. Your mind should have no room for worries when you come to grips with the knowledge of who you are because you belong to God. Be sure your assessment of yourself is in sync with what God thinks of you.

JANUARY 4

"The path of righteousness is like the morning sun, shining ever brighter till the full light of day." – Proverbs 4:18 NIV

𝐴 righteous person is one whose life has been redeemed by the blood of Jesus Christ. You cannot be righteous on your own merit because your righteousness is only valid if it is based on Christ's performance. What does that really mean? If your righteousness is based on your own performance, it is totally worthless. You are declared righteous when you acknowledge the sacrifice Jesus made on the cross for your sins and surrender your will to Him as your Savior. As a result, when the Heavenly Father looks at you, He sees Jesus. Because Jesus is perfect, God sees you as a perfect person. Yes, the path of a righteous person is very bright because his or her future is assured. It is in the bag, so to speak.

When you imagine the future, you see eternal life. This is a bright path. The wicked have no clue of what the future holds for them, because they have no connection with God, the Creator of the universe. The future is very dreadful for people whose hope is not in the Lord.

You cannot ignore the future by thinking that life is over when you die. Such reasoning is based on the idea that there is no resurrection after death. Because God raised Jesus from the dead, there is resurrection after death. If you were to deny God's existence, that would not nullify His sovereignty. Your own existence is evidence that God exists because He created you.

May your quest for wisdom help you to put your trust in God, for He oversees your destiny.

JANUARY 5

"Drink water from your own cistern, running water from your own well." – Proverbs 5:15 NIV

Today fidelity is viewed as a prudish word. Some people no longer believe in having one partner. Although they are married, they are still looking for somebody else. Ignoring fidelity is perversity and a lack of sexual morality.

Marriage is based on the commitment that you are together until death separates you from each other. You should not go out there looking for another person to satisfy your sexual desires. You should always run home to your spouse. Stop trying to get it from somewhere else. A healthy relationship is one that is based on trust and faithfulness. When you sow faithfulness, you reap peace of mind before God and your mate because you have nothing to hide. Your spouse should be able to look at your cell phone any time. You should have nothing to hide from him or her.

If you fail to drink water from your own well, you will end up creating resentments in your family. Your mate will no longer depend on you. The very foundation of your marriage, which is trust, will likely collapse. Your spouse should not have to worry about another person's interference. This is very troublesome for your partner, who expects nothing but your faithful commitment to the wedding vow.

Love and cherish your spouse so that he or she can be there for you. Don't spend your money on other women or men. Be wise. Try to preserve the bond of your marriage until death. This is the way marriage is meant to be. If you do that, you will enjoy peace and harmony in your household.

JANUARY 6

"But a man who commits adultery has no sense; whoever does so destroys himself." – Proverbs 6: 32 NIV

When you refuse to drink water from your own cistern, you become senseless according to the Scripture. It takes a prudent person to concentrate on creating a harmonious household. Today make a firm decision to be faithful to your spouse. A man or a woman who commits adultery is not wise. Your own reputation as a person depends on how well you manage your household. How logical is it to have intercourse with someone who is not yours? This is simply unacceptable!

You must know that adultery is a sinful act. Not only does it destroy your marriage, it also diminishes your friendship with the Almighty. If you are a child of God, your body is the temple of the Holy Spirit. He lives in you. Decide to honor God with your body.

An adulterous act is likely to impact negatively your relationship with God. As a Christian, you should not continue in adultery. The Holy Spirit, who lives in you, is sad when you persist in living in sin.

If you have fallen in the trap of adultery, do yourself a huge favor. Repent, ask God to forgive you, and stop practicing adultery so that your soul can prosper. Show that you are a sensible person, one who categorically refuses to plunge into the trap of adultery.

You know that you love yourself, when you avoid the path of adultery. Save yourself from destruction.

JANUARY 7

"Keep my commands and you will live; guard my teachings as the apple of your eye." – Proverbs 7:2 NIV

When you choose to obey God, you choose life. You know you choose the path of wisdom, when you live your life based on the teachings found in the Holy Bible. As you know, the apple of your eye is extremely sensitive. Certainly, you would not want any sharp objects to penetrate it. Similarly, you should guard God's teachings with extreme care in order to ensure that your lifestyle is guided by them.

The importance of living within the parameter established by the Holy Scripture is that it puts you on the path of eternal life. As you continue your journey through life, you should ensure that you have eternal life.

Nowadays, it is very difficult to live without health insurance. If you need insurance for your car, your house, and your life, why do you think that you don't need insurance for your eternal life?

Jesus came to provide you with free insurance. All you need to do is to surrender your life to Him and acknowledge that you have sinned and that you are not capable of saving yourself. "If you declare with your mouth, Jesus is Lord, and believe in your heart that God raised him from the dead, you will be saved" (Romans 10:9 NIV).

When you choose to keep God's commands and guard His teachings, you choose to live your life in accordance with the Holy Scripture. That's what it means to live for God.

JANUARY 8

"I love those who love me, and those who seek me find me." – Proverbs 8:17 NIV

*I*n this verse, wisdom is personified. Remember this devotional book is about searching for wisdom. If you love wisdom, you will enjoy lots of good things in life.

Wisdom is not reserved for an elite group of people. Wisdom is available to everyone who is willing to seek it.

When you seek something, you try to find it. Seeking is an active search for something valuable. You can tell something is valuable when its owner leaves no stone unturned to find it.

According to this verse, you are guaranteed to find wisdom if you are willing to seek it. When was the last time you asked God for wisdom? Asking God for wisdom is praying strategically. We should ask God to show us the gifts He has given us to serve His people.

If you are wise, you have better decision-making ability. You tend to avoid making foolish decisions. Unwise people make foolish decisions daily, and they tend to suffer because of their foolishness.

If you are wise, you don't have to ask God to deliver you from problems that could have been avoided in the first place. At least, you wouldn't have to do it as often as those who lack wisdom.

King Solomon had asked God for wisdom. The Scripture has revealed that he was the wisest king who has ever ruled in the Old Testament. God gave him wisdom from above because he asked Him for it. Today ask God to grant you wisdom.

JANUARY 9

"The fear of the Lord is the beginning of wisdom, and knowledge of the Holy One is understanding." – Proverbs 9:10 NIV

What does it really mean to fear the Lord? I want to point out that this verse is about the fear of the Lord, not your own fear or the fear of men. When we talk about fearing someone, we usually think about possible punishment or negative consequences.

The fear of the Lord has nothing to do with punishment. It is about love and respect for God. A good way to describe the fear of the Lord is to picture yourself standing in awe of God due to His Majesty.

God is so marvelous that we sense His awesome presence and power as we praise and worship Him. When we realize how awesome and powerful God is, we become wise altogether. It is such an eye-opener.

Because we were created to give glory to God, when we accept His sovereignty by showing Him love and respect, we prove that we are wise. Our knowledge of God is demonstrated by our attitude toward Him. The mere idea of loving and respecting God is proof of our knowledge. We worship God because we know Him.

When humans have a real encounter with God, they worship Him. God's fear or awesomeness is unimaginably great! His presence demands respect.

From a spiritual perspective, we are not considered wise if we do not acknowledge God. Knowing God is the genesis of everything that is good. Similarly, our understanding is not complete if it is not rooted in Yahweh, the true God.

JANUARY 10

"Lazy hands make for poverty, but diligent hands bring wealth."
– Proverbs 10:4 NIV

God expects us to work. Work is not one of the consequences of sin. Adam and Eve had worked the Garden of Eden before they disobeyed God. Of course, sin has rendered our labor difficult because our effort is not as productive as it should be.

We cannot expect God to bless us if we are not willing to work. We must participate in our own prosperity. It does not matter how rich your country may be, if you are not prepared to take advantage of the wealth of the land, you will continue to live in poverty.

Take time to figure out the best way to make money legally. Avoid being involved in corruption at all costs. Otherwise you may not be around to enjoy your wealth.

Capitalize on your youth by working hard while you are young, or while you are physically strong enough to work. It is better for you to work hard now and play later. Working is important if you would like to have financial freedom in your senior years.

Don't spend your time partying with your friends when you should be working. Be willing to work extra hours or a second job. There are twenty-four hours in a day. You only need 8 or 9 hours to rest.

Wealth is the fruit of diligent, honest work, unless it is inherited. It is not enough to just work; you need to work diligently. When you work with diligence, you get more done in less time, which may enhance your opportunities of amassing more wealth during your working years.

JANUARY 11

"For lack of guidance a nation falls, but victory is won through many advisers." – Proverbs 11:14 NIV

Given the complexity and diversity of opinions that exist within a nation, wisdom is a necessity. Those who are called to lead others should always seek guidance.

The role of advisers is to help leaders better understand the issues surrounding the circumstances of their leadership. They need assistance in their efforts to find viable solutions to difficult problems.

Be very cautious as you receive advice from your advisers, for many people in your entourage are ready to applaud you as you perform your duties, and there are some people who are looking for opportunity to cause your downfall.

Don't listen to only those who love you. You have a lot to learn from your opponents as well. Yes, it is painful to endure criticism from your adversary; your adversary will keep you humble and honest. When you are criticized, find out what you can change. If you can't change anything, at least try to improve on your performance.

Above all, ask God for guidance because advice from men is fallible. Seek wisdom from God and be sure He is your adviser for everything you do, including your business and your household.

If God is your captain, your ship will not sink. And if it does sink, know that your life is in His hands.

JANUARY 12

"In the way of righteousness there is life; along that path is immortality." – Proverbs 12:28 NIV

*I*f you want to live forever, you have a choice to make. You must choose the way of righteousness, which is the path of immortality.

What does it take to be a righteous person? As you read the Holy Bible, you will discover that righteousness can only be obtained through Jesus Christ. "This righteousness is given through faith in Jesus Christ to all who believe" (Romans 3:22 NIV). Your own goodness is not enough to get you to heaven.

As it is written: "There is no one righteous, not even one" (Romans 3:10 NIV). It is through Christ's righteousness you can be righteous or become immortal. What does that mean? This simply means that God accepts you as righteous through Christ's shed blood. He came down to your level in order to rescue you from sin and death.

When you surrender your life to Jesus Christ, you are considered dead to sin. As a result, you become alive in Christ. Your old life of wickedness is crucified with Christ. You are now connected with God through Jesus Christ, and God is now at peace with you. In the eyes of God, you are righteous, for He no longer judges you based on what you have done, but on the basis of what Jesus accomplished on the cross for you.

JANUARY 13

"Walk with the wise and become wise, for a companion of fools suffers harm." – Proverbs 13:20 NIV

Wise people have one thing in common; they tend to hang around people who are wise. This goes for successful people as well. If you only spend time with people who are less successful than you are, it is probable that you may end up being less successful in life. Success tends to produce success.

It is not beneficial to spend time with only senseless individuals. They are more likely to do something that may land you in jail.

Watch out for people who have no respect for the rule of law. They tend to hate structure. You may say that you're not breaking any law yourself, or you're not going to get caught. Don't be deceived. If you are caught with someone who is breaking the law, you may be accused of being an accomplice.

Does that mean you need to avoid dealing with unwise people altogether? No, you can still function with everybody. Be civil but avoid being a companion of fools. Having said that, you should not write them off completely. A miracle is still possible with God.

Finally, when fools refuse to change after many prayers and rebukes, you should limit your involvement with them. Such a person behaves like a loose cannon; there isn't much you can do to change their minds. Your best bet is to avoid being entangled with fools if you can. Be courteous with them, but for your own safety and well-being, avoid making deals with them at all costs.

JANUARY 14

"There is a way that appears to be right, but in the end it leads to death." – Proverbs 14:12 NIV

*B*ecause we are limited in our own understanding, we often misjudge things. What seems to be marvelous in our eyes may not be the case in God's eyes. As we try to decide which path to take, we need to think about the consequences of our actions. It is always important to reflect on the outcome of our actions. Otherwise the desires of the flesh will lead us toward the path of destruction.

If we cannot depend on our knowledge to determine what is right and wrong, it is obvious we need God's guidance. Without God's help, we cannot make the right decision, choose the right mate, the right career path, or follow the path of righteousness.

The world may lead you to believe that you don't need God in your life, in that you have everything under control. Don't succumb to Satan's tricks. Satan knows God exists, and he trembles at the thought of having to deal with Him in the end. Satan's destiny is very gloomy and bleak. There is no hope for him.

Be careful as you plan your life. Ask God to reveal His will to you. Be sure you choose the way that leads to eternal life, not to eternal death. If you trust God to lead you, you can rest assured that your life will have a happy ending.

JANUARY 15

"Plans fail for lack of counsel, but with many advisers they succeed." – Proverbs 15:22 NIV

When you set out to plan something important in your life, whether it be a new business, a new career, or a wedding, take time to pray about your decision. Don't rush into making important decisions so that you don't end up regretting it in the end.

In order to avoid making terrible mistakes, it's wise to ask people who know more than you about your plan. If you are young, talk to people who have ample knowledge and experience, especially people who are much older than you. Above all, look for people who respect and love God.

Strive for balanced decisions by consulting several people. In the medical field, it is often said that one needs a second opinion before deciding on surgery. It is okay to be redundant in decision making because this is an area where more means better. The more advice you receive on a project, the better you will be able to sort out the matter and come up with the best plan and/or decision.

Moreover, don't make any important decisions without consulting with God. God is sovereign, so He knows how your plan will end. He knows everything about you, and there is nothing that is hidden from Him. When you consult with God, you are basically telling Him that you are aware of His power over you. As a result, you can depend on Him for success.

JANUARY 16

"The lot is cast into the lap, but it every decision is from the LORD." – Proverbs 16:33 NIV

*A*s you start the New Year, you may have tons of things you would like to accomplish both personally and professionally. Those things you set out to achieve this year are not necessarily bad in themselves. However, it would be pure madness for you to think you can outsmart God through your smart planning and sheer intellectual exploits. Yes, the Lord has given you amazing ability to accomplish awesome things on earth, but your intellectual capacities are rather limited in both scope and breadth.

Acknowledging God is your way of telling Him you know who oversees your ship. The unimaginable power of God and His limitless, intellectual capacities make Him indispensable, no matter how you spin the facts.

Yes, go ahead and cast the lot, but turn to God for a smart decision that has the capacity to revolutionize your thinking, your accomplishments, your job, your marriage, and your destiny.

Does this mean that you should stop planning? No, God expects you to utilize your mind to plan and prepare your life to receive His limitless blessings. "Commit to the Lord whatever you do, and he will establish your plans" (Proverbs 16:3 NIV).

JANUARY 17

"The one who has knowledge uses words with restraint, and whoever has understanding is even-tempered." – Proverbs 17:27 NIV

When you enter a room, see if you can determine who has more or less knowledge. Sometimes, the person who has less knowledge tends to be the loudest one in the room. How is that? Well, he or she is trying to compensate for his or her lack of knowledge by being a chatterbox. That is not always the case, however.

A wise person takes time to think about what he or she is going to say. You don't just open your mouth and blurt it out. Mull over your thoughts. This is even more important if you are a leader. A leader has an audience, and the audience will parse every word he or she utters.

You should be careful even when you are talking in private. Over the years, many politicians have gotten in deep trouble due to lack of self-restraint. They have uttered things that have caused public outrage.

Remember your tongue can cause a great deal of damage to others. Think before you talk and choose words that will bring healing to your audience.

Above all, don't be quick to get angry. Be ready to give others the benefit of the doubt.

Understanding allows you to see the futility of the situation. Furthermore, if you take time to reflect on the issue, you will be able to keep your cool despite its gravity.

JANUARY 18

"The tongue has the power of life and death, and those who love it will eat its fruit." – Proverbs 18:21 NIV

*B*e careful with the use of your tongue. You can utilize it to bring comfort to others or destroy them. Imagine the number of people Adolf Hitler killed with his tongue. It takes one command from a whacky individual to send thousands to their death. Conversely, it takes the gentle words of one wise person to change the destiny of a nation. Ask God to grant you wisdom to use your tongue to bring healing and restoration to others.

Keep in mind that words have power. Yahweh spoke the universe into existence. Imagine how wonderful the world would be if humans could commit themselves to speaking words that edify others.

Due to the impact of the sinful nature, we are more likely to use words that bring others down. Therefore, we need to pray that the Lord will grant us wisdom to show empathy toward our brothers and sisters.

When the tongue is used wisely, it can bring tremendous blessings. Don't spend your time speaking negatively. When you get up in the morning, take time to speak something positive on yourself and your loved ones. See the world through God's eyes. Stand on His promises. With your tongue, you can declare war on the kingdom of darkness and proclaim freedom and peace of God upon the earth.

JANUARY 19

"Many are the plans in a person's heart, but it is the LORD's purpose that prevails." – Proverbs 19:21 NIV

Amid your hustle and bustle to piece together a viable plan for your life journey, it is the Sovereign God who holds the key to your destiny. It does not matter how smart you are as an individual, God will have the final word. Does that mean that you are basically helpless when it comes to life's issues?

The answer is no. You are not helpless in the game of life. God created you as a free-will individual. Your free will gives you tremendous opportunity to participate in the planning process. You are not a machine. What's important for you to realize is that your plan must be aligned with God's will for your life. What does it take then?

In order to align your plan with God's will, you need to acknowledge His plan for humanity. As a person, you were created to glorify God, and your plan must not prevent you from doing that. Regardless of your position in this world, you must always look to God for divine guidance. Don't be arrogant in thinking that you don't need God.

When the dust has settled, you will have to give God an account of your life. In other words, you need to know that your life is hidden in Christ. Without Christ's shed blood, you are not worthy to enter heaven. Your life insurance policy is in Jesus Christ. Therefore, don't allow Satan to harden your heart. Say yes to Christ today.

JANUARY 20

"Wine is a mocker and beer a brawler; whoever is led astray by them is not wise." – Proverbs 20:1 NIV

*T*here is nothing wrong in drinking a glass of wine or a beer from time to time. Apostle Paul advised Timothy to drink a little wine for the sake of his stomach (1 Timothy 2:23). However, you need to be careful so that you do not become an alcoholic. If you don't have what it takes to show restraints, you would do well to avoid drinking altogether.

In order to be a productive citizen, you need to remain sober. You cannot show up to work every morning with a hangover. This type of drinking habit is antisocial. If you go down that path, you will not only destroy yourself, you will put your own family in danger. Drink responsibly by waiting until you are off from work to drink. Think safety first.

If you are going to drink, be sure you call a taxi. Today there are several ride-hailing services that make it easier for you to get home safely. It is okay to park your car at the restaurant overnight. You can always call a taxi in the morning to take you back to your car. This is by far cheaper than paying a lawyer for a DUI.

I know your friends may entice you to do otherwise but be wise and listen to this sensible advice. It will save you a lot of headaches. Most importantly, it will save your life, your family, and your career as a professional.

Avoid being an alcoholic. If you have fallen into the alcoholic trap, seek professional help.

JANUARY 21

"Whoever pursues righteousness and love finds life, prosperity and honor." – Proverbs 21:21 NIV

This verse promises three specific blessings for those who are willing to seek righteousness and love: life, prosperity, and honor.

Righteousness is a virtue that can only be obtained from the Almighty God. We cannot declare ourselves righteous based on our performance. We totally depend on the sacrifice of Jesus Christ to pardon us, for we were completely disconnected from God as a result of Adam's and Eve's disobedience in the Garden of Eden.

In order to have life, we must become righteous. God will not accept us if we are unrighteous. There is no place in heaven for unrighteous people. The only viable way for us to become righteous is through faith in Jesus Christ, our Savior. This is an act of God.

In addition to righteousness, we also need to pursue love. God showed us how to love when He sent His Son, Jesus, to die on the cross for us.

Because God is love, we can love others when we allow God to love through us. Love is the evidence of God's presence in us. Love is also the fruit of the Spirit who lives in us.

If you want to have eternal life, live in prosperity, and be honored in the end, pursue righteousness and love that come from God.

JANUARY 22

"The prudent see danger and take refuge, but the simple keep going and pay the penalty." – Proverbs 22:3 NIV

*I*t pays to have foresight and forward-thinking ability. One thing imprudent people have in common is that they tend to be reckless. Even though they see danger, they keep going toward it.

To put it in a practical term, how can people continue to cheat on their mate when they know such behavior is going to destroy them, their family, and their reputation? They know full well if they keep peddling illicit drugs, they will end up in jail; yet they persist in doing it instead of getting a real job.

The Holy Spirit is not happy with us when we continue in disobedience. We should not keep on going on the path of death. The truth is that we need to be wise.

The idea of searching for wisdom is to find out how to make sensible decisions and live according to the precepts established in the Holy Scripture.

One thing is certain; there is no reward for continuous pursuit of godlessness. One day we will all have to give God an account of our journey on earth. If we choose to obey God and follow in the path of righteousness, we will spend eternity with God in the New Jerusalem.

JANUARY 23

"There is surely a future hope for you, and your hope will not be cut off." – Proverbs 23:18 NIV

*I*f your hope is based on the promises of God, you can rest assured that you will not be disappointed. No matter what you do, be sure you are not trusting in your own understanding. Your assessment of yourself is not always accurate. It is always good to allow the One who created you a chance to give you a better picture of your reality.

This does not mean that you are not supposed to use your brain. Basing your hope on God's promises means that you know that He is the captain of your ship. If you are going down, you want to make sure that your captain has solid mastery of the ocean as well as the ship. Otherwise you will not be able to withstand the tides. You will be swallowed up by life's adversity and the temptation of this world.

Knowing that your future will not be cut off should give you the moxie to push forward, even though your life's circumstances are hardly bearable. Please don't end your life. Continue to put your hope in God. Surely, He understands your trauma, and He will see you through.

God can turn your personal adversities into opportunities. Pray and ask God to strengthen you when you feel weak and disoriented. Nothing is hidden from God, and He sees your final destiny. You will win life's final battle if you walk with God.

JANUARY 24

"If you falter in a time of trouble, how small is your strength!" – Proverbs 24:10 NIV

When you place your faith in the Almighty God, you don't have to worry about the outcome of your circumstances. There is only one possible outcome for those whose faith is in the Lord. The result is victory.

You may not like the result in the end, but that does not mean that it is bad. God is sovereign, and He does not operate as the world does.

Because God always operates in the present, He knows when to pull the plug. Our timing may conflict with God's timing because we judge things in the natural order or based on our own understanding of time.

God sees things as they are. There is no future for Him. It is okay to question things as it is our nature to do so, but that does not make a difference in the spiritual realm.

Our best attitude is to allow God to direct us. That way, wherever He takes us, we know that the destination will be perfect. In time of trouble, don't falter. Just know that God is in control.

JANUARY 25

"Like a city whose walls are broken through is a person who lacks self-control." – Proverbs 25:28 NIV

Self-control is a very important skill to possess if you are going to survive in this world. Don't be ready to accept everything that you are proposed in this life. Have the courage to say no every now and then. In fact, you should take time to reflect on every decision you are making in this life. This is especially true if you are young. Your friends are constantly bombarding you with ideas. They are constantly inviting you to parties. Be careful not to be involved in anything illegal. One mistake is all it takes to render your life miserable. One DUI can cause you a lot of problems.

Be careful not to side with your friends when they are telling you to break the law. Always try to be a good citizen in your community. Respect speed limits and pay your taxes. It does not matter if everybody in the neighborhood is doing it. It is okay for you to be different.

Don't be afraid to be a leader among your peers. Your community needs you. When you say no to lawlessness, others take note. You may be the only beacon of light for your friends, so take your stand when you have a chance to do so.

Stand for justice when you see injustice. Raise your voice and speak up when the wicked are trying to triumph. You must not allow them to win. Remember you are the light of the world.

JANUARY 26

"As a dog returns to its vomit, so fools repeat their folly." – Proverbs 26:11 NIV

Spend a few moments to search your heart thoroughly today for things in your life that you know full well you have no business doing and ask God to give you enough courage to stop. Are you being unfaithful to your spouse? Do you harbor hatred against someone? Don't be a dog that returns to its vomit. Refuse to be a fool. Make a complete about face today.

There are certain habits that can only bring shame to your good name and your family. Muster enough moxie to stop your folly before it becomes too late.

Whatever is your folly, don't allow it to ruin your life. Be honest with yourself and assess the damage. Allow the Holy Spirit to woo you back to safety. Ask God to change your heart as you struggle to recover from your foolishness. Don't be a daredevil.

Bravery will not rescue you from the shame your foolish pursuit will bring on your family and friends. Have the courage to pause the clock and allow your conscience to tug your heart back to wisdom.

If you continue in the path of destruction, in the end you will suffer the consequences, and your loved ones will pay dearly. Listen carefully to the voice of the Holy Spirit and stop.

JANUARY 27

"As iron sharpens iron, so one person sharpens another." – Proverbs 27:17 NIV

*I*f you were to examine your life, you would quickly realize that many people have influenced your thinking, even your current view of life. This simply means that you should pay attention to the type of people with whom you hang around. If you allow people with a toxic attitude to sharpen your mind, your ideology or your belief system, your life is bound to be impacted negatively.

Try to choose your friends carefully because their behaviors may negatively impact your lifestyle, even on your chance of success in life.

Do not become entangled by the wickedness of this world. Above all, allow your mind to be sharpened by Jesus Christ and His wonderful teachings about eternal life. In the end, the outcome will be immortality.

Immortality should be your goal in life. This is the only aspiration that will follow you beyond the grave. Keep in mind that you cannot reach immortality without Jesus' sacrifice on the cross. Jesus died so that you can live forever.

God created you to live forever. However, living forever without God will be extremely miserable. You don't want that. You want to be sure that your name is written in the Lamb's book of life. The only way that can happen is for you to accept Jesus Christ as your Lord and Savior. If you have already done so, continue to live faithfully for God.

JANUARY 28

"Whoever conceals their sins does not prosper, but the one who confesses and renounces them finds mercy." – Proverbs 28:13 NIV

This key verse contains three powerful action words: conceal, confess, and renounce. This is a problem with two specific solutions.

First, let's examine the problem. The problem is the concealment of sins. Yes, it is shameful to tell others about the things you did in secret. However, if you really want to be set free, you have no choice but to confess.

There are two types of confessions: one you can do between you and God, the other with someone you trust. The ultimate confession is to come clean before God and ask Him to forgive you. Of course, you know that God is aware of your shortcomings. Nothing is hidden from the Almighty God.

Second, in addition to confession, you may find someone you highly respect and trust to reveal your sins and ask for prayer. This is not mandatory, but it does serve as an accountability system. It simply makes sense to seek wise counseling. Keep in mind that only God can set you free through the power of the Holy Spirit and the shed blood of Jesus.

The third element is to ask the person against whom you have sinned to forgive you. You also need to forgive yourself. Even after God had forgiven you, there is a possibility that you may still hold on to your guilty feelings.

Finally, you need to renounce your sins. You should not continue to repeat the same offense. Yes, God is merciful, but you need to try to honor and respect God.

JANUARY 29

"Whoever remains stiff-neck after many rebukes will suddenly be destroyed – without remedy." – Proverbs 29:1 NIV

*T*here is wisdom in learning from your mistakes. In fact, one of the characteristics of wisdom is the love of learning. You are not expected to be perfect in all your ways. On your journey through life, you will make mistakes. Each mistake will give you the opportunity to learn something new. That is why you depend on Christ's righteousness to make it to heaven.

Corrections often come by way of rebukes from others. Don't take offense when others rebuke you. You need to thank them. I am not talking about those mean folks who are out to destroy you for no reason. Some people are simply mean-spirited.

Your best counselor is the Holy Spirit. He has a way of rebuking you through your conscience. If you allow the quiet voice of the Holy Spirit to do its job, you will do just fine.

There are limits to your folly. If you refuse to abandon your bad habits, someday it will be too late to stop. You will come to sudden destruction.

The only remedy for your folly is to have the sense to stop it. There is no wisdom in your persistence in wrongdoing. Wisdom is to know when to stop.

Pray and ask God to show you which areas of your life need improvement. God can grant you wisdom and courage to make those changes.

JANUARY 30

"Every word of God is flawless; he is a shield to those who take refuge in him." – Proverbs 30:5 NIV

*I*f you doubt the veracity of God's word, I would like to direct your attention to what the Bible says about itself.

> "Above all, you must understand that no prophecy of Scripture came about by the Prophet's own interpretation of things. For prophecy never had its origin in the human will, but prophets, through human, spoke from God as they were carried along by the Holy Spirit." (2 Peter 1:20 and 21)

*T*he Bible is not a figment of someone's imagination. It is God's special message to humanity. God is the ultimate hiding place, a source of all comfort for the weary.

You can trust God with all you are, all you have, and all you hope to be in life. He is the Almighty God. And His sovereignty encompasses everything that you can ever imagine.

Allow God to be your compass as you journey through life. Make Him the focus of your existence by taking time to praise and worship Him daily.

Pray for wisdom so that you may continue to serve God, no matter what. You will never regret your decision to walk with God. Your friends may abandon you. Your own loved ones may give up on you, but God will never forsake you.

JANUARY 31

"Charm is deceptive, and beauty is fleeting; but a woman who fears the Lord is to be praised." – Proverbs 31:30 NIV

One thing you need to understand about external beauty is that it is temporary. Don't fall for it. Your partner may not remain skinny for the length of your relationship. It is natural for humans to get wrinkles as they grow older. If your relationship is only based on natural beauty, it will not last. That does not mean that you should marry someone you do not like. You should focus more on character and compatibility. If you cannot get along with your mate, beauty will not keep you together.

One of the criteria you should list when looking for a mate is a person who fears the Lord. This quality is not limited to women; it applies to men as well. If your mate does not fear the Lord, which is the beginning of wisdom in the first place, something fundamental is missing in the relationship.

Therefore, from the outset, look for a companion who respects and serves the Lord so that your relationship can be balanced. A balanced relationship brings harmony in the whole family.

Today's high rates of divorce have a lot to do with a lack of spiritual balance in the relationship. You may have the wealth of the world, but if you are not happy, your marriage will suffer.

If you are already in a relationship, please don't give up. Continue to make the best of it. If you are single, pay attention to these words of wisdom as you search for a companion.

FEBRUARY 1

"In him was life, and that life was the light of mankind."
John 1:4 NIV

The fall of Adam and Eve had plunged the whole world into utter spiritual darkness. Spiritually, it severed the very lifeline that God had established between Him and humanity. Jesus Christ came for a very specific purpose. He came to bring life by offering His own life on the cross of Calvary for us.

When we live in the absence of God in our lives, we are living in darkness. Jesus Christ is the very light of the world. We all need Jesus if we want to see. If we think we can see without Jesus, we are deceiving ourselves. There can be no light without Jesus. Jesus opens our eyes to see beyond this world. He helps us to understand that we were created in the image of God in that we have God's breath in us.

Jesus died for us all. No one should leave this world without hope, because we all have the same opportunity to reconcile with the Heavenly Father. We can have eternal life for free through Jesus Christ.

Eternal life is not something we can obtain through our personal efforts. It can only be obtained through faith in Jesus' birth, death, and resurrection. This is a personal experience, and it is unique for every individual. Faith is indispensable for that special connection to happen. We are spiritually dead, even though we appear to be alive in the flesh. For that reason, we must embrace Jesus Christ, the light of the world, so we can see and live forever.

FEBRUARY 2

"Yet to all who did receive him, to those who believed in his name, he gave the right to become children of God – children born not of natural descent, nor of human decision or a husband's will, but born of God." – John 1:12 and 13 NIV

We tend to worry less about who we are if we know beyond a shadow of doubt whose we are. In this passage of Scripture, John makes it perfectly clear that you belong to God if you have made the decision to believe in Jesus Christ, which seems to be the only prerequisite for claiming your full rights as a prince or a princess. Just in case you did not know, your Heavenly Father is the King of kings. "You are a chosen people, a royal priesthood, a holy nation, God's special possession, that you may declare the praises of him who called you out of darkness into his wonderful light" (1 Peter: 2:9 NIV).

It is not uncommon to come across children who do not have a clue who their father is. This goes for people who do not know who the Creator of the universe is. If you are an orphan, or you have lost your mom and dad, I would like to comfort you with the fact that you have a Heavenly Father, who loves you so much! He will never leave you nor will He forsake you. Decide to walk with Him as you journey through life, for He will guide you every step of the way.

FEBRUARY 3

"For the law was given through Moses; grace and truth came through Jesus Christ." – John 1:17 NIV

The purpose of the Law of Moses was to provide guidelines for the children of Israel. And God chose Moses to be the recipient. Just as speed limits are there to remind drivers of how fast they should drive, the law was designed to set the boundary for God's people and serve to remind them of their transgressions. Because the children of Israel were unable to comply fully with the Mosaic Law, God sent Jesus Christ, His Son, to die in our place.

In the Old Testament, the blood of animals was used to help the people expiate their sins. However, animal sacrifice was not enough to eliminate sins. For that reason, God decided to provide a permanent solution to sin, which is based on grace.

Grace means that we don't have to pay for our sins with the blood of animals. We have now a High Priest who can pay for our sins with His own blood on Calvary. The amazing truth about Jesus Christ is that He offers us salvation free of charge.

While we do not have to pay for our forgiveness, we must be willing to accept it. Jesus Christ is the source of truth. We can only come to know God through Jesus, the Guardian of grace and truth.

Jesus is the source of wisdom because He has been with the Father before the beginning of time. If you want to be wise, you must put your trust in Jesus Christ as your Lord and Savior.

FEBRUARY 4

"Jesus replied, "Very truly I tell you, no one can see the kingdom of God unless they are born again." – John 3:3 NIV

*B*ecause the kingdom of God is spiritual, we cannot enter it without a spiritual transformation. What does that really mean? This is an excellent question because even Nicodemus did not understand the concept of being born again. He was totally perplexed by Jesus' statement. He simply did not get it.

Similarly, in our own understanding, it is difficult to grasp supernatural concepts. Our thinking is limited to what we can conceptualize within the four known dimensions of the universe.

Being born again signifies being reconnected with God through the work of the Holy Spirit. Our spirits will continue to live forever beyond the grave. Therefore, we need to ensure that we are dead to the flesh and are made alive in Jesus Christ. The born-again experience is only possible through Jesus Christ. Jesus Christ came for this very purpose.

The mission of the Church is to encourage people to come to know this truth about Jesus Christ, the Savior of the world so that they will be able to see the kingdom. This should be the personal aim of every human being, which is to be ready to live in the kingdom. Preparation for the kingdom must be made while we are here on earth. It will be too late after death.

FEBRUARY 5

"For God so loved the world that he gave his one and only Son, that whoever believes in him shall not perish but have eternal life." – John 3:16 NIV

We should not go to Hell, because we now have a way out. There is no doubt that God loves us. The fact that Jesus came down to earth as a baby, shed His blood on the cross, and resurrected on the third day, God settled once and for all the sin issue. The door to paradise is wide open for us if we choose to believe in Jesus.

The crux of the matter is our personal choice. Keep in mind that God did not create us to function like a machine. A machine does not have a conscience. Conversely, God created us with a free will. Our free will gives us autonomy over the decisions we make in life. We cannot be forced to believe in God.

Considering this verse, we are responsible for the ultimate outcome. If we go to Hell it will be our decision, not God's. As far as eternal life is concerned, God has taken care of it through Jesus Christ. It has been paid for by the blood of Jesus Christ.

It is up to us to listen to the voice of the Holy Spirit and accept Jesus Christ, the Lamb of God. He is the ultimate sacrifice for sins. There is no other sacrifice left.

Now the Holy Spirit has the mission of convincing us so that we can see the need for Jesus Christ. Let us ask God to open our eyes so the devil does not blind us to the fact that we are hopeless without Jesus Christ, the Savior. Let us choose to believe so we will not perish. Eternal life is made available through Jesus Christ.

FEBRUARY 6

"Whoever believes in the Son has eternal life, but whoever rejects the Son will not see life, for God's wrath remains on them." – John 3:36 NIV

As a free-will individual, you can certainly choose life or reject it. However, one thing that is not negotiable, according to this verse, is that God has provided a specific solution for the problem of sin and the question of eternal life. It is obvious that you have a major decision to make as you journey through life.

Eternal life is important in that it gives you the opportunity to dream beyond the grave. I don't know how often you reflect on your life beyond death. With all sincerity, I can tell you that there is nothing more important than your eternal dwelling place. You should think more about your eternal destiny than your eventual retirement, albeit its crucial importance for your personal well-being. If you happen to live longer than most people, you may have a chance to live 25 to 35 years past retirement. In terms of quality of life, perhaps you will enjoy 20 to 25 years of those 35 years in retirement.

This little exercise is to help you to wake up from your sleep and think more logically about your existence. Do not allow the worries of this life to keep you from planning for your future. Yes, it is a good idea to save for your retirement and long-term care. It is also essential to plan for your eternal life. And the way you do that is by accepting Jesus Christ as your Lord and Savior. By doing so, you will avoid God's wrath. If you have already given your life to the Lord, continue to put your trust in the Lord and enjoy the peace that surpasses understanding. Jesus loves you!

FEBRUARY 7

"God is Spirit, and his worshipers must worship in the Spirit and in truth." – John 4:24 NIV

The fundamental truth about God is that He is Spirit. We, humans, were created by God. This means, we have a spiritual element in us.

Why is it important for us to worship God in the Spirit? We have to wordship God in the Spirit because this is the only way we can have access to Him. If we worship in the flesh, our worship is not going to reach God. There is no connection between material and immaterial.

Worshiping in the Spirit does not necessarily mean speaking in a heavenly language, even though it may be at times. This simply means we must focus our attention on God. Often, we are praising and worshiping God while our minds wander. We need to pay attention to what we are doing. We need to give God our undivided attention by allowing our spirits to adore God.

Our bodies and souls must submit to the Spirit through our spirits. Remember we have a body, a soul, and a spirit. Salvation happens in our spirits, not in our bodies and souls. That's why we have the potential to sin, even after salvation, for our bodies and souls are vulnerable.

We worship in the Spirit when our spirits control our bodies and souls, not the other way around.

FEBRUARY 8

"Very truly I tell you, whoever hears my word and believes him who sent me has eternal life and will not be judged but has crossed over from death to life." – John 5:24 NIV

*J*esus sums up the message of salvation in thirty-one words. If you are not sure about what it takes to have eternal life, you now have the truth right here before your eyes. It is no longer a secret. Salvation lies in the hearing of the word Jesus Christ and in believing the Father who sent Him. You have here the basic requirement for obtaining the miracle of a born-again experience.

Now, in order to have eternal life, you must put your faith in Jesus. Through the ministry of the Holy Spirit, God nudges and encourages you to put your trust in Him. You cannot obtain eternal life by works. This is an act of faith that is based on God's grace and favor.

When you have eternal life, you are safe from eternal punishment. God will not judge you for your sins, because Jesus took upon Him all your sins. Additionally, you will also overcome death in the end.

The real death is not when you stop breathing. Yes, this is physical death, a simple transition to eternal life or eternal death. If you have put your trust in Jesus' word and the One who sent Him, you have eternal life. You will not receive eternal death, which is the eternal punishment after the judgment of the Great White Throne. See Revelation 20:11-15.

FEBRUARY 9

"I am the bread of life." – John 6:48 NIV

Bread is such a common food item; it is often used as a synonym for food in general. If you are the breadwinner in your family, you are responsible for providing for your family by making sure they have enough to eat regularly. Bread may look slightly different in every country, but everyone knows what bread is.

Despite the popularity of bread, there is no place in the world where you can buy living bread. Jesus is not just ordinary bread. He is the bread of life, the living bread that came down from heaven. By using this metaphorical word, Jesus wants us to understand that we cannot survive spiritually without Him. He came and died in our place.

Have you eaten the bread of life? If you have, you can be sure that you have eternal life. Until you have consumed the bread of life, you are spiritually dead because you have no connection with the Heavenly Father. Jesus came to satisfy your spiritual hunger. You can eat all kinds of bread, but they cannot satisfy you spiritually.

You may think that you are not hungry because you have been eating natural bread. However, know that natural bread can't sustain you forever. That's why you must keep going to the store and buying more bread.

Make Jesus your Savior by accepting Him if you have not yet done so. Eat the bread of life so you can live forever.

FEBRUARY 10

"Whoever eats my flesh and drinks my blood has eternal life, and I will raise them up at the last day." – John 6:54 NIV

In this verse Jesus uses a different figure of speech. He wants us to eat His flesh and drink His blood. He is not trying to turn us into cannibals. He is referring to the sacrifice that He was going to offer in order to pay for our sins.

In the Old Testament, there was one way that the children of Israel used to expiate or cleanse their sins. They had to offer animal sacrifices. They also had to go through a high priest. They couldn't do it themselves.

Jesus Christ presents Himself as both the sacrifice and the High Priest. This is extraordinary. That's awesome! That means we don't need to go through someone to get to Jesus. We can call upon Him directly and be saved.

Jesus literally gave His life for us. God basically came down to our level when it was impossible for us to get to Him ourselves. The death of Christ was the ultimate sacrifice that God could make to redeem us.

Today we need to simply acknowledge the works of God and accept the gift of eternal life. We don't have to work for it. It is totally free. The only requirement is to open our hearts and let Him in.

Not only did Jesus die for you, He also overcame death for you. Because He is no longer in the tomb, He will be able to raise you up in the last day. You will live beyond the grave because of what Jesus did for you. Continue to put your hope in Jesus Christ.

FEBRUARY 11

"The Spirit gives life; the flesh counts for nothing. The words I have spoken to you – they are full of the Spirit and life." – John 6:63 NIV

One thing we need to keep in mind is that when we are talking about Jesus Christ, we are talking about preparation for the supernatural world. We are not dealing with anything finite. Because we live in the flesh, we tend to focus more on things that have to do with this world. By doing so, we often neglect the most important thing in life, which is preparing for eternity. We know it is important to go school, have a job, and raise a family. Nevertheless, amid all these important life's obligations, we must not lose sight of our priority.

Our priority is eternal life, and there are no two ways about it. We need to do all we can with God's help to provide for our family, but we also need to fix our eyes on Jesus, the Author and Finisher of our faith.

When Jesus came, He spoke words of life. Here, we are talking about ῥήματα (rhēmata), which refers to the active, living words animated by God's Spirit and/or anointing, not λόγος (logos), which is associated with God's creative, divine "Word" used in John 1 verse 1.

Jesus spoke words that were completely aligned with the Holy Scripture, and they were full of life. Jesus Christ came to do the will of God, not His own will. Therefore, when you listen to and apply God's words regularly, you can live according to God's will, for God's words contain the spiritual guidance you need to live a godly life.

FEBRUARY 12

"Whoever believes in me, as Scripture has said, rivers of living water will flow from within them." – John 7:38 NIV

*J*esus continues to use practical metaphorical terms to help us understand the necessity of accepting Him as our source of life, meaning our Lord and Savior. Initially, He describes Himself as the bread of life, and then He invites us to eat His flesh and drink His blood. Now, we see Him as rivers of living water. One thing we can expect from rivers is fresh water that flows continuously, refreshing everything in their surroundings.

Eternal life begins with believing in Jesus with all our minds. We must allow the Holy Spirit to draw us closer to God. Without this supernatural intervention, there cannot be salvation. Only God's Spirit can change us.

When we are connected with God, we are alive, and our spirits are in control of our journey through life. We are not living according the desires of the flesh. We can please and bring glory to God because we have God's Spirit living inside of us.

We cannot love as God wants us to love if we do not have the Spirit of God living inside of us. That's why there is so much hatred in the world today. God's Spirit is not present in those individuals, and the devil inhabits their minds. In lieu of living water, their hearts are completely dry.

Now eternal life is made available to you by virtue of your belief in Jesus. Allow the rivers of living water to flow from within you.

FEBRUARY 13

"So if the Son sets you free, you will be free indeed." – John 8:36 NIV

Genuine freedom is found in Jesus Christ. If you have committed your life to Jesus Christ, you are a free person, and no one can enslave you if you do not surrender yourself. You are free forever, so don't allow Satan to enslave you.

There are many people who are living in captivity, even though they do not know it. They do not have the freedom that comes from Jesus Christ.

What does it take to be free indeed? To experience real freedom, you must acknowledge that you have sinned and have been disconnected from God. Imagine that you are drowning, and there are a bunch of people around you. What will happen to you if you do not call for help immediately? Well, you will come to a sad conclusion. You will drown.

Similarly, unless people realize that they are living in sins, they will never repent. As a result, they will die in their sins. It is very sad for a person to die in sin. Jesus' presence on earth was to set people free from the bondage of sin. He came to set the captive free by giving them a second chance to get connected with God.

Please do not make the tragic mistake that many people have made in life. Allow Jesus to enter your heart and set you free. If you have already given your life to Jesus, you are free indeed. Continue to enjoy your freedom in Christ and share your wonderful experience with others so they can put their trust in Jesus as well.

FEBRUARY 14

"Very truly I tell you, whoever obeys my word will never see death." – John 8:51 NIV

$\mathcal{A}$s you search for wisdom, you will discover that your current life's experience is temporary. Real life does not begin until you are living in eternity with God.

Jesus confirms that physical death is not something to fear because it is not permanent. When you die, you will take your permanent form. Keep in mind you will live forever one way or the other. You will either live with God in the New Jerusalem, or away from God in Hades. That's why it is so important for you to determine where you will spend eternity. This is a very serious matter.

Life begins with obedience. You have a decision to make while you are still in your physical body. If you have been reading this devotional book, by now you know that Jesus came to die for you. However, you need to accept Him in order to be saved. Because God created you with a free will, God will not force you to accept Him. Although you were created to glorify God, God did not choose to make you a robot.

For your worship to be genuine, it must be a voluntary act. Would you like your spouse to behave like a machine? As of the time of this writing, humans are experiencing with dolls. I don't think a doll will be able to satisfy a person's longing for true love. Similarly, God wants you to volunteer your worship. Choose to obey the word of Jesus so that you will never see death.

FEBRUARY 15

"Very truly I tell you, "Jesus answered, "Before Abraham was born, I am!" – John 8:58 NIV

When we try to understand God from a natural standpoint, we tend to get confused. God cannot be figured out. We are limited to a four-dimensional world: width, breadth, height, and time. We can only perceive three of the four dimensions.

When it comes to time, we don't have much control over it. Our minds cannot fully understand a timeless reality, where everything operates in the present.

With God, there is neither a past reality nor a future reality. In God's mind, the concept of time does not exist as we perceive it. Over the years, mathematicians have made tremendous progress in quantum mechanics. Nonetheless, there is so much to learn about the universe. It is not possible for us to explain the origin of God, because in order to do that, we must refer to a time reference, something that does not exist from the vintage point of eternity. Perhaps you may think of eternity as a parallel universe that is operated by unknown laws of physics. Whatever the case may be, this is an experience that is beyond our current cognitive ability.

God, being the Creator of the universe, knows everything there is to know. There is no future for Him. He knows you before you were born, and He has complete control over your destiny. Jesus uses the present tense of the verb to speak about His existence. "Before Abraham was born, I am." Allow God to figure out your destiny. Do what you can today. God will take care of your tomorrow if you put your faith and trust in Him.

FEBRUARY 16

"He replied, "Whether he is a sinner or not, I don't know. One thing I do know. I was blind but now I see!" – John 9:25 NIV

*I*t is one thing for someone to tell you about God. It is another thing when you have an encounter with Him. Until then, your experience with God is not real.

For your testimony to be convincing, you must have your own experience with Yahweh, the true God. You cannot experience God through your family. Salvation is a personal experience, not a collective one.

The man who was born blind had a real encounter. His parents couldn't convince the Pharisees of the fact that their son was born blind. The man's testimony was very persuasive! Basically, he told the Pharisees, I don't care if you doubt Jesus' power to heal. I know for fact that He healed me because I can now see.

The most powerful testimony you can share with people who are not Christ's followers is to let them know about what God has done for you. You don't need to argue about the existence of God, for God can defend Himself. If your God has not done anything remarkable in your life, you will certainly have a hard time persuading other to put their faith in Him.

Just like the young blind man, I was spiritually blind because I did not know Jesus as my Lord and Savior. Now I know Jesus Christ is my Lord and Savior. I hope you too have your own experience with Jesus.

FEBRUARY 17

"I am the gate; whoever enters through me will be saved. They will come in and go out, and find pasture. The thief comes only to steal and kill and destroy; I have come that they may have life, and have it to the full." – John 10:9 and 10 NIV

*T*he battle between good and evil is real. Satan's goal is to thwart God's ultimate plan by luring people into the wrong path. Satan knows God's solution to sin because he had been with God prior to his fall. He knows that he has lost the battle, but he is trying to fight until the end.

The path to eternal life is through Jesus Christ. God sent Jesus Christ into the world to seek and save the lost. No one can be reconciled with the Heavenly Father without going through Jesus. The truth is that we have been separated from God due to the fall of Adam and Eve. Since Jesus Christ is the substitute for Adam, we must accept His ultimate sacrifice on the cross of Calvary to regain our spiritual footing.

The thief is Satan, God's main adversary. He has three objectives in mind: steal, kill, and destroy. We need to be wise so that we do not allow the enemy to hoodwink us.

Although Satan is not the true shepherd, he poses as one, so be very careful. He is an impostor, a fake shepherd.

The truth is that people cannot enter heaven through the devil's gate. The devil's gate leads to eternal punishment. Conversely, those who enter through Jesus' gate will be saved, and they will not have to face eternal death. They will be spared from God's wrath.

FEBRUARY 18

"Jesus said to her, "I am the resurrection and the life. The one who believes in me will live, even though they die; and whoever lives by believing in me will never die. Do you believe this?" – John 11:25 and 26 NIV

As you search for wisdom, I hope you will discover that there is more to life than what you are currently experiencing on this planet. This life is only a foretaste of what is to come. The real life is hidden in Jesus Christ.

If you have surrendered yourself to Jesus, you don't have to worry about anything. Continue to live your life as you wait for the day when you will leave this earth.

Jesus makes it very clear in those two verses that you have nothing to fear. In fact, you have His guarantee that you will not see death. Here, Jesus is referring to eternal death reserved for those who have refused to believe in Him as their Lord and Savior.

Keep in mind that God can forgive all sins, but there is one thing God is not willing to do. If you die without accepting Jesus as your Lord and Savior, there is no more sacrifice left for you. The death of Jesus on the cross of Calvary was God's greatest sacrifice for humanity.

You cannot be forgiven without Jesus' shed blood. If you confess your sins, God will forgive you if you have put your faith in Jesus. The solution is to believe in Jesus. If you have not accepted Jesus as your Lord and Savior, consider doing so this moment. If Jesus is your Lord and Savior, rejoice. You have nothing to fear. Your name is written in the Lamb's book of life.

FEBRUARY 19

"Then Jesus cried out, "Whoever believes in me does not believe in me only, but in the one who sent me." – John 12:44 NIV

Jesus represents God, the Father. There should be no confusion between God and Jesus. Jesus is God. He and the Father are one.

People often confuse the idea of trinity, or God in three persons. In the Godhead, you have the Father, the Son, and the Holy Spirit. They are co-equal. You cannot have one without the other. If you have the Son, you have the Father. Similarly, if you know the Son, you know the Father.

The fundamental truth about Jesus is that He is the sacrificial Lamb, the One who can save us. Jesus' mission was very specific in that He came to seek and save the lost (Luke 19:10).

If you want to make peace with the Father, you must accept Jesus. You cannot be forgiven without His shed blood. This is what makes Christianity so different from the world's regions. Religions present you with a list of things you must do in order to be acceptable to God. God in Jesus accepts you just as you are, and His gift is free of charge.

When it comes to eternal life, you only need to accept the gift. You are not required to pay for your sins through your good deeds. Yes, you should produce good works after you have received Jesus, but such good deeds will not enable you to enter heaven. The only way to heaven is by faith in Jesus Christ and through grace.

FEBRUARY 20

"A new command I give you: Love one another. As I have loved you, so you must love one another." – John 13:34 NIV

Have you ever wondered how much you should love others? Jesus gives us a pretty good idea about how much we need to love others. How much do you think Jesus loves you? Try and put yourself in Jesus' shoes for a few minutes. Jesus is God, but He decided to put His Deity aside to take upon Himself the sins of humanity. Can you imagine for a few minutes how humiliating it was for Jesus to become human? The Bible says that human is a little lower than an angel. A good human example is a prince or a king that decided to become a common person. That means the king must lay aside his throne, crown, and all the privileges that come with his kingship. Jesus did a whole lot more than an earthly king who decided to abdicate his throne in order to come to our rescue. I said all of this to explain the depth of Jesus' love for us. He truly loves us.

We too should demonstrate similar love for others. Jesus gives us a new command. Yes, the Bible contains the Ten Commandments in Exodus 20. Jesus did not say that those commands are null and void. What He was saying was that we need to love others as He loves us, as a measure of our commitment to Him.

If you think about it for a second, love summarizes all the Ten Commandments. We will not kill others or steal from others if we genuinely love them. All these wars around the world would cease automatically if love were to become the focus in everything we do.

FEBRUARY 21

"Do not let your hearts be troubled. You believe in God; believe also in me." – John 14:1 NIV

*O*ne thing that distinguishes believers from non-believers is the way they conduct themselves in times of adversity. Believers tend to go to God in prayers seeking comfort and wisdom instead of despair. Keep in mind that believers are not exempt from problems.

Jesus reminds us to believe in God. He also reminds us to believe in Him. There is a reason for the second reminder. Jesus said in verse 6 of this same chapter that He is the "way and the truth and the life." It is not enough to say that we believe in God in general. The essential is to base our belief in God through what Jesus did on the cross. Everything rises and falls on Jesus' birth, death, and resurrection. It is our faith in Jesus and the grace of God that save us.

When we place our faith solidly in God based on what Jesus did for us, we have no fear of what tomorrow may bring. The traumatic things that occur in this dangerous world do not faze us. They have no bearing on our heavenly focus. Yes, we are not exempt from physical pain. Nonetheless, we are neither hopeless nor helpless. Our hope is in God, and our help is from Him. We know He will never abandon us, no matter what.

From time to time, our eyes and hearts may remind us of our trouble, but our spirits will remain steadfast through our faith in God's wonderful promises.

FEBRUARY 22

"If you love me, keep my commands." – John 14:15 NIV

Although Christianity is not based on our performance, we know that Christians should live their lives in such a way that they can attract others to Christ. Keeping Christ's commands is based on a single condition. It is hinged on love.

Because God did not create us to function as a machine, we have certain freedom to do what we want. Worshiping is part of the freedom God gave us.

One day I was having a conversation about Jesus with a young man. He asked me: "Why did God create us if He had known long before creation that we were bound to self-destruction?" I turned around and asked him, "How good do you think it will feel if your wife only tells you she loves you only when you force her to do so?"

You see, it is the same with God. For our love for God to be worth something, it must be voluntary, not forced. Yes, it hurts God to watch us destroying ourselves when He could stop us in a second. As the saying goes, "You can't have your cake and eat it too."

If we want to have the freedom of choice, we must be willing to accept the ultimate consequences. Sometimes, the consequences come instantly, especially when we are caught breaking the law. Sometimes, the consequences are delayed.

When you are faced with temptation, put your love of Jesus to the test. I am not saying that you are not capable of sinning, for that would be a lie. However, your love for Jesus should remind you why you choose to suffer for Him.

FEBRUARY 23

"Peace I leave with you; my peace I give you. I do not give to you as the world gives. Do not let your hearts be troubled and do not be afraid." – John 14:27 NIV

As Jesus was preparing to accomplish His mission on earth, He began to comfort His disciples, because He knew life on earth would be tough. He spoke to them about the coming of the Holy Spirit that would be with them permanently. The Holy Spirit plays an important role in our daily spiritual support system and our victory over the adversary.

Jesus came to bring us spiritual peace. While world peace is important, we know that it is not achievable given the multiple hot spots around the world. Jesus wants us to know that world's peace is not the same as His. He reminds us again not to let our hearts be troubled.

The enemy often puts fear in our hearts. We need to pray for protection from fear. It does not matter the daily threats we receive from Satan. We know that he does not have the last word. Amid the storm, we know that the Holy Spirit is with us. Therefore, we know God is with us through the Holy Spirit.

Jesus gives us His peace by way of salvation. Knowing where we are going to spend eternity is key because such knowledge can help us deal with fear and life's uncertainties.

FEBRUARY 24

"If you remain in me in my words remain in you, ask whatever you wish, and it will be done for you." – John 15:7 NIV

*I*mage yourself operating at a spiritual dimension, where you become at one with God. At that level, you are no longer operating according to the demands of the flesh. Although you are living in a physical body, your actions are divinely guided. The guidance we need is found in Jesus' words and the assistance of the Holy Spirit. This is not impossible, because we have a spiritual component in us.

Does that mean that you are perfect? If perfection means sinless, then the answer is no. Perfection for God is viewed through Jesus. It is never yours in the first place. In this case, Jesus is saying if you live your life based on His guidance, when you pray for something you will get it. Why? It will be possible because what you wish will be something that God wishes. When there is spiritual harmony between you and Jesus, you are now operating in the realm of possibility, not impossibility.

When we pray outside of the will of God, there is no spiritual harmony. We often pray for things that are not aligned with what God wants for us.

Jesus wants us to align our lives with Him by remaining in Him so that the desires of our hearts can be in sync with His desires. Miracles happen when this kind of spiritual harmony is present.

FEBRUARY 25

"Until now you have not asked for anything in my name. Ask and you will receive, and your joy will be complete." – John 16:24 NIV

*I*n this verse, Jesus revealed the key to effective Christian prayers. I have a lot respect for Virgin Mary for her obedience to God and the honor God has bestowed upon her to have been chosen to be the earthly mother of Jesus. However, we should not pray in her name. Similarly, we should not pray in the names of Saint Peter, Saint Paul, Saint Thomas, or any other Saints. We are recommended to pray in the name of Jesus.

When we pray in the name of Jesus, the Heavenly Father hears us based on what Jesus did on the cross of Calvary for us. Jesus is the bridge that connects us with God. Without Jesus, we are completely separated from God. The death and resurrection of Jesus made it possible for us to receive forgiveness. That's why it makes sense for us to approach the Heavenly Father through Jesus Christ.

When we come to the Heavenly Father in the name of Jesus, the Son, we are telling Him that we have accepted the sacrifice He made for us. Jesus is the expression of God's love for humanity.

In the Old Testament, the Israelites could not approach God without the sacrificial blood. Similarly, we can't come to God in any other name but Jesus. Without Jesus, our prayers are simply unacceptable. Therefore, let us come boldly before the Heavenly Father in the name of Jesus, our Savior.

FEBRUARY 26

"Now this is eternal life: that they know you, the only true God, and Jesus Christ, whom you have sent." – John 17:3 NIV

I do not know your heart's desires or your life's aspirations. One thing I do know, however, is that eternal life should be the number one goal of us all. Frankly, I cannot think of anything that is more valuable than the hope of spending eternity with the Creator of the universe.

If you have any lingering doubt about eternal life, know that it consists of the genuine knowledge of the Father as well as Jesus, the ultimate gift from the Father Himself. Now, keep in mind that we cannot have access to the Father without the Son of God – Jesus Christ. This is where most people get confused. They think it is okay to ignore Jesus in their quest for eternal life. It is simply impossible.

As Jesus was about to finish His mission, He prayed that we know the Father, the only true God as well as Jesus Christ. If you surrender your life to God by accepting His gift of salvation through Jesus, you have eternal life. If you have not, then I invite you to make this important decision this minute. You will never regret it.

May you continue to pursue God on your journey through life, for there is nothing in this world that is more important than the acquisition of eternal life through Jesus Christ, the Savior of the world.

FEBRUARY 27

"Jesus said, "My kingdom is not of this world. If it were, my servants would fight to prevent my arrest by the Jewish leaders. But now my kingdom is from another place." – John 18:36 NIV

Despite numerous prophecies about the birth of Christ, the Israelites did not fully understand the spiritual dimension of God's plan for humanity. They were basically looking for a king that would come to deliver them from the Roman yoke of slavery. However, God, in his sovereignty, was not thinking about an earthly kingdom. He had a greater purpose for humanity. Sometimes, we want a quick fix for our problems.

The disruption caused by the fall of Adam and Eve needed a more drastic solution, not just a simple change in a government system. We should not be surprised to hear Jesus talk about His kingdom, because He is the King of kings.

For God to establish His kingdom on earth, the current system must be changed from a natural environment to a spiritual one. God will replace this earth with a new one so that His kingdom will take full control of the universe.

When God's kingdom is fully established on the new earth, evil will disappear, and Satan will not have any authority over the new kingdom. Jesus Christ, the Savior of the world, will be in control. This will be the final demonstration, the outcome of everything God has been working on since the beginning of the process to restore order into the universe.

FEBRUARY 28

"Then he said to Thomas, "Put your finger here; see my hands. Reach out your hand and put it into my side. Stop doubting and believe." – John 20:27 NIV

*I*n John 19, we read about the crucifixion, death, and the burial of Jesus. In this verse, we read about Jesus' victory over the grave, how God raised Him from the dead.

Christ's resurrection was not a symbolic victory. This was God's complete triumph over the entire system. Christ's resurrection marked the beginning and the end of the kingdom of darkness. With this stunning victory, we now have hope. We too will be able to overcome death in the end.

Amid news of the resurrection of Jesus was the problem of unbelief among the people. Even though Jesus had demonstrated His power over death when He raised Lazarus from the dead, Thomas was one of those who were reluctant to believe the news.

Today people continue to doubt the resurrection of Jesus, His power to forgive sins and grant eternal life to those who believe. Jesus wants everyone to know that He is alive. He invites us to believe Him instead of doubting.

In order to receive eternal life, we must believe in the birth, death, and resurrection of Jesus. These three elements are the bedrock of Christianity.

Because Jesus triumphed over death, we too will triumph over death. In fact, the whole idea of believing in Jesus is to ensure that we are prepared for eternity. Let us believe in the power of Jesus to save us.

FEBRUARY 29

"Jesus did many other things as well. If every one of them were written down, I suppose that even the whole world would not have room for the books that would be written." – John 21:25 NIV

Since you only get to read this passage every four years, I would like you to take this opportunity to reflect on this month's devotions. The Gospel of John is somewhat different in that it keeps the focus on Jesus as the Son of God. Unlike Matthew, Mark, and Luke who put the emphasis on Jesus, the Son of Man, or the humanity of Jesus, John wants us to see Jesus as the Son of God, the Messiah.

It was important for God to send us the Messiah because we needed someone who would point us to the truth about God, and no one was in a better position to do so than the Son of God.

In the Gospel of John, Jesus made it clear to us that He is the One. Jesus was with His Father before the beginning. He said, "Before Abraham was born, I AM" (John 8:58 NIV).

The question of time is not a factor with Jesus. We can put our trust completely in Him because He knows everything about us. We cannot keep any secret from Him, because He knows it all.

The essential factor is that Jesus is the way, the truth and the life. If we believe this absolute truth, we have everything we need to know for eternal life. We just need to believe in Him.

MARCH 1

"For the Lord watches over the way of the righteous, but the way of the wicked leads to destruction." – Psalm 1:6 NIV

When we choose to walk on the path of righteousness, the Almighty God watches over us. This type of protection is not earned; it is freely given because it is based on God's divine plan. The requirement for God's protection is based on our knowledge of God's provision and our willingness to accept God's gift.

God's gift of salvation is clearly demonstrated in Jesus. God sent His Son to die on the cross for our sins. Jesus' death and resurrection have paid for our passage to eternity. The Holy Spirit speaks to our conscience and shows us the necessity to turn to God. Once we have become aware of God's solution to sin and have been drawn by the Holy Spirit, we are now responsible for our destiny. We cannot say that we do not know about Jesus Christ.

Although God provides salvation freely, some of us will not make it to heaven. We can choose to believe in Jesus or continue to ignore all about God and His plan for salvation. By doing that, we opt for the path of the wicked and punishment God has determined for the wicked.

The way of the wicked leads to destruction because it is not protected by God. There is no protection outside of God's will. God knows us and everything about us, but He has chosen not to encroach on our freedom. This is the way God meant to deal with us.

MARCH 2

"Serve the Lord with fear and celebrate his rule with trembling."
– Psalm 2:11 NIV

*I*f we were to stop and meditate on God's sovereignty for a few minutes, we would conclude that the Almighty God is able to do amazing things. We would marvel at His sheer power and might as well as His unlimited knowledge. In addition, we would quickly come to the realization that He has the final word.

In the Old Testament, God was viewed as the God of vengeance, and the Israelites had experienced His wrath firsthand, shortly after their exodus from Egypt. God demonstrated His fierce anger, and about three thousand of the people died because of their involvement in the worship of an idol, the golden calf (Exodus 32:28).

In the New Testament, God is seen as the God of mercy, who pardons the sins of those who repent. Yes, there is no need to tremble the way the Israelites did. Nonetheless, we need to know that God does not condone sins. As a matter of fact, God wants to put an end to sin by sending Jesus to eliminate, once and for all, the root cause of sin. God wants to give us a new heart, a new future, and a new dwelling place, where there will be no place for sin.

Considering God's mercy, we can now approach God with confidence instead of fear and trembling. Jesus made it all possible by His shed blood. Let us serve the Lord with Joy and a sense of gratitude for His compassion and grace.

MARCH 3

"From the LORD comes deliverance. May your blessings be on your people." – Psalm 3:8 NIV

David knew a thing or two about the need for deliverance. From an early age, he learned how to overcome personal adversities. He had faced Goliath, the scary giant. Even after he had conquered Goliath, Saul, his own father in-law wanted to kill him.

Whatever is the source of your menace, God alone can deliver you from it. God brings lasting peace. When you think about God, think about the eternal aspect of His deliverance, albeit the importance of your current situations.

Deliverance from sin remains one of our most important needs in life. This is a problem that we cannot overcome on our own. David was a king, which means that he could do whatever he wanted; yet he concluded that he was powerless. He was running from his own son, Absalom.

What do we do when we are unable to help ourselves? The answer is Jesus. God can make a way where there is no way. Reliance on God does not mean inaction. It simply means that we know He is in control of our circumstances.

We should do whatever we can to run from danger, without losing sight of our real Protector, just like David. Yahweh is in control, no matter what. His blessings are available to us through Jesus.

We have something that the Old Testament folks did not have. We have God's grace. We also have His mercies, which are new every morning.

MARCH 4

"In peace I will lie down and sleep, for you alone, LORD, make me dwell in safety." – Psalm 4:8 NIV

Yes, you are living in a very dangerous world. The wicked are working arduously to inflict the maximum amount of pain on you. Therefore, you should pray this prayer before you go to bed, because you need the firm assurance that the Almighty God is watching over you.

Even in your sleep, Satan may try to attack you. It is important that you pray and seek the Lord daily. Ask God to protect you from your foes. The enemy knows that you are a spirit living in a body. He knows that he can affect you while you are sleeping if God is not with you.

Be cautious so that you do not willfully give Satan an inroad in your life. When God oversees your security, you are safe indeed. The adversary may try to reach you, but God will not allow anything to touch you without His permission.

In our frailties, we often want to know where God was when this or that was happening to us. However, God in His sovereignty has power over everything.

If something occurs to us, it is not because God is incapable or absent. We may not understand the circumstances of our sufferings, but God does know.

Again, it is important that we understand that nothing can happen to us without God's permission. A very good example is Job's personal adversities and the traumas he had to endure in his family as well as in his own body. At the end of his pain and losses, God restored him and blessed him beyond measure.

MARCH 5

"Hear my cry for help, my King and my God, for to you I pray." – Psalm 5:2 NIV

*I*f you have chosen to surrender yourself to God, you can unashamedly approach Him with full confidence when you need Him. David, a person of authority, a king himself, knew who oversaw his life. He acknowledged his King and his God. He knew that the Almighty is the King of kings.

It does not matter how prestigious your position is in society, you must know whose you are. Without such important knowledge, you are basically in a spiritual crisis. A key insight from this verse is that we should turn only to God in prayer. God is our source of refuge in times of trouble.

In order to speak with God, like David did, you must have a relationship with Him first. If you are an outsider, you do not have any right to address God in this manner. You can still call on God for salvation, however.

In the New Testament, Jesus invites us to pray to God in His name. Jesus' sacrifice on the cross has opened a new way to approach God. If you have accepted Jesus as your Lord and Savior, you can now approach God boldly in the name of Jesus.

Discovering Jesus is discovering the fountain of wisdom. The world may not understand the value of knowing God, but there is nothing that is more precious than knowing where you will spend eternity. Call upon the LORD, your King and your God because He alone can hear your cry for help.

MARCH 6

"The Lord has heard my cry for mercy; the Lord accepts my prayer." – Psalm 6:9 NIV

After David had pleaded for mercy, he was relieved to know that God has heard his cry. How beautiful it is to know that God has heard us, especially when we are going through trials.

One thing we need to know is that God is merciful and is ready to forgive us if we are willing to come to Him. The Heavenly Father has shown His mercy when He decided to send Jesus to die in our place. We should not be reluctant to call on God in Jesus' name in times of distress, for God is our source of refuge.

People often turn to illicit drugs or alcohol for solace. God should be our first choice. A few days before I wrote this passage, I was on a plane to Orlando from Dallas Fort Worth. Shortly after take-off, the plane went through some very bad turbulence. The young man who was sitting on my right was very scared. He started cursing using four-letter words. Conversely, my wife was calling on the name of Jesus on my left. She was saying, "Have mercy Lord!" "Help the pilot stabilize the plane." Suddenly, the plane stopped shaking, and everything was calm again.

God oversees all your life's circumstances. You can call on Him any time. God has provided you with free access to His throne in the name of Jesus. You don't need a go-between to reach out to God. You can call on Him right now.

MARCH 7

"I will give thanks to the Lord because of his righteousness; I will sing the praises of the name of the Lord Most High." – Psalm 7:17 NIV

There are many reasons for which we should give glory to God. For instance, we should thank God for His grace and mercy. It takes grace and mercy for God to reverse the eternal punishment that we deserved. Given the gravity of our disobedience, the chaos our sins have generated in the universe, and the filthiness of our sinful nature, Hell was what we truly deserved. But God demonstrated His love toward us by paying for us with the blood of His Son.

In addition to the above blessings, the main reason we should glorify God is for Who He is. God created us to bring glory to Himself. We are the object of His praise. God takes pleasure in us when we acknowledge His sovereignty. God knows everything about us, and nothing is hidden from Him.

David's praise is focused on God's righteousness. God has done everything right, and no one can find fault in Him. He is a perfect God in every sense of the word.

David also praised God for His name. The name of the Lord is powerful. Even in the natural realm, if a person is very influential, his or her name means something. If you know someone who is very important, you may consider using his or her name as one of your references. God's name gets things done. Satan knows how powerful God's name is. When we confront Satan in the name of Jesus, he must flee.

MARCH 8

"Lord, our Lord, how majestic is your name in all the earth!" – Psalm 8:1 NIV

*J*ust as David marveled at God's name, so should we stand in awe of His name. In Psalm 7 David praised God for His righteousness. In this verse, he contemplated God's majestic name by bragging about God's popularity and His vast array of power upon the entire universe. When we imagine what God can do, it is a miracle that God even thinks about us.

Considering such knowledge of God's greatness and majestic power that lies in His name, we should not take God's compassion and love for granted. We should show our gratitude to God by glorifying his name and make Him known as much as we can and every time, we have a chance.

God created the universe and everything that is in it. Scientists may not agree about the origin of the universe, but the Scripture says that God is the Creator. We have a decision to make. Are we going to believe the Holy Bible?

Despite God's greatness, He still pays attention to our needs. Although God created angels to be slightly higher than us, God does not see our inferiority to His angelic beings as a reason to forget about us humans. On the contrary, He took it upon Himself to rescue us despite our stubbornness. His response is marvelous! He sent His Son, Jesus, to die for us. How majestic is your name, our Lord!

MARCH 9

"I will give thanks to you, LORD, with all my heart; I will tell of all your wonderful deeds." – Psalm 9:1 NIV

*F*or the past two days, you have had a chance to focus on God for Who He is. You have been meditating on God, just like David did. Think for a few moments how often we allow our minds to forget about all the worries of this world.

We are so busy working; we hardly have time to meditate on God and His goodness. Despite our hectic schedules, it is important that we find time to praise Him, and we must do it with all our hearts.

Our hearts belong to God. When we allow God to have first place in our lives, we can experience God's majestic power.

It is not enough for us to praise God with all our hearts; we also need to find the opportunity to tell others about God's deeds. What has God done for you?

Think about the opportunity to breathe with ease. The fact that you can breathe is a huge blessing! Allow your mind to take pleasure in knowing God.

Meditate on God's grace. Meditate on God's mercies and His love for you. God will not forsake you nor will He abandon you. He loves you so much!

Reach out to others with confidence and tell them about all God has done for you.

MARCH 10

"Why, LORD, do you stand far off? Why do you hide yourself in times of trouble?" – Psalm 10:1 NIV

Sometimes, we might think God is absent when we observe what the wicked are doing in society. This is the way we tend to feel. We, humans, are limited in knowledge and foresight, so we are not able to perceive the full scope of God's plans.

Although our enemies may win some battles, God is always in control of the war. Because of God's sovereignty, it is impossible for Him to lose control. What we need to know is that God chooses the hour of His intervention.

Why did David react this way about the perceived victory of the wicked? In order to understand David's emotional reactions, we must put ourselves in his shoes. David was not different than us. If we had been in his place, our reactions would have been the same.

When it comes to the enemies, God will deal with them in due time. Satan knows that his time is up. In the meantime, he is trying everything in his limited power to cause as much trouble as he can.

In the end, God will have the upper hand. Satan, with all his followers, will be destroyed. Therefore, we do not have to lose heart when we witness Satan's temporary success. God will never allow Satan to win in the end. The mere fact that Jesus resurrected from the dead, God has squarely won the war, so rejoice in the Lord!

MARCH 11

"When the foundations are being destroyed, what can the righteous do?" – Psalm 11:3 NIV

When we observe the public displays of godlessness in this world, we are wondering what has happened to the foundations of our faith. Today the voice of the Church of Jesus Christ is being drowned by the noise of the wicked.

As time goes on, we are seeing the boldness of Satan in every aspect of life. Some local churches no longer uphold the absolute truth, and Scripture is being reinterpreted to please the desires of the flesh.

What can the righteous do as Satan is trying to silence the Church? I believe it is time for the Church of Jesus Christ to lift the standard of righteousness and assert the absolute truth about Jesus. It is also time for the Church to ask God for wisdom in order to discern what is going on in the world and uncover the dirty tricks of Satan.

Our foundations are laid on the absolute truths found in the Holy Bible, with Jesus Christ as the cornerstone. Jesus came, died on the cross for our sins, and God raised Him from the dead on the third day, and He is alive forevermore. This is the truth we need to continue to uphold.

David did not have a chance to experience victory in Jesus. Today our foundations are firmer because of Jesus Christ's victory on the cross. For that very reason, we do not have to be afraid of Satan's continued attacks because he cannot destroy the cornerstone upon which the Church is built. The foundations of the Church of Jesus Christ are super solid.

MARCH 12

"And the words of the Lord are flawless, like silver purified in a crucible, like gold refined seven times." – Psalm 12:6 NIV

*B*efore you can have silver and gold, you must dig for nuggets or lumps of valuable metal or mineral that is found in the earth or a gold mine. A crucible is a pot used to burn the dross from the gold nuggets. This process is designed to purify or refine the nuggets to turn them into gold bullion or gold bars. This precious metal can be used to create all kinds of costly items.

David compared the words of God to gold and silver because gold and silver are flawless. The refining process does not allow flaws to exist in the nuggets, because it eliminates them through fire. Just like gold and silver have gone through a refinery process, God's words have gone through the test of time. The Bible has been a bestseller for many generations. There are no flaws in God's overall message.

Since God's words are flawless, we need to find out what God has promised us. It is also important that we understand the guidelines found in the Bible, especially what we need to know about eternal life.

Through the Bible, God wants us to know that He loves us so much that He sent Jesus to die in our place. By believing in Jesus, we have eternal life. With the hope of eternal life, we know that we will spend eternity with God in the New Jerusalem.

MARCH 13

"But I trust in your unfailing love; my heart rejoices in your salvation." – Psalm 13:5 NIV

God's love for us will endure forever. God's love does not depend on our own efforts; it is unconditional. The Bible says that God loved us so much. And He has shown His love for us by sending Jesus to die on the cross for us.

God did not send Jesus to die for us based on our goodness. In fact, we did everything to show God that we have nothing good in us. We rejected God's guidelines for holy living. When God realized that the world was in a downward-spiral, in His divine counsel, He concluded that the solution was to provide a way out for humanity to become reconciled with Him through a redemptive process. He bought us back.

Because God's love is not based on our own efforts, He does not need our help to maintain it. If God can maintain His love commitment toward us, then His love is unfailing.

Salvation belongs to God. Salvation is found in no one else. Jesus is the source of salvation. If you put your faith in Jesus by accepting His solution to sin, you can rejoice in the fact that your future is secured.

When the time has come for you to travel to eternity, you can go with confidence. You will be able to face God by faith through grace in the Lord Jesus Christ, the Savior.

MARCH 14

"The fool says in his heart, "There is no God." They are corrupt, their deeds are vile; there is no one who does good." – Psalm 14:1 NIV

*I*n your search for wisdom, I hope you have already discovered that God is in the center of life. Life without God is like a ship without a captain. And a ship without a captain cannot reach its destination. It will simply drift to destruction.

The fool who concludes that God is not in control of the universe is on his or her sure path to destruction.

People who deny the existence of God act without restraints. They behave like there is no tomorrow. They think they rule the world and that no one can ever stop them in their wickedness. Make no mistake about it. God controls the universe and everything that is in it.

As you read this verse, allow the Holy Spirit to draw you closer to God. Don't allow Satan to deceive you into believing that there is no God. Your very life depends on God. And when the dust has settled, God will call you into account.

Remember God loves you so much that He sent Jesus to die in your place. As you surrender your life to God, He will continue to guide your steps. Your future is secured in God. When you leave this earth, you can be sure that you will not be alone. You will triumph beyond the grave because the Holy Spirit dwells in you and will be with you forever.

MARCH 15

"LORD, who may dwell in your sacred tent? Who may live on your holy mountain?" – Psalm 15: 1 NIV

Sometimes, the best way to come to our senses is to ask some thought-provoking questions. Seriously, will we ever be ready on our own to dwell in God's presence? Will God allow us to face Him based on our own righteousness? The answers to those questions are obvious. We are not prepared to face God in our own strengths. We will always need God's help.

It does not matter how good you are. I understand that some people are simply wicked. They are full of wickedness and hatred. However, the fact that you are not like those evil people, that does not make you ready to live in eternity. You still need God's grace.

God knew it was impossible to meet those requirements. That's why He sent Jesus. Jesus had a very specific mission. He came to set the captive free (Luke 4:18 and 19).

Everyone who is living outside of God's will is a captive. The day you surrender your soul to God through Jesus, you become a free person. Satan no longer has access to your spirit. Satan may try to attack your body, but your spirit is not accessible to him. God will not allow Satan to attain you. You are in God's hands forever (John 10: 28).

The fact that you are being attacked daily is proof that you belong to God. You and God have a common enemy, and his name is Satan.

MARCH 16

"Keep me safe, my God, for in you I take refuge." – Psalm 16:1 NIV

One thing you can be sure of is that God will be there when you need Him if you have made Him your refuge. A refuge is designed to keep people safe from danger. The refuge contains safe places, where the enemy cannot penetrate.

When a country is in war, its people tend to leave the war zone to find a place to live. Sometimes, people leave their homeland altogether. Refugees are protected by international laws. While they are living in the refugee camp or have been granted refugee status, they are protected.

God is our refuge. Our enemy is Satan, and he would like to destroy us. If we are not with God, Satan can do whatever he wants with us. Many people have fallen in the trap of Satan, and they have a hard time getting out without a breakthrough from God.

Be careful not to allow the enemy to take over your life. God wants you to be free, so don't allow Satan to have access to your life, your family, and your business. Pray and ask God to protect you every day.

If you trust in God to protect you, don't try to have contact with Satan. If you do that, you will open the door to the enemy to grab hold of your soul.

Serve God wholeheartedly. Don't serve God nonchalantly. You are either in or out. You cannot serve God and the devil at the same time. Be like David. Say to God that He is your refuge.

MARCH 17

"Though people tried to bribe me, I have kept myself from the ways of the violent through what your lips have commanded." – Psalm 17:4 NIV

*B*ecause you are living in a sinful world, you can sin. As a matter of fact, you do not have to make any effort to do what is wrong. You can do bad things naturally.

Although it is hard to live a life of integrity, you should strive to live your life in such a way that God can receive praise and honor through your lifestyle.

Remember as a Christian you are the temple of the Holy Spirit. God lives in you through the Holy Spirit, even though you may not always feel His presence.

David depended on God's words. What God has commanded you to do is found in His words. Spend time learning about God's precepts. If you are serious about seeking wisdom, you would want to spend time reading the Bible. You may find it useful to read the entire chapter where this key verse was taken.

This devotion is designed to keep your mind on God daily, but it is not a replacement for your in-depth Bible reading.

Therefore, take time to read the Bible and meditate on God's words daily.

MARCH 18

"The LORD is my rock, my fortress and my deliverer; my God is my rock, in whom I take refuge, my shield and the horn of my salvation, my stronghold." – Psalm 18:2 NIV

David knew that he could totally trust in God in times of danger. He has experienced God's power throughout his life. From the moment David joined in the service of the Lord to his actual acceptance in Saul's household, the enemy was there trying to thwart his dreams. In fact, the enemy was trying to eliminate him altogether.

When you decide to surrender yourself to the Lord, you instantly become a target for Satan's persecutions. Since Satan is not in God's camp, he hates everything that belongs to God. In this connection, you need to depend on God's daily protection.

In battle, a shield keeps soldiers from taking bullets. You too need the shield of faith to protect you from the killing arrows the evil one throws at you every day. You are not immune from attacks, but when you do get attacked, God is there to protect you.

God has shown his interest in saving us, for we did not influence his grace. God decided to send the Deliverer despite our willful transgressions of His principles.

With God, salvation is made available to us. Some people will go to Hell because of their stubbornness, not because of a lack of space in eternity. There is room for everyone.

God is your rock. You can trust Him to protect you. You may call on Him any time in the name of Jesus.

MARCH 19

"The heavens declare the glory of God; the skies proclaim the work of his hands." – Psalm 19:1 NIV

When I contemplate the beautiful stars and the wonderful landscapes throughout the world, I am completely at awe of God's creative works. God possesses the power of imagination and creativity, and everything He created is wonderful.

If we fail to glorify God, nature will take our place. All the scientific studies about creation continue to display God's greatness. The more we probe the universe, the more we will discover God's magnificence. Whether we know it or not, we came from God and our lives find meaning through God.

As you search for wisdom, may your greatest discovery be your acknowledgement of God's handy works. When you come to the full realization that you are dead and your life is hidden in Christ, then you become a member in God's family.

The world in its pursuit of knowledge ignores the Creator by attributing creation to a random occurrence. People ignore the redemptive works of God and worship images or material possessions. But those who are wise know that God created them for His own glory.

Considering this verse, you should allow your life to be an object of God's praise. You were created to bring glory to God along with creation.

MARCH 20

"Some trust in chariots and some in horses, but we trust in the name of the Lord our God." – Psalm 20:7 NIV

Back then, people did not have tanks and war planes to fight. For that reason, horses were very valuable. Today we have stealth fighting jets and all kinds of nuclear weapons to wage wars. Nevertheless, we should not trust in our modern arsenals either.

The name of the Lord, especially the name of Jesus, is the most powerful weapon we have. In the name of Jesus, we can overcome unsurmountable obstacles.

The name of Jesus is a master key. It can open all locks. If you are looking for a solution for an impossible problem, your best bet is to turn to God. Not only can you trust God with your daily issues, you can also trust Him with your destiny. In fact, only God knows your destiny. You have no clue about your tomorrow. You can do everything to get ready for your life's journey, but the essential is to prepare for your eternal destiny by trusting God.

It does not matter what happens to you in the future, God will be there waiting for you. God already has your future under control. That's why He is the Almighty.

There is nothing that is hidden from the Sovereign God. Everything is in the open. Trust in the Lord with all your heart and surrender your worries to Him because He will not disappoint you.

MARCH 21

"Though they plot evil against you and devise wicked schemes, they cannot succeed." – Psalm 21:11 NIV

*I*t is useless to plot against the Sovereign God, for no one can attain Him. Likewise, if you make God your refuge, your enemies will not be able to reach you either. They can reach you only if God allows them, like in the case of Job. Rest assured. If God allows them to reach you, He has a higher purpose for you. Somehow, you will come out a winner.

When it comes to God, there cannot be losers. God always wins, even when He appears to be losing a battle. The crux of the matter is that God is always in control of the universe, no matter what.

In the natural, you may not be satisfied with the current situation, but you should never give up hope. Your assessment of things is different from God's assessment. When you see death, God sees it as a simple transition into eternity, where there is peace and joy from everlasting to everlasting.

You see, everything is clearly resolved in the spiritual realm because God is not limited by time. The notion of time does not exist in God's sphere. God can clearly see the beginning and the end of your daily struggle.

God is already in your future waiting for you. The idea of trusting God with your life simply means that you should not worry about anything. Everything is taken care of, from beginning to end. You have nothing to dread, because in God there is no surprise. The solutions to your problems are already there, so trust God.

MARCH 22

"All the ends of the earth will remember and turn to the LORD, and all the families of the nations will bow down before him, for dominion belongs to the Lord and he rules over the nations." – Psalm 22:27 and 28 NIV

$\mathcal{A}$s you search for wisdom, your intellect will continue to grapple with your spirit as to the relevance of your faith in God. You see, your spiritual journey is far deeper than your intellectual capacity. The whole idea of having faith in the first place is to be able to grasp supernatural truths. Regardless of the level of your education, you must try to live by faith if you would like to understand God.

In the final analysis, there will be a full revelation of knowledge. Right now, the four known dimensions of the universe will not allow you to grasp timelessness. Your mind has been trained to think limitedly, so it is difficult to even imagine the immense ability of the Almighty God in all His plenitude. That is why you need to exercise your measure of faith so you can connect with God.

Some People think that science is incompatible with God. Science showcases the omniscience of God. In your entire search for wisdom, know that every knee will bow before the Almighty God.

MARCH 23

"The LORD is my shepherd, I lack nothing." – Psalm 23:1 NIV

A shepherd's role is to ensure that the sheep have plenty to eat and drink. The shepherd must ensure that the sheep are safe as well.

In this world, there are so many things that could cause you to worry. Everywhere you go, you are trained to watch your back because you don't know who is about to harm you. The fear of the unknown tends to cause people to doubt their very future; however, when you think about the fact that Jesus Christ is your Shepherd, you have nothing to fear. You lack nothing.

Not having enough to eat is a big problem for certain people and nations. Poverty is causing a lot of sufferings around the world. In the natural realm, we are not promised that we will never lack anything but rest assured that God will never abandon you in life.

In the spiritual realm, God has all your needs under control. You don't have to worry about anything. I know it is easier said than done but try to trust God for all your needs.

One of your greatest needs is forgiveness- the *sine qua non* for salvation. If your sins are forgiven, you have everything. You see, you can't enter heaven if your sins are not forgiven. Jesus Christ, the Great Shepherd, came to resolve your sin issues.

Even though you walk through the valley of death, you have nothing to fear. Why? If you happen to die, God is waiting for you on the other side of the grave to welcome you to His presence.

MARCH 24

"The earth is the Lord's, and everything in it, the world, and all who live in it; for he founded it on the seas and established it on the waters." – Psalm 24:1 NIV

There are many arguments among those who believe in creationism, intelligent design, and natural selection or undirected evolution or big bang.

Those who believe in the Almighty God know that He is the Creator of the universe. I, for one, believe that God is the Creator of the universe. There is no way there could be so much order without a designer, and the intelligent designer is Yahweh, the true God.

Because I believe in science and the Bible, I know that the Bible was not designed to explain science. In the scientific realm, scientists conduct observations, hypothesize, and try to come up with ways to either prove or reject hypotheses.

If you take time to observe the universe, you will find out that everything is rather consistent. There is more order in the universe than there is disorder.

The Bible says that nature reveals the glory of God (Romans 1:20). If you look at creation and think, you will begin to see evidence to support the notion of an intelligent design. Of course, intelligent design has been rejected as pseudoscience or false science.

Whether you believe God or not, the time will come when you will encounter God. Be sure your encounter happens on this side of the universe. If it happens after death, it will be too late for you.

MARCH 25

"In you, LORD my God, I put my trust." – Psalm 25:1 NIV

As you search for wisdom, you will conclude that life without a solid faith in God is very shaky. One thing you should realize is that life is very short.

If you spend your life gathering only material possessions, in the end you will find out that you have not accomplished much. Your time down here will come to an end.

If you put your trust in the Lord, then you have something that will never end. You can now count on eternal life.

Eternal life opens a new way of looking at life. Now you no longer depend on your life on this planet. You now know that God oversees your future.

Your trust in God can help you in your approach to life. When you feel discouraged, you know you can come to God in prayer and ask Him for divine guidance. It is amazing how God can come alongside of you through the power of the Holy Spirit in moments of adversity.

In a world full of worries, trust in God to help you to keep your sanity. The enemy is working day and night to wreak havoc in our family, job, church, and government. If you put your trust in God, you can rest assured that things will be all right.

You may suffer for a while, but don't lose hope, for God will see you through if you don't give up. Therefore, make a firm decision to put your whole trust in God today.

MARCH 26

"Test me, LORD, and try me, examine my heart and my mind; for I have always been mindful of your unfailing love and have lived in reliance on your faithfulness." – Psalm 26: 2 and 3 NIV

As you trust in the Lord, your God, it is easy to be honest with God. This type of honest conversation with God requires a relationship with Him. If you don't have a relationship with God, you can invite Him into your life right now so He can be your LORD as well.

Since God knows all about you, you should feel comfortable telling Him everything. Before you were born, God knew you. He knows about your past, present, and future. There is nothing you can think about or do that has not already been known by God.

From time to time, it is good to ask God to examine you. At least once a year, most people in developed countries pay a visit to their primary care physicians. They want to be sure that everything is functioning well and that they don't have any physical ailments.

In the spiritual realm, you should visit with God about your spiritual life and life's journey. You want to be sure you are headed in the right direction and that nothing is keeping you from having a fruitful relationship with God.

One thing you should know is that God is faithful, even when you are unfaithful. In fact, God is the only constant in your life. Yes, you can rely on God as you journey through life. Your friends may give up on you, but God will remain faithful. He is always there when you need Him. Trust God with your whole life.

MARCH 27

"The LORD is my light and my salvation – whom shall I fear? The LORD is the stronghold of my life – of whom shall I be afraid?" – Psalm 27:1 NIV

When you feel insecure in life, it is okay to run to God for protection. The enemy enjoys darkness because it provides special cover for dirty tricks. Light is a huge deterrent to sinful acts because other people can see what is going on. If God is your light, then your life is safe.

Salvation provides a sense of peace and security. The only way you can be sure of your salvation is to surrender your life to God and ask that He forgive your sins by the blood of Jesus Christ. God sent Jesus to die for you so you can be sure of your salvation.

Although God is your light and salvation, the enemy is not going to leave you alone. In fact, you become a real target when you surrender your heart to the Lord. You need to be reminded from time to time that God is your stronghold.

When the devil comes to attack you, he must go through God in order to reach you. God cannot be defeated by Satan. There are times that Satan appears to be wining, but in the end, you will have final victory.

Don't allow Satan to trick you into believing that he will win. He has lost the battle when the Heavenly Father raised Jesus from the dead. Satan will never be able to recover from that loss. Don't be afraid of anything. God is with you.

MARCH 28

"To you, LORD, I call; you are my Rock, do not turn a deaf ear to me. For if you remain silent, I will be like those who go down to the pit." – Psalm 28:1 NIV

When all is dark and uncertain, your best place of refuge is to call on God, your LORD. Yes, you should do everything humanly possible to resolve the issues, but in order to maintain your balance, you need God's help. Trusting in God in times of distress will give you a sense of serenity.

Sometimes, things do not look promising at all. When your doctor tells you that you have cancer, your mind starts spinning ninety miles an hour. Even though you know there is a good chance you're going to kick that tumor, the thought of the opposite outcome can easily drag you into despair and depression.

See God as your rock. Those moments of intense trials will shake your spiritual foundations. Your faith in Christ will be tested in every sense of the word. Knowing that God will be there for you should give you a sense of stability. You need faith to sustain you. Faith will enable you to hope for physical restoration, even though the diagnosis sounds bleak.

Be honest with God. It is okay to be frank with to God. God knows about your doubt and fear. Revealing all your life's uncertainties to God is one way of saying that you are not keeping them to yourself.

Remember God knows all your needs before you come to Him with them. Let God know that you depend on Him for salvation and healing. Of course, God can use your doctor to treat you.

MARCH 29

"The LORD gives strength to his people; the LORD blesses his people with peace." – Psalm 29:11 NIV

There is no doubt that God makes it rain both on the garden of the wicked and that of the righteous, because He is a just God. However, God reserves special blessings for His people.

If you belong to the Lord, you should know that God knows about your daily activities. Your life is in God's hands and He knows your needs. When you come to the Lord in prayer, you acknowledge that you are His.

If you are lacking in strength, you can ask God to strengthen you. Special strengths come from the Lord, not from your material possessions or from your intellectual capacity.

One of the benefits God's children enjoy immensely is peace. Although they are not exempt from natural disasters, they are in a better position to manage fear and life's uncertainties if they put their trust in God. Though you don't know what tomorrow holds, you should know that God holds your tomorrow. And if God holds your tomorrow, you have nothing to worry about.

No matter what is going on around you, have peace that surpasses all understanding. You may not know about the outcome of your situation, but God will see to it that you are victorious in the end. Therefore, do not allow the enemy to steal your joy. Rejoice in God's strength and peace.

MARCH 30

"For his anger lasts only a moment, but his favor lasts a lifetime; weeping may stay for the night, but rejoicing comes in the morning." – Psalm 30:5 NIV

The good thing is that God is more prone to forgive us than to punish us. Despite our rebellious nature, God is ready to forgive us if we are willing to ask Him for forgiveness. Of course, God is not happy with our transgressions, because they anger Him. However, God is willing to forgive us right away. His anger does not last. Aren't you glad that God's favor lasts much longer than His anger?

When you pray today, ask God to grant you favor with everyone with whom you come in contact. If you have God's favor, you have everything you need in life. God's favor will cause even your enemies to help you.

Because you are a child of God, you have something that unbelievers do not have. Rely on God to come through for you after a night of agony.

You are not exempt from some nights of weeping, but you have hope that God will take care of you in the morning. You have assurance that God will never forsake nor abandon you.

If you are going through some tough moments right now, don't lose hope. Keep your hope in God, for His promises are certain, and His love for you is real. Your own family may reject you, but God will not leave you in the lurch. He will find a way to come to your rescue.

MARCH 31

"Be strong and take heart, all you who hope in the LORD." – Psalm 31:24 NIV

*I*t is perfectly fine to call on God in times of distress and cry out to Him for mercy and grace. Since you know that everything is wide open before God, you do not have to be afraid to discuss your problems with Him. When you are talking to God, tell Him what you are feeling.

While nonbelievers try to come up with their own solutions to their problems, believers involve God as they try to find solutions to their problems. They know that they should not lose heart in the process.

As a witness for God, it is important that you give God a chance to display His power through you so that unbelievers will be able to see Him at work in your life. Be strong, even though the ground is shaking from under your feet. Expect God's intervention in your situation.

God knows how to bring you the breakthrough you are seeking. He wants you to prepare your heart and trust Him for a miracle.

If everything is falling apart around you, know that God is ready to intervene. Don't allow the enemy, Satan, to cause you to give up trusting God with all your heart. Remember you are commanded to be strong because your hope is in the Lord.

APRIL 1

"Blessed is the one whose transgressions are forgiven, whose sins are covered." – Psalm 32: 1 NIV

Carrying a spiritual burden can be very depressing. The way to find peace of mind is to know that you are in the clear with God. God has provided a way out for everything that may not be going well in your life. You should not carry your guilt. Jesus died for you.

You can come to terms with the Heavenly Father by confessing your transgressions to Him. He is merciful and full of compassion toward you. There is nothing you can do that cannot be forgiven, unless you categorically refuse to accept God's solution for your sins.

God's only solution is found in Jesus. There is no more sacrifice left for you. If you do not accept God's way of forgiveness, you will surely die in your transgressions.

Praise God! You can be liberated of all guilt. Jesus loves you and is always available to forgive you if you acknowledge Him as your Lord and Savior.

God, thank you so much that I am no longer a slave to sin and death. Thank you for providing forgiveness for my sins free of charge. Today I surrender all my transgressions to you. I lay them at your feet knowing that the blood of Jesus is enough to erase every sin that I have ever committed. Amen.

APRIL 2

"For the word of the LORD is right and true; he is faithful in all he does." – Psalm 33:4 NIV

*I*f you are going to stand on God's promises, you need to believe that God's word is right and true. What makes God different from a mere mortal is the fact that He is sovereign. God in His sovereignty defies all boundaries. Everything is possible with God.

In addition to knowing that God is what His word says that He is, God does everything right. You cannot find fault in God.

You may not be able to comprehend every aspect of God's creation. When you are not able to understand everything about God, it is okay to question things. David did plenty of questioning in his own experience with God. Job questioned God during his excruciating pain. Although Jesus had no doubt of God's plan and love for Him, he wanted to have confirmation during the intense suffering and feelings of abandonment He felt on the cross.

Questioning is part of our human experience. God, however, has the answers to all our questions. His word is right and true. You can trust God with your life and destiny.

APRIL 3

"The lions may grow weak and hungry, but those who seek the LORD lack no good thing." – Psalm 34:10 NIV

How refreshing it is to know that God is in the business of taking care of His children. Like children who depend on their parents to provide for their needs, so we are in the hands of God. Jesus urges us to seek Him in saying, "But seek first his kingdom and his righteousness, and all these things will be given to you as well" (Matthew 6:33 NIV).

The secret in this quote is that our duty is to seek the Lord. If we don't want to be hungry like the lions, we should seek the Lord. Often, we would like to run to the Lord when we are in trouble, but deep down, we are not always eager to spend time with Him. It is important to run to God in times of trouble, but it is even more important for us to show the desire to communicate with Him on a regular basis. Do not allow your hectic lifestyle to consume you. Allow a few moments of reflection on God and His goodness daily.

When we have God, we have everything we need. You may still experience difficulties in the natural realm but rest assured that you need nothing when Jesus Christ is with you. You can always count on Him to come through for you.

APRIL 4

"Contend, LORD, with those who contend with me; fight against those who fight against me." – Psalm 35:1 NIV

As a servant of the Lord, there are days that you will find yourself in intense battle with Satan. Satan often uses people to attack others. Be on your guard so that you will be able to recognize the onslaught of the enemy.

The fiercest struggles are not always visible. Your mind is the battle ground for the enemy. Watch out for bad thoughts and ideas that keep crossing your mind. If you are going to do something bad, it will come by way of a thought or an idea. Be sure to turn every thought into something positive or rebuke it outright.

One good way to combat Satan is to turn his idea against him. For example, if the idea is about infidelity, you need to quickly remind Satan that your body belongs to the Lord and that you will not allow him to defile it. Begin immediately a worship session. Give praise to the Lord for victory over temptation and sin. Satan does not like it when you worship, so if each temptation is turned to a worship opportunity, Satan will be reluctant to attack you.

Allow God to fight your battle. If an individual wants to persecute you, turn him or her to the Lord. The battle is not yours. It is the Lord's battle.

If you try to fight alone, you will not be able to withstand the enemy. Without God's help, you are powerless. Always invite God to fight for you instead of worrying about your own fight. This is the key to victory in Jesus.

APRIL 5

"Your love, LORD, reaches to the heavens, your faithfulness to the skies." – Psalm 36:5 NIV

When we are going through difficult times in life, we might be tempted to doubt God's love. This verse makes it clear that God's love has no limits. We can always count on God's love to come through for us. In fact, God demonstrated His love toward us by sending Jesus to die for us (Romans 5:8).

Today if you doubt God's mercy and grace, know that God will never leave you nor will He abandon you. You can put your trust in the Lord and be confident that you will be victorious, no matter what. Your victory may not be what you expect, but God will do what's best for you. He knows your needs and has what you need.

God will never disappoint you. He is faithful. Your family and your friends may let you down from time to time, but God will always be there when you need Him.

You may be asking yourself why all your prayers have not been answered. One thing you should know is that God's thoughts are higher than yours. Isaiah 55:8 says it this way: "For my thoughts are not your thoughts, neither are your ways my ways" (NIV).

Sometimes, in our carnal minds, we may be praying for selfish reasons. God knows what we need and will be sure that our needs are met according to His will for our lives.

APRIL 6

"Take delight in the LORD, and he will give you the desires of your heart." – Psalm 37:4 NIV

Often, we come to the Lord just to ask for something, not just for Who He is.

God does not lack anything. He has access to everything we need. If we surrender ourselves to Him in earnest, He will take care of us. Jesus encourages us to seek God first (Matthew 6:33).

Our faith in the Lord makes it possible to have access to miracles. When we spend time worrying about our circumstances instead of trusting God to resolve them, we find ourselves trusting in people. As believers, we should always pray for God's favor every day.

Do you need a job? Go to the Lord and praise Him for a good job. Rejoice in the fact that you can come to the Lord with your needs. Trust God to open many doors for you while you are actively seeking. Would you like to find a good spouse? Trust God to show you someone.

While you are seeking and knocking, thank God for His provision. You don't have to wait until you have received the results to praise God. By faith, begin to tell God how much you appreciate Him for what you prayed for. Whatever is your problem, trust God to provide you with a practical solution.

APRIL 7

"I confess my iniquity; I am troubled by my sin." – Psalm 38:18 NIV

Before we can experience peace with God, we must be willing to confess our sins. The Holy Spirit constantly draws us to God through conviction. If we refuse to hear the voice of the Holy Spirit after many rebukes, our hearts will eventually be hardened, like in the case of King Pharaoh.

In the Old Testament, it was not possible to receive forgiveness without the blood of an animal. Today we have hope in the sacrifice of Jesus Christ. 1 John 1:9 says: "If we confess our sins, he is faithful and just and will forgive us our sins and purify us from all unrighteousness" (NIV).

If you feel troubled by your sins, it's time to confess your sins to God. God is merciful and stands ready to forgive you, but you need to acknowledge that you have done something wrong. Without confession, there is no forgiveness. And without forgiveness of sins, there is no salvation. And without salvation, there is no eternal life.

Now no animal's blood is necessary. Forgiveness is found in the shed blood of Jesus. Jesus paid for our sins once and for all. All we need is to put our faith in Him. Without faith in Jesus, it is not possible to be saved.

When we allow the Holy Spirit's voice to pierce through our stubbornness, God intervenes and wipes out our sins.

APRIL 8

"Show me, LORD, my life's end and the number of my days; let me know how fleeting my life is." – Psalm 39:4 NIV

Life on this earth is momentary. We were meant to live here forever. However, Adam's and Eve's disobedience has caused us to take a long detour toward eternal life. Yes, we will end up living forever, but first we need to transition from a mortal body into an immortal one.

This type of spiritual transformation calls for physical death. Therefore, as David did, from time to time we need to stop and think about our days. They are numbered for sure.

Although your days are short, you don't need to lose hope, because there is something far better waiting for you on the other side of the long detour.

When we think of eternity, there is cause for rejoicing. Without the hope of eternal life, this life would be very disappointing.

We are constantly fighting evil in this world. As we are approaching Jesus' return, Satan is desperately trying to destroy as many souls as he can. The world is plunging deeper and deeper in wickedness.

Pray that the Lord will protect your mind from evil thoughts. Ask God to draw you near to Him. May the Holy Spirit continue to help you overcome the power of Satan as your time on earth gets shorter.

Don't be discouraged as you continue to serve the Lord. There is hope for you in God, and nothing is more precious than the knowledge that God is on your side. Don't worry about your last days. God is watching over you.

APRIL 9

"Many, LORD, my God, are the wonders you have done, the things you planned for us." – Psalm 40:5 NIV

*T*ake a few moments to think about the wonders of the Lord in your life. You are a unique individual, and no one is like you in the whole world. You are special, aren't you? You may not think so as often as you should, but you really are.

One of the wonders of God is that He loved you so much that He sent Jesus, His Son, to die in your place. Despite your personal feelings this minute, God loves you so very much, and His love for you is incomparable.

Because there is no one like you, God's love for you is not the same as the love He has for others. That's what makes it so awesome!

The truth is that you have not seen anything yet. Wait until you get to heaven. You are going to have the time of your life. Imagine this. You will not have to suffer any pain. There will be no reason to worry about anything in your life. Everything you need will be readily available to you. God will be there with you, so you will have no reason to look for God. He will be with you always.

Can you imagine a place where there is no illness? You will be able to enjoy yourself without having to worry about sinning. Sin will be vanished for eternity.

When we think about all these marvelous things, we can't help but wonder. God is amazingly wonderful.

APRIL 10

"Blessed are those who have regard for the weak; the LORD delivers them in times of trouble." – Psalm 41:1 NIV

Although God is in a position of authority, He does not take advantage of our weaknesses. On the contrary, He bends over backward to come to our rescue. People who take advantage of the weak are mean. They are heartless bullies. They feel good when they hurt others. They think they are strong, but they are simply feebleminded folks. Your greatness is shown in the extent you are willing to show mercy and kindness to the weak.

In your daily dealings with people, ask God to give you many opportunities to speak for those who cannot speak for themselves and do as much good you can. You show that you are comfortable in your own skin when you show kindness to people who are serving under your leadership.

This is not an easy task, for it takes will-power to do the opposite of what your mind or your body is telling you to do. Because of sin, you are more prone to do what is wrong than doing what is right. In fact, Satan is willing to help you when you want to do what is wrong.

To the extent that you are willing to support the weak, God will also come to your rescue when you are in trouble. God can help both the strong and the weak. Only God has the ultimate power over every being. Pray and ask God to help you become a more compassionate person.

APRIL 11

"As the deer pants for streams of water, so my soul pants for you, my God." – Psalm 42:1 NIV

*I*f you are not careful, your daily concerns will leave no room in your mind for God. The sons of Korah remind you of the importance of your desire for God, even when other things are trying to keep you too busy to find time for God.

When the enemy threatens to destabilize you, remember God is your refuge. Allow the Holy Spirit to tug on your heart so that you can turn your attention to God daily. Yes, I know it is very hard to find time to pray and think about spiritual things. It is so easy to go on for days without thinking about God, even for a few moments. The truth is that it is not difficult to do the wrong things in life.

The enemy will even help you out so that you can continue doing the wrong things. Allow your soul to pant for God. It is good to exercise and eat every day so you can have physical strength to carry out the duties of the day. Similarly, it is important for your soul to be nourished spiritually.

When your soul is spiritually fed, the enemy is not able to distract you easily. Yes, it is okay to want to accomplish great things in life, but in all your searching, allow God to occupy the first place in your mind. May God continue to be your priority as you journey through life.

APRIL 12

"Why, my soul, are you downcast? Why so disturbed within me? Put your hope in God, for I will yet praise him, my Savior and my God." – Psalm 43:5 NIV

*I*t is permissible to question your own state of mind. If you know the Lord, He is always with you, no matter what you are going through. You may not always feel God's presence in your life. When that happens, it is not unusual for you to start doubting your own spiritual stability.

As your mind wanders, allow your spirit to connect you with God so that you can regain your sense of spiritual stability. As a human being, you are both physical and spiritual. Your spirit is the most stable part of you; your body is the weakest part of you. Your soul governs your thought process or your intellectual activities.

From time to time, your body must do what your mind tells it to do. For example, when you are tempted, your mind begins to think about the object of your temptation by trying to come up with the best way for the body to carry it out. It is important that you do not spend too much time thinking about it. Otherwise your body will end up doing the very thing you have been imagining.

The key to overcoming temptation is to allow your spirit to take over your mind and body. Your spirit is strong and can resist the devil. However, it is important that you submit yourself to the Lord (James 4:7).

APRIL 13

"Awake, Lord! Why do you sleep? Rouse yourself! Do not reject us forever." – Psalm 44:23 NIV

*I*t is not unusual for us to react to God the same way we would react to a human being. This shows our lack of understanding of God in all His attributes. This was exactly what the sons of Korah were doing in this verse. Of course, they were skilled musicians whose duties were to sing and play instruments before the King and the LORD. During difficult moments, they would cry to Yahweh for a supernatural breakthrough and deliverance.

One thing you should know is that God will never sleep, and His eyes are always upon you. Your reactions may not match your knowledge, however.

We often get scared when we are in trouble. As a result, our minds get carried away. We may say things that do not reflect our beliefs and knowledge of God.

God may appear to be absent from the scene when you really need Him, but do not lose heart. He promised to be with you.

Even though you cannot see Him, He is right there with you. Pray that you will continue to hold firm, even when you are going through tough moments. God is faithful. Trust in His power to save.

APRIL 14

"Your throne, O God, will last for ever and ever; a scepter of justice will be the scepter of your kingdom." – Psalm 45:6 NIV

Be glad that you belong to a kingdom that will never end. In this verse, the sons of Korah sang about the kingdom of David, but the prophetic application has to do with the kingdom of Christ to which you belong from a spiritual standpoint.

God's actual physical kingdom on earth is yet to be established. Now, it exists in heaven. In the Lord's Prayer, Jesus prayed for God's kingdom to come (Matthew 6: 9-13).

Someday God will establish His eternal kingdom on a new earth. He will live among His people forever and ever. If you have given your life to Jesus to be your Lord and Savior, you belong to the eternal kingdom mentioned in this verse.

One thing you should know is that justice will reign forever in God's kingdom. You will never have to complain about injustice. Jesus, your just Judge, will represent you before the Father.

The enemy, Satan, will not be able to pose any threat to God's children. God will put an end to all the plans and actions of the enemy forever. If you are suffering injustice today, take courage. You will soon forget your sufferings.

APRIL 15

"He says, "Be still, and know that I am God; I will be exalted among the nations, I will be exalted in the earth." – Psalm 46:10 NIV

Amid your personal adversities, God is saying to you that He is God. He is God over the entire universe. He is also God over your life. Therefore, rest assured that God is in control of your destiny.

God, your Lord, is ready to take charge of your issues. Allow Him to penetrate your thought and mind. Invite God into your life, your family, and your job.

Your promotion in life depends on God. Your enemies may want to harm you, but they will not be able to touch you unless God gives them authority over you. And if God allows them to have access to you, there must be a special reason for it. In the case of Job, God had allowed Satan access to his family and his body, but in the end, God restored him beyond measure.

In life, you are not promised an issue-free life, but God has promised to be your God amid your issues. The battle may last for a while, but don't lose heart, because victory rests with the Lord.

No one can outsmart God regardless of their knowledge, influence, and their power. Yahweh cannot be contained nor can His power be squashed. Be still and know that Yahweh is your God.

APRIL 16

"For God is the King of all the earth; sing to him a psalm of praise." – Psalm 47:7 NIV

Wisdom allows your conflicting mind to conclude that Yahweh is the King of all the earth. This is huge news! Imagine how peaceful it is to know that it does not matter how boastful a country's ruler may be, God is his King, too.

Peace of mind lies in the fact that we know our God is bigger than any other gods, rulers, and kings. Therefore, it does not matter if they plan to destroy us, God will defend us.

A fundamental conclusion that we can draw from this biblical truth is that Satan, the father of lies, is not in control of the universe. Yes, it can wreak havoc in our lives if we allow him to do that, but he is not in control of our destiny.

Finish this reflection on God's word today by praying this prayer: God, I am so glad that you oversee this earth. You are King. You are not just King of all this earth; you are also my King.

Today I surrender all things to you, my Lord. Allow the Holy Spirit to guide my thoughts so that they can also bring me back to you when my mind tries to drift way.

Thank you, Lord, for Who you are. You are so awesome in my life!

Lord, embolden me so I can share your love with confidence. Thank you so much, Lord, for all you are doing in my life. And I pray in the name of Jesus. Amen.

APRIL 17

"For this God is our God for ever and ever; he will be our guide even to the end." – Psalm 48:14 NIV

*N*o one deserves your praise more than the Almighty.

God created you to bring glory to Him. Regardless of how painful your circumstances may be, God remains the primary focus of your existence. Everything becomes insignificant when they are viewed through the lens of God's sovereignty and grandeur.

Today join in with the sons of Korah to praise the Lord, your God. Allow the Holy Spirit, the Comforter, to soften your heart and mind this very moment. Let go of your worries and surrender your destiny to the Lord. Acknowledge the Lord as your God for ever and ever.

If you are not sure where life is taking you, allow God to be your guide. If you make Him your trusting guide, He will lead you toward the path of righteousness.

When the dust has settled, the only thing that will be worth something is your hope in the Almighty. He knew you before the foundation of the universe, and He cares deeply for you.

Society may reject you, but God will always be there to accept you as you turn to Him for help.

APRIL 18

"People who have wealth but lack understanding are like the beasts that perish." – Psalm 49:20 NIV

As you journey through life, it's okay to make as much money as you can. However, be sure that your wealth is not elevated above Yahweh, the true God.

Use your wealth to bless people. Be a good steward of what God has given you. Do not squander God's blessings on things that have no eternal impact.

Strive to create a balance between your efforts to gain wealth and your service to the Lord. Work hard to make money, but do not allow your pursuit of wealth to take the place of your praise and worship. Take time off to worship the Lord, as least once a week.

It is so easy to get swallowed up by earthly pleasures and the desires of the flesh. Try to honor God with your body. Don't allow pornographic images take control of your soul.

If you are struggling with things, you know, that are not pleasing to the Lord, ask the Holy Spirit to give you strength to overcome those desires. Ask a trusting friend to become your accountability partner. Be sure your friend is a committed believer.

Finally, ask God to grant you wisdom and understanding so that you will be able to use your wealth for His glory. Keep in mind that everything you are and everything you have belong to God.

APRIL 19

"I have no need of a bull from your stall or of goats from your pens, for every animal of the forest is mine, and the cattle on a thousand hills." – Psalm 50:9 and 10 NIV

God is autonomous. He has everything that He will ever need to function. He never lacks anything. When you bring your tithes and offerings to the Lord, you do so to show obedience. It is one way of saying that you know who owns everything.

When you come to the Lord in worship, you are acknowledging that you were created to honor God for Who He is.

We praise and worship God because we belong to Him. Nature and everything that is in it gives glory to God. If we fail to praise God, even the rocks will cry out (Luke 19:40).

These verses help us to understand that God has everything we need. When we ask God for something, we can have confidence that He is able to give us what we need.

Sometimes, we hesitate to approach God with our needs. And when we pray to God for something, we do not always have faith that we will receive it. Jesus encourages us to ask whatever we need in His name. "If you remain in me and my words remain in you, ask whatever you wish, and it will be done for you" (John 15:7 NIV).

If we take care of the "if factor" in this verse, the rest belongs to God. Sometimes, we have a problem remaining in God. Our flesh is not predisposed to obey God and walk in the way of righteousness.

APRIL 20

"Restore to me the joy of your salvation and grant me a willing spirit, to sustain me." – Psalm 51:12 NIV

Do you remember how excited you felt on the day you surrendered your life to God? I remember vividly the joy I felt knowing that my sins were forgiven. I felt so close to God and my mind was in total peace.

David probably felt the same way when God granted him favor by making him the man after God's own heart. However, David fell into sin by committing adultery with Bathsheba. As a result, he felt so far away from God's presence.

God was never far away from David, but David's heart was far away from God. While our spirits are always in touch with God, we do not always feel God's presence in the flesh. Our flesh is not necessarily connected to God. We relate to God through our spirits. When we sin with our bodies, which are the temple of the Holy Spirit, we become uncomfortable with God. The same situation had happened in the Garden of Eden when Adam and Eve disobeyed God. Suddenly, Adam, who had walked and talked with God in the garden, resorted to hiding from God's presence.

Don't be afraid to come back to God after you have let Him down by sinning. God is always willing to listen to your heart's cry for forgiveness.

Instead of going deeper in sin, try to climb back up from your hiding place and come back to Jesus and ask Him for mercy. Surely, God will forgive your sins and restore the joy of your salvation once again.

APRIL 21

"For what you have done I will always praise you in the presence of your faithful people. And I will hope in your name, for your name is good." – Psalm 52:9 NIV

When things are not going your way and you need a breakthrough, it is time to examine God's goodness in your life. Begin by giving thanks to the Lord for all He has done for you. When you start analyzing all God has done for you in the past, suddenly, your faith in God becomes stronger.

God has done great things for us. He has granted us hope of eternal life when we were completely separated from life. We were headed directly to Hell full speed ahead. Jesus came and mended our relationship with Yahweh. Now, we can say, by the blood of Jesus Christ on the cross, we have eternal life.

There is a reason we should praise God in the presence of faithful people because they, too, need to experience God's goodness. They need to know that God can rescue them in times of distress.

David experienced God's goodness because He delivered him from Saul's death trap so many times.

God's name is a tower of refuge. Don't be afraid to call on the God of Abraham, who is Yahweh, or the God of Israel. God's name is different from any other names.

When you call on His name, things happen in the spiritual realm that can alter your situations in the natural realm. God's name is good. His name is Yahweh, the true God.

APRIL 22

"The fool says in his heart, "There is no God." They are corrupt, and their ways are vile; there is no one who does good."
– Psalm 53:1 NIV

*T*his devotional book is designed to help you discover wisdom, and one of the signs of wisdom is to acknowledge that there is a divine plan for your life. If you are one of those people whose hearts are closed to God, I pray that the Holy Spirit will soften your heart and open your eyes so that you can see God's marvelous plan for your life. If you are born again, I praise God for you. Jesus loves you so much!

Yes, the fool fails to see any divine plan for this universe. It is easy for the fool to acknowledge that we are all animals and that we will all perish after death. But I am telling you right now that it is not so. Your death does not put an end to your existence. You will continue to live well beyond your grave.

Therefore, it is important that you surrender your life to God if you have not already done so. If you have given your life to the Lord, continue to serve Him faithfully.

Do not allow Satan to deceive you so you give up along the way. Pray that the Holy Spirit will make you brave so you can share God's love with others.

APRIL 23

"Surely God is my help; the Lord is the one who sustains me." – Psalm 54:4 NIV

*I*n this world, you will have difficulties. Things will not always go your way, because you are living in a sinful society. However, despite your trials, you are never alone.

It is easy for us to become consumed by our problems and forget who is in control of our circumstances. Nevertheless, when things get tough, we need to remember that God is our help. It is a huge deal to have God as our Helper. If we were to take time to analyze the implications of having God on our side or being on the side of God, we would have no time at all to plunge into depression. Next time you find yourself depressed; meditate on God as your Helper. It does not matter how much the enemy would like to devour you; he simply cannot overcome you if you are on God's side.

God is not only your Helper; He is also there to keep you. He will see to it that you will not fail as you strive to maintain your steps along your journey through life. Yes, your life may not be problem-free, but you will not be left to defend yourself all alone.

God will fight alongside of you all the days of your life. Therefore, keep your eyes on God, your Maker. He will not abandon you along the way. Surely, He will turn His eyes toward you with compassion and grace. He will give you the strength you need to overcome your personal adversities.

APRIL 24

"Cast your cares on the Lord and he will sustain you; he will never let the righteous be shaken." – Psalm 55:22 NIV

When you are going through tough times, remember God's promises. Although you believe in God, you will still face with adversities in life. This is just the nature of the world in which you live. When you leave this world to live in the presence of God forever, you will never have to face difficulties.

Since you are God's righteous in Jesus, God's eyes are on you consistently. In the flesh, God's presence is not perceptible. That's why it is important to anchor your faith in Jesus Christ.

Do not allow Satan to rob you of your joy. Ask God to restore unto you the joy of your salvation, just as David did when he faced sorrow after his mishaps with Bathsheba.

You do not have any guarantee of a problem-free life, but you are guaranteed final victory with God's help. This is the only certainty you have, and this should help you a whole lot as you suffer in the flesh. You see, your life on this earth is temporary.

The bulk of your hope should be placed on God. Do not rely on your personal achievements to carry you through. Put your trust in God for your deliverance. God will not abandon you, no matter what.

APRIL 25

"When I am afraid, I put my trust in you." – Psalm 56:3 NIV

*I*t is so refreshing to know that we can just run to God when we are afraid. God is powerful enough to defend us. The battle belongs to the Lord, so give Him a chance to show His sovereignty.

If you are feeling a bit insecure right now, put your trust in the Lord because He knows how all will finish. I know how difficult it can be to live in uncertainties but rest assured that things will turn out okay in the end if God is in control of your circumstances.

I find it comforting to be able to go to God because I know He has my back. I do not even care if I come out of the situation alive. I know if I do not come out alive, somehow, I will wake up in the presence of God. You see, I do not have a reason not to surrender all to God.

Sometimes, we are paralyzed by fear of man. We should, instead, pay attention to our relationship with God. The only thing that really matters is our personal relationship with God.

If our destiny is not secured in Jesus Christ, we have no future. In all our hustle and bustle, we need to fix our gaze on God. Don't worry about what human beings think of you. Instead, be sure to honor God with your life and your wealth.

May God give you strength not to lose heart when you are faced with a scary situation. God is with you, even though you cannot see Him. He will never forsake you nor will He abandon you. Give thanks to the Lord for being your refuge.

APRIL 26

"For great is your love, reaching to the heavens; your faithfulness reaches to the skies." – Psalm 57:10 NIV

*I*f you have any doubt whatsoever about how vast God's love is, think about the ultimate sacrifice God made for us to have access to eternal life. Satan's grand scheme was to thwart God's plan by poisoning the mind of Adam and Eve. In so doing, Satan had caused tremendous chaos on earth by destroying the wonderful relationship that had existed between God and us. Now, God had to find an alternative to mend His relationship with humanity and reopen access to a sinless existence. And this has shown how loving God really is.

There is no reasonable way to gauge God's love for us. When we think about the suffering and subsequent death of Christ, God had spared no effort in lavishing His love upon us.

If you are feeling a bit isolated or unloved right now, comfort yourself with the assurance of God's love. God loves you with an endless love, and you can count on His love because He is faithful.

His faithfulness is as infinite as His love for you. When you're going through dark moments in your life, remember God will not forget about you. Hang in there and trust in God's faithfulness. It's so vast that it can reach to the skies.

APRIL 27

"The righteous will be glad when they are avenged, when they dip their feet in the blood of the wicked." – psalm 58:10 NIV

*I*t is not up to you to punish the wicked. God has set a time for the wicked to receive their just punishment.

Eternal punishment is reserved for Satan, not for human beings; however, Satan is in the business of destroying human beings. Keep in mind that Satan is God's archenemy. He is doing everything in his power to disrupt God's kingdom as much as he can. In the end, Satan will not be able to overcome God.

There will come a time when Satan will pay for his mischief. He knows that so well that he was trying to disrupt God's plan when Jesus Christ was about to start His mission on earth. Jesus' mission was to take upon Himself the punishment of the world. Satan offered Jesus Christ the kingdom of the world.

Until Christ's death and resurrection, Satan had authority on earth. But, all of that changed when God raised Jesus from the dead. Upon Jesus' resurrection, authority was conferred on Him. "Then Jesus came to them and said, "All authority in heaven and on earth has been given to me" (Matthew 28:18 NIV).

If you do not give Satan authority over you, he does not have it. On your own free will, you can open the door for Satan to penetrate your soul. If you do that, you will become his slave until you have turned to God for forgiveness of your sins through repentance.

APRIL 28

"You are my strength, I sing praise to you; you, God, are my fortress, my God on whom I can rely." – Psalm 59:17 NIV

*I*f you are feeling weak and debilitated right now, know that God is your strength. This is a huge deal to have this kind of backup. This means you do not have to worry about life's burden, because you do not depend on your own strength to carry it.

Considering the knowledge of God's strength, what you can do now is to praise and worship God. We praise God for all He can do for us despite our limitations. We do not need anything to praise God. This is something we can do, no matter what. We praise God in Good times; we praise Him in bad times.

Not only is God our strength, He is also our protection. Sometimes, we worry about the danger we can see, but God protects us when we are not aware of it.

We can depend on God's protection because He cannot be overcome. Satan can persecute us, but He is not allowed to touch us if God does not give Him permission.

If God permits something to happen to us, it is because He knows that we will come out of it victoriously. Not all bad experiences are detrimental. Negative experiences can teach us wisdom if we are willing to learn. What is important is not to make the same mistake repeatedly.

Praise God for being your strength and your fortress. Yes, you can count on Him with your life. Your future is in God's hands.

APRIL 29

"With God we will gain the victory, and he will trample down our enemies." – Psalm 60:12 NIV

*I*f you are going to experience victory and success in life, there is one thing that you must keep in mind. You cannot afford to face your enemies by yourself. You may think that you don't need God and that you are safe. However, you are powerless in the face of your enemies.

Trust God to carry out your victory. God may seem to be too far away, but that is not the case. As a matter of fact, God is always near you in times of distress. Allow the Holy Spirit to open your eyes so you can see God's provisions. He is ever-present and is ready to step in and trample your enemies.

It is not up to you to fight the enemies. Your job is to remain connected with your Heavenly Father. He knows what to do and will not allow your enemies to have the upper hand.

Your enemies may appear to be winning, but this is not the case. God has an element of surprise, and Satan will not be able to get away until God has put an end to his rebellion. No more triumph for the enemies, for God will be in control of the entire universe.

Knowing that God oversees every aspect of your life, rejoice and ask God to be in control of your family, your job, and your destiny. With God, you will never be without hope as you journey through life.

APRIL 30

"I long to dwell in your tent forever and take refuge in the shelter of your wings." – Psalm 61:4 NIV

When I was growing up, I had many things on my bucket list, including completing my doctorate. Nevertheless, out of all the things on my list, the priority is to spend eternity in God's presence.

As you meditate on this verse, I pray that the Holy Spirit will bring you closer to God. This does not mean that you should give up on your aspirations. Yes, go ahead and be all you can be in life, but please do not allow the worries of this world to keep you from serving God. Always strive to leave room for God in all you do.

When our lives are put on the scale, the only thing that counts is eternity. Therefore, our greatest desire should be focused on where we want to be after our journey on earth. Everything else is temporary.

Your earthly accomplishments do not quite measure up when they are viewed through the lens of God's eternal plans for your life. Continue to work hard to reach your potential while you are here but do keep God in the forefront.

The safest living environment is where God dwells. One day, everything will change forever. We will no longer suffer from physical ailments. God will keep us safe under His wings. God is our eternal refuge.

MAY 1

"My salvation and my honor depend on God; he is my mighty rock, my refuge." – Psalm 62:7 NIV

When we realize that God is our salvation and our honor depends on Him, we become liberated. We no longer see ourselves as victims. If we do not get promoted at work, we do not blame others. Instead, we ask God for guidance as to where we should go and apply for a new job, or simply ask God to grant us favor with our existing supervisor.

When your promotion time has come, no one can stop it from happening. God can help you to break through natural barriers, whichever nature they might be.

God is responsible for your salvation. All you need is to acknowledge Him as your source and accept His provision for salvation. It is through Jesus Christ, His Son, God has provided the path to salvation.

There is no alternative for salvation. If you refuse to accept the gift that God has provided, there is no more sacrifice left for you. Jesus' death on the cross is God's ultimate sacrifice for humanity. Through Jesus, you can have peace and joy.

In addition to your salvation, your honor depends on Christ. And it is because you are loved by God and that you are no longer a slave to sin.

From time to time, Satan may try to remind you that you are worthless, but don't listen to him. His plan is to demoralize you so that you lose your sense of worth. You have value in God's eyes because you have been bought by the blood of the Lamb.

MAY 2

"On my bed I remember you; I think of you through the watches of the night." – Psalm 63:7 NIV

David had some bad experiences with idle thoughts when he had committed adultery with Bathsheba. This time, he chose to do otherwise.

If you are lying in bed and cannot fall asleep, you should focus your mind on God. David was in the desert of Judah, away from fresh water, but he decided to focus his mind on God. I can only imagine how thirsty for fresh water he was. However, he realized that God's presence was better than fresh water. His soul was thirsty for God.

It is important that you focus on God when you find yourself in a desert or alone. This habit may prevent the enemy from taking advantage of your loneliness to sow seeds of destruction in your mind.

Being alone can be fruitful if you use the time to think creatively. If you are not praying or praising the Lord, try to think about things that can alter your life. For example, you may find it beneficial to think of a new job or business. That may be a good time to think about some great strategies to put your life in order.

Do not allow the enemy to coax you into doing something illegal or falling into sin. Spend your sleepless moments meditating on God's word, praising Him for all He has done for you, and the many blessings He has in store for your life.

MAY 3

"The righteous will rejoice in the LORD and take refuge in him; all the upright in heart will glory in him!" – Psalm 64:10 NIV

*I*f you have placed your faith and trust in the Almighty God, you can depend on His promises. It does not matter how bold your enemies are, they don't have any power over you.

I know as humans; we tend be afraid when we see the external demonstration of our enemies. Being afraid is one of many aspects of the human reality.

Now pray this prayer. Lord, I know things are difficult for me right now. My enemies seem to be winning the battle. However, deep down, I know you are more powerful than my enemies.

Please grant me courage and strength to withstand in the face of constant attacks. Lord, open the eyes of my foes so that they can see your marvelous walls of protection around me.

Help me not to give in to fear, because you will never forsake me, nor will you abandon me. Thank you, Lord, for being my refuge. I trust in your unfailing love. Amen.

Give glory to God for His amazing love and protection. Through Christ, you will have victory over your enemies. God knows your heart and your situation, and He has it under full control. May God continue to watch over you and guide your steps.

MAY 4

"When we were overwhelmed by sins, you forgave our transgressions." – Psalm 65:3 NIV

We are serving a compassionate God. In lieu of destroying us from the face of the earth, He willingly sent Jesus Christ, His only Son, to die on the cross for our transgressions.

God came down to our level when we could not get up to Him. Such an extraordinary action has clearly proved that God loves us indeed! There is no other way to explain God's love. God made the ultimate sacrifice for our sins through the birth, death, and resurrection of Jesus Christ.

If you are living in guilt and condemnation right now, accept God's forgiveness through Jesus Christ. Christ died so that you can experience forgiveness. No matter how terrible your past might have been, God is ready and willing to give you a new beginning. Ask God to forgive your sins and give you strength to live for Him.

Please say this prayer:
Lord, thank you so much for sending Jesus to die for me. Today I accept your forgiveness through the blood of Jesus Christ. I accept the freedom that comes from acknowledging you as my Lord and Savior. I am free because of your love. Thank you for your forgiveness.

Allow the Holy Spirit to draw you closer to God. Continue to trust God for your forgiveness. Enjoy God's spiritual blessings and freedom that come from knowing Jesus Christ.

MAY 5

"Shout for joy to God, all the earth!" – Psalm 66:1 NIV

When we witness the marvelous things that God has accomplished on the earth on our behalf, we can't help shouting for joy. God's intent was for the whole earth to bring glory to His name. However, we know Satan has been working very hard to prevent the world from worshiping God. In the end, Satan will lose the battle because nothing can stop God from achieving His goals.

This verse refers to God's deliverance of the children of Israel when He saved them from Pharaoh's powerful chariots. "By day the LORD went ahead of them in a pillar of cloud to guide them on their way and by night in a pillar of fire to give them light so that they could travel by day or by night" (Exodus 13:21 NIV). All these miraculous deeds caused them to shout for joy, and they wanted the whole earth to join in with them.

When you experience God's miracle, do not be afraid to shout for joy. God is pleased when we show gratitude for His favor and grace. Moreover, when we showcase God's mercies, we encourage others to join in with us.

If we are reluctant to show our enthusiasm for what God has done for us, nonbelievers will not come to Him.

Let's keep on bragging about God's grace. We know He is compassionate because he spared nothing in sending Jesus Christ to die for us. Part of being wise is to ensure that we spread the gospel so that many people will be able to hear about the marvelous things God has done for us.

MAY 6

"May God be gracious to us and bless us and make his face shine on us – so that your ways may be known on earth, your salvation among all nations." – Psalm 67:1 and 2 NIV

Today as you meditate on these two verses, ask God to bless you so that you can be a blessing to others.

If we are going to make a difference in this sinful world, we need God's grace and blessings. Around the world are many nations where the good news about God must be preached. Those nations need the message of salvation.

In your prayers, ask God to bless you financially so that you can support many missionaries around the world. You may not be able to go to those countries yourself. However, if you are blessed with financial resources, you can make it possible for others to go.

For people who are lost to come to God, they need to see God on our faces. We need to be sure that our behaviors are not impacting the gospel negatively. As we deal with the world, they need to see something different in us. Our lifestyle needs to display God's love.

You are God's witness in your community, at work, and everywhere you go. Allow God to shine on your face, in your language, and in your business dealings.

Do not make it harder for others to accept God by your negative attitude. Ask God to give you wisdom so that you can make a difference in someone's life in your sphere of influence.

MAY 7

"A father to the fatherless, a defender of widows, is God in his holy dwelling." – Psalm 68:5 NIV

Have you ever felt alone? Know that God is always there for you. You are never alone in this rough life. Seek God because He is there and can be found.

If you have lost your father to death or your father is there, but he is not much of a father to you, take comfort in knowing that God is your Heavenly Father. He is there to lavish His love on you when you feel unloved.

If you have no spouse, or the one you have is not treating you as he or she should, God is there to defend you. God will never leave you nor will He abandon you. Don't lose heart.

How awesome it is to know that God is mindful of us. God is not just sitting there enjoying His throne and kingdom away from all the chaotic situations that are taking place on this planet. He is right here with us amid the circumstances.

It is important to know that God lives in us through the Holy Spirit. He knows all our twists and turns. Before we open our mouths to pray, God knows our thoughts because He knows everything.

Today rejoice in the fact that God cares about you, even when no one else does.

Thank God for His constant care and protection. With His help, you will continue to experience victory on your journey through life until you have finished the race and joined Him in eternity.

MAY 8

"Answer me, LORD, out of the goodness of your love; in your great mercy turn to me." – Psalm 69:16 NIV

Until we are willing to get rid of our pride and all those things that make our hearts so puffed up, we are not quite ready to experience God. A true encounter with God is one that brings us to our very minimum so that we can experience the fullness of God. It is neither by might nor our intellectual capacity that we will get to experience God's divine presence. It is when we are in our lowest place fighting the enemy with our last breath that we get to know the mercy of God.

When we have nothing left to brag about, God then can show His wonderful love. It is when we are in difficult trials, we become aware of our own inadequacy. At this level, we have no other place to turn to but to place everything in the hands of God, the Author and the Finisher of our faith.

It is only by God's love we can expect to get out of this mess triumphantly. We know God loves us so much because He has demonstrated it through His Son. No one has ever loved us in such an extravagant way. Through God's love, we have been able to live a productive life.

If God answers us through His love and mercy, we can count on Him to sustain us until the end. We know that God does not treat us according to what we deserve. He will protect and preserve us until the end. Therefore, rely on God to protect you today.

MAY 9

"Hasten, O God to save me; come quickly, LORD, to help me."
– Psalm 70:1 NIV

Don't be ashamed to call on God in times of distress. God is your first source of rescue.

In an emergency, we may not have any other source of rescue but to call on God. If you are trapped in an elevator and there are no communications with the outside world, you may make a lot of noise so that others can hear you but call on God for a miracle. You are on a flight and all sudden you start having very bad turbulences; you need to call on God for protection. You are told that you have but a few weeks to live, it is time to call on God for a miracle of healing.

It does not matter what's going on in your life, God remains your true source of refuge. That does not mean you should not recognize other sources of help. Do not view going to the doctor as a sign of unbelief.

It is okay to see a doctor for the symptoms you are having. Doctors are instruments in God's hands. It is God who gives them the ability and knowledge to diagnose and cure diseases. God oversees the universe, and everything belongs to Him.

Calling on God simply means that you recognize His authority over you. God has sovereignty over the entire universe. Nothing can budge without His permission; even the enemy cannot do anything without God's permission.

MAY 10

"As for me, I will always have hope; I will praise you more and more." – Psalm 71:14 NIV

You have something special going for you if your hope is in the LORD. It is special because you will never be put to shame, no matter what. Serving God is a sure shot! It does not matter the outcome of your daily battle; you will have the upper hand in the end because victory always rests with the LORD.

Having such a great hope of being on the side of victory, you can't help praising the LORD. You praise God because you know that you have already won. Jesus Christ won the battle fair and square when God raised Him from the dead on the third day.

Satan's goal was to put an end to God's plan, but he failed miserably. Because Satan lost the battle, you know who the winner is. His name is Jesus Christ, the Savior of the world.

Christ's win made it possible for us to have peace with the Heavenly Father. The divide that was created by the fall of Adam and Eve in the Garden of Eden can now be closed on the cross.

Today thank God for the hope of eternal life. Don't be discouraged if you are going through a tough time right now. Put your hope in God. He knows your situation and can see you through. Pray for a breakthrough, and do not give up hope.

MAY 11

"Praise be to the LORD God, the God of Israel, who alone does marvelous deeds." – Psalm 72:18 NIV

*I*n the Old Testament, the people did not know God's name, so the God of Israel was one way to indicate the only true God. Later, God was revealed to His people as Yahweh.

In the case of Moses, God revealed Himself to him as "I Am that I Am." Today we do not have enough knowledge to provide infinite details about God's origin; however, one thing we do know is that He is the Alpha and the Omega. He is the Beginning and the End.

Because God is the Author of everything that exists, everything that has breath must worship Him. We worship Yahweh because of Who He is. Of course, we praise God for all He has done for us, but we still need to praise God just for Who He is.

God has no competitors. Satan is not God's competitor, because He can't win. To qualify as a competitor, one must have a chance of winning. In the case of Satan, he is no competitor. He is just an impostor. He would like you to believe that he is able to beat God, but this is just a lie from the pit of Hell. He couldn't win, he can't win, and he won't win.

Considering God's sovereignty, we can declare that He alone is able to do marvelous things. He alone can give us eternal life, and His promises are yes and amen! Praise the LORD! And Praise Him forever and ever. Amen.

MAY 12

"Whom have I in heaven but you? And earth has nothing I desire besides you." – Psalm 73:25 NIV

We should not allow our temporary nature to take the place of what was designed to be eternal, because we were created to live forever.

If we comb through all the hustle and bustle of the temporary world, we will come to one conclusion. We all long to live forever. While we enjoy making a difference down here, which is one of many reasons we should wait for God to call us home, we should never allow our carnal desires to supplant God's plan for our lives. We should not commit suicide, because we are not in control our destiny.

There are many things on earth, but they are not worth much, because they have no eternal values. The pleasure of this world will not withstand the test of time.

There is nothing wrong if you enjoy your short time here, but please do not let your enjoyment keep you from serving your Creator. Know whose you are amid all the confusion that is taking place on earth.

God will not close His eyes forever. The day will come when we all must give an account on how we have spent our time down here. Let us look forward to spending our eternity with God in paradise, where Jesus Christ will be crowned as the King of kings.

Praise God! We have so much to hope for. Our minds are on the Lord, and nothing on earth is good enough for us.

MAY 13

"It was you who set all the boundaries of the earth; you made both summer and winter." – Psalm 74:17 NIV

*D*espite what the world may think about the universe, the Bible makes it quite clear that God is its Chief Architect. Genesis 8 verse 22 reads: "As long as the earth endures, seedtime and harvest, cold and heat, summer and winter, day and night will never cease" (NIV).

If you are not sure if God created the universe, then you may not be sure that God is able to take care of you either.

Over the years, Satan has used some scientists to discredit God by denying the biblical information about creation. For those who believe in God, creation is not a farfetched story. It is well within the power of God to create everything that exists, including the universe.

Believing that God is the Creator of the universe gives us the hope that He can help us in times of need. There is nothing that our God cannot do. He can do everything.

When you see changes in the weather, you are being reminded that God is in control. Giving God glory for His works is vital. That's why the enemy has been trying to find a way to poison the minds of humans by using scientific knowledge wrongly in order to confuse people. I think science is very cool. When science is viewed from a godly perspective, it shows how great God is.

It is perfectly fine to believe in God and in scientific discoveries. Given the sovereignty of God, He can control the entire universe and everything that is in it. As a result, God is in control of your destiny.

MAY 14

"It is God who Judges: He brings one down, he exalts another."
– Psalm 75:7 NIV

It is very interesting to watch how God works out everything. In our finite minds, it is very difficult for us to figure it all out. Things do not always work out the way we would like them to. Therefore, our analysis of things is not always accurate. Don't be discouraged, for God is not going to leave you behind. Trust God to fight your battle. Although it may appear to delay, do not give up hope.

When the expected results are different, we need to acknowledge that God is in control of our circumstances. Always give God room to maneuver. You will be surprised how it's all turned out.

Sometimes, we are surprised to see the enemy experiencing success. God sees the future and knows how the movie is going to end. Allow God to be God.

Don't be jealous when you see the enemy is making progress. God can use your enemy's success to bless you. The world is all connected. If your enemy is successful, you will benefit from it as well. For instance, the taxes your enemies have paid may be used for your community's development.

Keep in mind your blessings are from the Lord. He will determine the day of your deliverance. It is not up to you to decide, because God is the Judge.

MAY 15

"It is you alone who are to be feared. Who can stand before you when you are angry?" – Psalm 76:7 NIV

When we think about the limitless power of God and what He can do, we understand that it is only by grace that we are able to stand before Him. Had God not chosen to demonstrate His compassion toward us by sending Jesus Christ to die in our place, we all would be doomed forever.

What makes God so amazingly awesome is that He has power over our bodies, our souls, and our spirits. He has complete authority over us both on earth and in eternity. It is He who knows our coming and going. Our destiny depends on Him.

We often fear people who only have control over our bodies. Our spirits are the most important part of our beings. People can destroy our bodies, but they cannot destroy our spirits (Matthew 10:28). The spirits of those who have sincerely surrendered themselves to God are sealed and protected by God forever.

In order to find protection from the fierce anger of God, we must accept Christ as our Lord and Savior. Jesus Christ is the only effective antidote to sin. We cannot be forgiven without the precious blood of Christ.

When God looks at us through Jesus, His Son, He can accept us as righteous despite our imperfection in the flesh. Praise God! We do not have to stand before Him when He is angry. Christ can pacify God's anger for us by His own blood.

MAY 16

"I cried out to God for help; I cried out to God to hear me." - Psalm 77:1 NIV

*I*t is not a sign of weakness to cry out to God for help in times of distress and personal adversities. On the contrary, it is a sign of strength to run to God. When you cry out to God and acknowledge His power to save you from danger, you are telling Him that He is your source of life.

God wants us to rely on Him completely for protection. That does not mean that we are not responsible for anything. We still need to get out there and get a job or deal with the chaos of this life. However, we need to trust God for our health as well as for wisdom so that we can handle whatever life may throw at us. We need God to sustain us daily because Satan is trying his best to defeat us through temptation.

We need to depend on God for our spiritual needs. We do not need to worship images or adore other gods. There is only one true God, and His name is Yahweh, the God of Israel. When we need help, we can call on His name with confidence knowing that He is able to hear us when we pray in the name of Jesus, His Son.

God is not far from us, because He lives in us through the Holy Spirit. Therefore, when we call on God, He can hear us. The Holy Spirit translates our groaning into beautiful prayers to God. As a result, God can grant us what we need. God knows what we need, even before we call on Him for help.

MAY 17

"My people, hear my teaching; listen to the words of my mouth." – Psalm 78:1 NIV

There is wisdom in God's teaching. In God's teaching, we find the necessary advice to live for Him. Today God speaks to us through the Holy Bible as well as through the ministry of the Holy Spirit. Make it a habit of reading and meditating on God's words daily so that you know how to handle each situation you encounter for the day. Life is full of challenges, and you need divine guidance to sort things out without losing your sanity.

You know that you are blessed if you are counted among God's people. By virtue of creation, we all were created in God's image, but sin had placed a wedge between God and His beautiful creation. In this connection, we need the Savior to reunite us with God's plan and set our feet on the path of righteousness once again.

By God's grace we all have an equal opportunity to be called God's people. We have access to God's grace through Jesus Christ.

God wants us to listen to His teaching because in it, there are important guidelines for Christian living.

If you are among God's people, live your life according God's teaching. That's what sets you apart from those who have no relationship with God. You are God's witness if you hear His instruction and apply it daily.

MAY 18

"Help us, God our Savior, for the glory of your name; deliver us and forgive our sins for your name's sake." – Psalm 79:9 NIV

Because nonbelievers tend to judge the effectiveness of God by observing the way believers live their lives, it is important that we trust God to meet our needs so that we do not dishonor God's name. If we are committed to testifying of God's goodness and mercy, we should be the recipients of God's mercy and goodness. Our behavior should be indicative of God's sovereignty. That does not mean that we must defend God, because He can defend Himself. It simply means that we can call upon God because of our relationship with Him.

God is our Savior, so we do not have other sources of support. We should not go to Satan when we are in distress, because we do not have a relationship with him. Moreover, God does not approve of such practices.

If you have submitted your life to the Lord and have accepted Jesus Christ as your Lord and Savior, trust in Him to resolve your issues.

Don't succumb to temptation by communicating with other gods. While there is only one true God, there are many idols that people worship as gods.

Although those idols are not necessarily God's rivals, they can prevent you from having fellowship with God. That's why Yahweh had warned us of other gods as well as communications with the spirit world. If you are a child of God, you should avoid consulting a medium. Go to God in prayer if you are confused about certain aspects of your life's journey.

MAY 19

"Restore us, LORD God Almighty; make your face shine on us, that we may be saved." – Psalm 80:19 NIV

Our greatest spiritual restoration occurred when God decided to send Adam's replacement. Adam's broken relationship with God had created a spiritual gap that could not be bridged without a major divine intervention. God had a stake in the brawl because His creation was in jeopardy. Jesus' presence on the scene was God's own way of shining His face on us.

Without the birth, death, and resurrection of Jesus, the gap between humanity and God could not be bridged. The incarnation of Jesus made it possible for us to be redeemed by His blood on the cross. After the death and burial of Jesus, the light of salvation shone brightly on the third day. Today we know that God is ready to accept us back into the fold.

God is willing to accept everyone who wants to accept His solution to sin. Broken relationships can be restored by calling upon the name of Jesus.

If you feel spiritually broken today, ask God to mend your spirit. Call upon the Almighty for strength to go on, even though things may look bleak in the natural. God can help you with a breakthrough for your difficult circumstances.

Ask the Almighty to shine His face on you today. True restoration can only come from the Almighty.

MAY 20

"Hear me, my people, and I will warn you – if you would only listen to me, Israel!" – Psalm 81:8 NIV

*I*n the Old Testament, God is often portrayed as stern and demanding. However, if you think of it, God was always wooing His people by trying to draw them closer to Him. God's mercies were there despite the Israelites' reluctance to be faithful to God.

The people were not listening to God. They were quick to worship idols. If we are not careful, we will allow other gods to take the place of the true God in our lives.

You may not be worshiping idols like some of the people used to do in the Old Testament, but you may allow the worries of this world to occupy first place in your heart. Anything that is considered more important than God is an idol.

You need to allow God to be your priority. I understand how difficult it is to meditate on God's words daily. The purpose of this devotional book is to help you keep your mind on God while you are busy meeting your needs.

We hear God when we read His words and find time to allow the Holy Spirit to communicate with us. If only we would make room for God in our lives. God is interested in interacting with us. We just need to allow Him to have His say in our daily matter.

If you are born again, God lives in you through the Spirit. God is not far from you. You don't have to open your mouth to communicate with God. Just acknowledge God when you feel the urge to do so.

MAY 21

"Defend the weak and the fatherless; uphold the cause of the poor and oppressed." – Psalm 82:3 NIV

*R*egardless of your political views, if you are born again, you are called to defend the poor and the oppressed. You may think you are doing God a favor by denigrating the oppressed. Nonetheless, this is not the way God sees it.

God has a soft spot for the oppressed because His people were oppressed by the Egyptians and Babylonians for years. Yahweh empathizes with the poor.

God loves the poor because they remind Him of how humanity had been before He sent Jesus. The poorest experience one can have is to be separated from God. There are no adequate words that can describe the trauma of living apart from God.

We had been so poor before we came to know Jesus. Jesus' presence in us has made us rich. We are spiritually rich. We have everything we need in Jesus.

Ask God to give you a soft spot for the poor among us and the people who do not have a voice. There are many weak and fatherless people in our society. Some of those oppressed people are immigrants who live in our society. We need to remember God's people had been immigrants in Egypt and Babylon. Allow God to love the poor and the oppressed through you.

MAY 22

"Let them know that you, whose name is the LORD – that you alone are the Most High over all the earth." – Psalm 83:18 NIV

Generally, Christ's followers do not pray for vengeance. There are times we need God's intervention to defeat our enemies. Keep in mind that our enemies today are all those things Satan is using to manipulate society so that we do not have any passion or respect for God anymore. We need to get on our knees and ask God to intervene so that people can recognize the Almighty God.

Satan knows how to adapt in every society. Satan can take many forms. For instance, in Haiti, Satan has used witchcraft and sorceries to keep people from God. In developed countries Satan has used material possessions, knowledge, erroneous religious practices, and sensuality to enslave people. Some rich people do not think they need God. And sensual pleasures have kept people from pursuing purity and holiness.

As Christians, we need to ask God for wisdom in order to unmask the tricks of Satan. Satan has one goal in mind, which is to keep people from acknowledging God.

If Satan can keep you busy amassing wealth and enjoying sins, he can keep you from honoring God with your life. Today pray and ask God for wisdom so you can continue to serve God.

MAY 23

"Better is one day in your courts than a thousand elsewhere; I would rather be a doorkeeper in the house of my God than dwell in the tents of the wicked." – Psalm 84:10 NIV

Allow your spirit to meditate on this verse for a while. Surely, there is nothing on earth that can replace your faithfulness to God. As you continue to search for wisdom, you will discover that God is the end of your quest. When you find God, you find everything.

Jesus reminds us that we have nothing to worry about when we surrender everything to God. He said, "But seek first his kingdom and his righteousness, and all these things will be given to you as well" (Matthew 6: 33 NIV).

All we need is God. As we turn our attention to God, suddenly, the college degree we are pursuing becomes possible. As we turn our attention to God, He makes a way out of no way for us to pay the debts that have become an albatross around our neck. The situation that was declared impossible is now possible because we surrender it to God.

When you side with God, you take the best course of action. No matter how luxurious life may look on the other side, it is much better to stick with God through thick or thin.

God's way is a better way to live your life. You may be happy for a while living the world's way, but in the end, you will regret wasting your time gratifying the desires of the flesh. Remain in God and ask Him to give you strength to live for Him.

MAY 24

"Surely his salvation is near those who fear him, that his glory may dwell in our land." – Psalm 85:9 NIV

For those of us who have surrendered ourselves to God, we stand in awe of Him. The fear we have for God is not one that makes us scared. It is the awesomeness we sense when we reflect on God's greatness.

There is no doubt that God is ready to save us as we turn our hearts to Him with respect and reverence. God is majestic and His presence is magnificent! There is no one like Him.

In order to have access to God's salvation, we must revere God by accepting His gift of salvation. In the New Testament, God offers salvation through Jesus Christ's death and resurrection. "Salvation is found in no one else, for there is no other name under heaven given to mankind by which we must be saved "(Acts 4:12 NIV).

The best way to honor God is to say yes to Jesus, His Son. And the best way to show His glory in the land is to be a witness for Him among the lost. Because God lives in us through the Holy Spirit, we can show His glory by our lifestyle.

Today ask God to grant you wisdom so that others may see God through you. It is good for you to witness when you have a chance. The way you live your life can draw people to God as well. If you are on fire for God and your lifestyle is bad, people will not accept your words. Show God's glory on earth in everything you do.

MAY 25

"Teach me your way, LORD, that I may rely on your faithfulness; give me an undivided heart, that I may fear your name." – Psalm 86:11 NIV

Without divine guidance, it is difficult for us to serve God faithfully. God can direct us in the way of righteousness. When we live according to God's teaching, our actions reflect God's way of life. Our analysis of life is based on things that have eternal ramifications, not on things that satisfy the desires of the flesh.

The worries of this world tend to divide our hearts. We must focus on God's way. By praying and asking God to assist us in our effort to please Him, we can fix our eyes on Him.

When it comes to salvation, God can sustain us. Keep in mind, salvation is not part of our daily struggle. In other words, we are not struggling daily to remain saved. Our daily struggle has to do with our daily walk with God.

Although we belong to God, we continue to face daily temptation. Even Jesus Christ was not immune to temptation. We should pray and ask God to teach us His way so that we do not succumb to temptation.

Satan is doing everything in his power to dislodge God's people from the kingdom. God's way will guide us as we continue to live for Him and wait for the eventual Rapture of the Church.

MAY 26

"The LORD loves the gates of Zion more than all the other dwellings of Jacob." – Psalm 87:2 NIV

*I*n the Old Testament, God dwelled in places. Today God dwells in His people. This is a huge difference between the Old Testament and the New Testament.

The gates of Zion were special because God chose to dwell there. You, too, are a special dwelling for God if you open your heart to Him. God can dwell in everyone at the same time because He is omnipresent. That means He can be in more than one place at a time.

At salvation, God enters the believer through the intervention of the Holy Spirit. He continues to live in the believer forever. God's intervention happens in the spiritual realm, which makes it possible for the individual to be transformed or changed. This miraculous transformation is called a born-again experience.

Through the born-again experience, you become a symbol of the gates of Zion, a place where God wants to dwell. Praise God for the opportunity to be united with God through Jesus Christ and by the Holy Spirit's intervention.

Allow God to dwell in you so you can serve Him with all your mind and all your heart. May you be a dwelling place for the Almighty forever. Amen.

MAY 27

"LORD, you are the God who saves me; day and night I cry out to you." – Psalm 88:1 NIV

*I*t is important to call on God when you are in distress. Of course, you do not have to wait until you are in distress to call on God. You should call on God daily to acknowledge His sovereignty over your life, or praise and worship Him for Who He is.

There is not a specific time to cry out to God. You can do it any time. The best thing is to be sensitive to the urge of God's Spirit who lives in you. Often, you will feel the urge to acknowledge God in your life. It does not have to be a special meeting place.

At work, or wherever you may be, allow God to talk to you through the quiet voice of the Holy Spirit. Remember salvation happened in your spirit. Your body and your soul are not necessarily subdued. That's why you struggle with certain ideas or thoughts. You must constantly control your body and soul. When your body and your soul control your actions, you are very susceptible of falling into sin. Your spirit must rule your body and soul, not the other way around.

The key is to live according to the mandate of the spirit, not according the constant urges of the boy and soul. When you do that, God can guide you through life. This only works if your spirit is born again. God is in the business of saving people. Praise God for salvation through Christ, the Messiah.

MAY 28

"I will sing of the LORD's great love forever; with my mouth I will make your faithfulness known through all generations." – Psalm 89:1 NIV

*T*hose of us who have tasted God's goodness, we tend to have a burning desire to share our experience with others. If you do not feel the same about your encounter with God, pray and ask God to give you a special desire to make His name known. Spreading the good news about the faithfulness of God is one of the duties of Christ's followers.

It is important to sing God's great love because others need to know about it. When we think of the benefits of knowing God, it is impossible not to have a special desire to let other people know about it. I know it takes a lot of guts to share your faith with others because of the stigma of being called a Jesus' freak. However, you should consider it a privilege to be a witness for God. You want others to have the same exciting experience of being sure of their future salvation. The greatest gift you can give someone is to introduce them to Jesus, the Savior of the world.

Today many people do not want to believe that there will be a place called the New Jerusalem, or a new earth for that matter. They tend to believe that there is no life beyond the grave. Do not be deceived in believing that you do not have to give an account to God for your life. There is more to life than what you are experiencing now. Pray and ask God to give the desire to embark on the mission of making Him known among your friends, your neighbors, and the world around you.

MAY 29

"Before the mountains were born or you brought forth the whole world, from everlasting to everlasting you are God." – Psalm 90:2 NIV

This prayer of Moses is a reminder of God's creation. God is not only in control of the universe, He created it. This is a very controversial topic among scientists because there are those who believe that the universe came about by chance or by natural selection.

Despite the controversies surrounding this topic, it is important that you come to grips with the reality of this verse. You must choose whether you are going to accept God as the Creator. Your ultimate view of this topic will determine how you approach God. If you believe that God is the Author of everything, then you are more likely to rely on Him for your destiny.

God has neither beginning nor end. The chicken or the egg causality dilemma does not work with God. Let me remind you that your mind cannot grasp fully the concept of timelessness, because it is beyond the four known dimensions of the universe. You must think outside the universe's box in order to comprehend God fully. Therefore, in order to believe in God as the Creator of the universe, you need a leap of faith, not a quantum leap.

In this prayer, Moses acknowledged God as the Creator of the universe. And you?

Remember from everlasting to everlasting, He is God. Praise God for the opportunity to grasp something so profoundly marvelous!

MAY 30

"Whoever dwells in the shelter of the Most High will rest in the shadow of the Almighty." – Psalm 91:1 NIV

Whenever you are afraid, think of this verse. It does not matter how terrible your situation may be, you can always count on the Almighty if you choose to dwell in His shelter. This is a choice you must make if you have not yet done so.

When you are resting in the shadow of God, you are safe. I know you are living in a fallen world, where the enemy is trying his best to harm you. However, God has His eyes on you.

Surrender everything to God before you go to bed at night so that He will send His angels to watch over you while you are sleeping. There are times Satan sends wicked people to break into people's home and harm them. You need to rely on God to protect you. Do consider purchasing a good alarm system for your home. There are things you can do as well.

In the morning, ask God to accompany you as you leave your home. You need God's favor on the road as well as at your job. We should leave nothing to chance. We need to allow God to permeate every aspect of our daily activities.

In the shadow of the Almighty, there is peace of mind. You do not have to worry about your safety if you trust God to watch over you. God will also watch over you beyond the grave. When your time has come to travel to the other side, God will be there to transition you to eternity.

MAY 31

"How great are your works, LORD, how profound your thoughts!" – Psalm 92:5 NIV

*I*n order to remember the grandeur of God, it is imperative that we take a few minutes to ponder about God's works from time to time, because we are inclined to elevate ourselves and forget whose we are.

Although we are not able to fathom the magnitude of God's works, our frequent reflections on His handy works may help us to understand how much we are dependent on Him.

Creation provides us with thousands of things at which to marvel. It is difficult to observe the beauty of the landscapes around us and the vast oceans around the world without thinking about the Creator. Our own existence is a mind-blowing feat because none of the living creatures are like us.

We are endowed with intellectual capacities to create phenomenal things that are often unthinkable. If we were to choose to ignore our Creator's works, we would certainly undermine our very existence.

God's thoughts are profound because they are higher than ours. If you have ever questioned God's motive, here is what He wants you to know. God said, "As the heavens are higher than the earth, so are my ways higher than your ways and my thoughts than your thoughts" (Isaiah 55:9 NIV).

JUNE 1

"Your throne was established long ago; you are from all eternity." – Psalm 93:2 NIV

Someday God's throne will be on earth according to the Scripture. And I heard a loud voice from the throne saying, "Look! God's dwelling place is now among the people, and he will dwell with them. They will be his people, and God himself will be with them and be their God" (Revelation 21:3 NIV).

It will be a glorious experience living with God in eternity. The issue of death will disappear. We will not have to suffer pain. Satan, God's archenemy, will be cast in the lake of burning sulfur, where he will stay forever. He will no longer be able to tempt us.

God is not limited by time, so it is not possible for you to figure Him out based on your intellectual capacity. However, you can still put your trust in God because He has demonstrated His love for us in the Scripture.

Don't allow your limited understanding of the afterlife to prevent you from believing in God. You have nothing to lose by believing in God. If you fail to trust in the Lord while you are still in the body, you will not be able to live with God in eternity.

You have everything to lose by refusing to believe in God. If you have not done that, be sure you put your trust in God by accepting Jesus Christ as your Lord and Savior today.

JUNE 2

"The Lord knows all human plans; he knows that they are futile." – Psalm 94:11 NIV

God can read our minds. We cannot hide our thoughts from Him. That means we can speak to God without opening our mouths, thereby keeping Satan out of the loop.

Why are human plans futile? They are futile because they are not based on eternal outcomes. When we make plans, we are trying to obtain finite outcomes. In the spiritual realm, God's plans have eternal outcomes.

Because God knows everything, when you are making plans, be sure you include Him in them. It is okay to change your plans from time to time in order to allow God to intervene in your life.

God wants you to trust in Him for guidance. If God is involved in your plans, the outcomes will not be pointless. "Trust in the Lord with all your heart and lean not on your own understanding; in all your ways submit to him, and he will make your paths straight" (Proverbs 3:5 & 6 NIV).

When you plan without God, you are trying to lean on your own understanding. Your own understanding is limited and is often misguided. You need to trust in God to guide you along the way so that the outcomes of your plans can be in sync with His will. Because life is short, you should invest in plans that are productive, not futile.

JUNE 3

"Come, let us bow down in worship, let us kneel before the LORD our Maker; for he is our God and we are the people of his pasture, the flock under his care." – Psalm 95:6 and 7 NIV

*I*f you acknowledge that God is your God, then you need to be willing to worship Him as such. Bowing down or kneeling before God is one of many ways that you can worship Him. This is a willful act. You can also worship God with your lifestyle. People may come to God by watching the way you live your life. Moreover, you can use your knowledge as well as your financial resources to bring glory to God.

We worship God because He is our Maker. As God's people, we are not afraid of kneeling before Him. In fact, God created us to praise and worship Him.

If we do not worship God, we are not fulfilling our purpose. As a result, we will end up worshiping false gods. We cannot live without worshiping. It is part of our nature to do so. That's why people around the world worship images, animals, and people, among other things. They just must worship someone or something.

We worship God because He is our God. We also worship God because He takes care of us every step of the way. God watches over us, even when we are not aware of His protection. We need to approach God with thanksgiving for all He has done for us.

JUNE 4

"Let the heavens rejoice, let the earth be glad; let the sea resound, and all that is in it." – Psalm 96:11 NIV

God is the Creator of the heavens and the earth, so they all reflect God's glory. God's glory is not limited to human activities, albeit the importance of human worship.

Creation reveals God's glory as well. All the trees in the forest sing praise to the Lord. The sea and everything in it proclaim God's magnificence. The birds of the air rejoice in the presence of God.

If nature can give glory to God, we, humans, cannot ignore God's influence over our lives. We should be ashamed of ourselves if we do not do so. As the Scripture says, "For since the creation of the world God's invisible qualities- his eternal power and divine nature – have been clearly seen, being understood from what has been made so that people are without excuse" (Romans 1:20 NIV). We do not have a valid reason to refuse to serve God.

We tend to enjoy our autonomy and ignore our dependence on God. However, if we really think about it, we are not as independent as we may think. We depend on God for our breath of life.

We have no idea what tomorrow will bring. We are living from second to second because we do not have any control over our destiny. Let's be wise and join in with creation to glorify God.

JUNE 5

"For you, LORD, are the Most High over all the earth; you are exalted far above all gods." – Psalm 97:9 NIV

*I*f you had the opportunity to know the true God, would you serve the false gods of this world?

Growing up in Haiti, I witnessed the worship of idols. People would sacrifice chickens and pigs as a sign of worship to demonic spirits. They call this practice voodoo. Deep down in their hearts, those Haitians know the God of light, but they remain slaves to the voodoo's spirits.

The Most High is the God of Abraham, the God of Jacob, and the God of Israel. He is Yahweh, the true God. If you have committed your heart to Yahweh, then your God is above all gods.

Keep in mind that the gods cannot save anyone. Only the true God can save people through Jesus Christ, the Son. Jesus is the Messiah, the Anointed One. He shed His blood on the cross for us so that we can have eternal life. As a result, we can become kings, priests, and prophets with Jesus through the anointing of God's Spirit who lives in us.

If you are going to spend your energy in worship, be sure you worship the Almighty God. You want to be sure that your God is above all gods. Do not spend your time and energy worshiping the gods that cannot save you. Jesus is the Savior.

Exalt the God of all the earth. He can rescue you in times of distress. Furthermore, the Almighty God loves you and wants to be part of your existence as you journey through life.

JUNE 6

"The LORD has made his salvation known and revealed his righteousness to the nations." – Psalm 98:2 NIV

*E*verything about God, the Creator of the universe, is carefully orchestrated. Following the fall of Adam and Eve, God announced His plan of salvation for His people. Speaking to Satan, who took the form of a serpent, God said, "And I will put enmity between you and the woman, and between your offspring and hers; he will crush your head, and you will strike his heel" (Genesis 3:15 NIV). Here, God announced the victory of Jesus Christ over Satan.

Jesus' death and resurrection opened the door for the whole world to make peace with the Heavenly Father. And through Jesus, you can become God's righteous. You cannot be righteous by your own efforts, but you can be declared righteous by virtue of your faith in Jesus. This is an act of God.

Jesus is the revelation of God on earth because it is through Him that God's love is fully demonstrated. Unless you put your faith in Jesus Christ, you cannot experience the true love of God. "For God so loved the world that he gave his one and only Son, that whoever believes in him shall not perish but have eternal life" (John 3:16 NIV). This provision is for the whole world, not just for a nation. If you are part of humanity, you are included. Therefore, your salvation lies in your decision to accept God's plan of salvation.

JUNE 7

"Moses and Aaron were among his priests, Samuel was among those who called on his name; they called on the LORD and he answered them." – Psalm 99:6 NIV

*I*n the Old Testament, the priests were anointed to represent the people before God. They were not allowed to approach God on their own. As priests, they were obligated to set themselves apart for service, and they were from the Levitical lineage. As the people's representatives, God answered them when they called on Him.

In the New Testament, God has transferred the priesthood from the Levitical lineage to Melchizedek's order. Since the priesthood is solidly handed over to Jesus Christ, the High Priest from above, you are now a priest as well.

You do not need a mediator to communicate with God. You can call on God any time provided you remain in Jesus Christ, the High Priest of the new covenant. "But you are a chosen people, a royal priesthood, a holy nation, God's special possession, that you may declare the praises of him who have called you out of darkness into his wonderful light" (1 Peter 2:9 NIV).

Since you belong to the royal priesthood of the new covenant, you have God's anointing to carry out the works of the Lord. This special privilege is available to all God's children because Christ's Spirit dwells in them. Apostle Paul said, "And if anyone does not have the Spirit of Christ, they do not belong to Christ" (Romans 8:9b NIV).

JUNE 8

"For the LORD is good and his love endures forever; his faithfulness continues through all generations." – Psalm100:5 NIV

What sets the living God apart from all the gods that people worship around the world is that He is a good God. When you think of God, think of His goodness.

God is light, and in Him there is no darkness at all. Because of God's immense power, people tend to think of God as a God of vengeance. God's vengeance is not His priority. God is in the business of loving people. God did not create humans so He can punish them. Punishment is only reserved for Satan and those who have chosen to disobey God.

God's love is not a temporary phenomenon that comes and goes. The love of God will remain forever. Since God's nature is love, He cannot stop loving. God will continue to love you, even when you stop loving Him. God is constantly wooing His people.

If you have surrendered your heart to the Lord, continue to rely on His eternal love. He will never leave you, nor will He abandon you in times of distress. Even when you are unaware of God, He is still with you. He will continue to be with you forever.

There is no place you can go where God's presence is absent. God is always there, even when you do not feel it. You can rely on God's faithfulness, no matter what. Remember God's Spirit dwells in you if you have surrendered your heart to Jesus.

JUNE 9

"I will not look with approval on anything that is vile. I hate what faithless people do; I will have no part in it." – Psalm 101:3 NIV

As time goes on, people are becoming less and less interested in godliness. Holiness is no longer seen as a worthwhile pursuit, because more people are willing to accept the ungodly way of life.

Despite the reluctance to pursue holiness, God's people are to remain faithful to God's words. God's people are not to hate people. They are called to hate the sinful actions that are happening around them.

If you love the people and hate their sins, you will show compassion toward them by sharing the love of Jesus with them instead of hating them with a passion. This is what sets God's people apart from religious zealots. Religious zealots do not want anything to do with people who are living in sins. Imagine what would have happened to us if God had decided to abandon us altogether due to our sinful nature.

While you are to try to love those who are evil, you are to avoid participating in their sinful activities. This is another characteristic of a truly born-again person. Although they know their righteousness is based on what Jesus did on the cross, they resolve to live a godly life as they wait for the appearing of Jesus Christ. They act that way because they want to draw more people to Jesus Christ.

JUNE 10

"Hear my prayer, LORD; let my cry for help come to you." – Psalm 102:1 NIV

The LORD is the source of refuge for those who have accepted Jesus as their Lord and Savior. Do not hesitate to approach God with your needs in the name of Jesus Christ, the Savior of the world. As Jesus declared to His disciples, "You did not choose me, but I chose you and appointed you so that you might go and bear fruit – fruit that will last – and so that whatever you ask in my name the Father will give you" (John 15:16 NIV).

If you have surrendered your heart to the Lord, Jesus has authorized you to call on His name. As a child of God, you have His favor. And because you have God's favor, you may call on Him in times of distress and expect Him to hear you. If He is not your Lord, make Him your Lord so you can have all the privileges that come with His name.

Lord, I thank you for the opportunity to call on your name and expect your intervention. Thank you for your favor and your compassion.

I know you can answer my prayers, not based on my own efforts, but because of your favor and your grace.

Thank you, Lord, for your mercy and compassion. Thank you, Lord, for shedding your blood on the cross for me. Most importantly, thank you for being there for me.

JUNE 11

"Praise the LORD, my soul; all my inmost being, praise his holy name." – Psalm 103:1 NIV

*Y*ou must command your soul to submit to the Lord. It does not happen automatically. Sometimes, your soul is more willing to do what displeases God. Yes, your spirit is willing to worship God because it is the part of you that has been impacted by salvation. You are more complex than you think. What do you mean? Well, your body and your soul are still susceptible of falling into sin. Really? Yes. What can I do about it?

It is not easy, but you can overcome the desires of the flesh if you allow your spirit to guide your body and soul. Born-again individuals succumb to temptation when they allow their body and soul to dominate them. Keep in mind that your soul includes your emotions and your intellectual capacities.

What is the key to overcoming temptation? First, you need to submit yourself to the Almighty. Second, you need to be very mindful of your thoughts. Satan usually starts by planting a bad idea in your mind. Through your soul, you begin to wrestle with that idea. God's Spirit, who lives in you, will make you aware of the danger of that idea and warn you.

Since you are not a machine, the Holy Spirit will not stop you. You must use your knowledge of God to fight the idea so that you can experience victory. If you do not do that, you will continue to ruminate that bad thought until you surrender yourself to it. You'd better watch out!

JUNE 12

"I will sing to the LORD all my life; I will sing praise to my God as long as I live." – Psalm 104:33 NIV

Serving the Lord is a lifetime commitment. Once you have come to understand the benefits of serving God, there is nothing on earth that can replace such a milestone in your life. Serving God is a larger-than-life endeavor. This is exactly what this book is all about.

It does not matter how successful you are in this life. Unless you live for God, you will be a loser in the end. If you have made God your Lord and Savior, you may now go ahead and conquer the world. Rejoice because your destiny is now in God's hands. You have nothing to worry about, even though the earth shakes and crumbles. The LORD is now your refuge and your safety.

Based on your assurance in the God of Jacob, you can't help praising the name of the Lord as you live. As a matter of fact, your praise to the Lord will continue well beyond your life on this planet. After your physical death, you will continue to give praise to the Lord in your glorified body.

In the second coming of Christ, your spirit will have a glorified body that will never be decayed. In that new body, you will be able to enjoy fully all the benefits God has in store for you.

Now you have limited access to your spiritual benefits. You have not seen anything yet. Everything God has for you will be readily available to you in heaven. Therefore, praise the Lord with your life. Keep in mind that you will live forever.

JUNE 13

"Give praise to the LORD, proclaim his name; make known among the nations what he has done." – Psalm 105:1 NIV

*I*n addition to praising the Lord, you are encouraged to proclaim His name.

Your pursuit of wisdom should empower you to win the lost souls for Christ. "The fruit of the righteous is a tree of life, and the one who is wise saves lives" (Proverbs 11:30 NIV).

Despite the worries of this life, wisdom enables believers to see life through God's eyes. Without such a divine endowment, you are not capable of sifting through life successfully.

Believers proclaim God's name because they want people who are living in the darkness to come to know the God of light. God has done something remarkable when He demonstrated His love toward us by sending Jesus Christ, His Son, to die in our place. This was indeed an extraordinary demonstration of love and grace. Such knowledge must not be hidden from the world.

We need to proclaim loud and clear God's immense love. God did not spare anything from us. He has given it all to us unreservedly. Jesus gave all He got to prevent Satan from having the upper hand. And He did it when the Heavenly Father raised Him from the dead. This is what we need to let others know. God has done so much for us for which we must be grateful.

JUNE 14

"They forgot the God who saved them, who had done great things in Egypt, miracles in the land of Ham and awesome deeds by the Red Sea." – Psalm 106:21 and 22 NIV

God had displayed tremendous power in Egypt to deliver the Israelites from the yoke of slavery. God spectacularly parted the Red Sea so that the people could walk on dry land, thereby avoiding the Egyptian massacre. Yet they managed to forget all those miracles while they were in the wilderness. As a result, they were not able to reach the Promised Land. From the older generations, only Joshua and Caleb were granted the opportunity to enter Canaan because they had put their faith in God to deliver them. The rest of the people wondered in the wilderness for forty years and died there.

Today remember what God did for you so that you do not end up falling in the same trap in which the Israelites had fallen in the Old Testament. God sent Jesus to die on the cross for you. Through His death, Jesus has paved the way for you to live forever with God in the New Jerusalem, where there will be no sickness and death.

Words cannot describe such a marvelous gift of eternal life. There is nothing that can be compared with the hope of glory. This is so indescribably awesome! God did all of this to show His love for you and me.

Ask God to give you strength and wisdom so that you can share His love with others.

JUNE 15

"Give thanks to the LORD, for he is good; his love endures forever." – Psalm 107:1 NIV

There are so many reasons for which we need to give thanks to the Lord, and one of those reasons is because He is good. Goodness is an inherent attribute of God. In fact, only God is inherently good in every sense of the word. As humans, we may display certain characteristics of goodness, but we are not essentially good. The reason is that our sinful nature has rendered us vulnerable to evil tendencies.

Therefore, we totally depend on Christ's righteousness to satisfy God's prerequisites for heaven. God will accept us in heaven because when He looks at us, He will see us through Jesus Christ's righteousness. Christ's righteousness neutralizes the impact of our own righteousness, which falls short of God's criteria for eternal life.

Considering God's goodness, we need to give thanks to Him. His goodness has caused Him to show mercies to us, even though we did not deserve mercy. God came down to our level when we could not reach His standards on our own.

God's goodness is complemented by His eternal love. Through His love, Christ suffered crucifixion for us. It takes love to keep God from destroying us from the face of the earth in a twinkling of an eye.

For that reason, give thanks to Lord for His goodness as well as His love that endures forever.

JUNE 16

"Be exalted, O God, above the heavens; let your glory be over all the earth." – Psalm 108:5 NIV

When God is elevated, the power of darkness must go. By His omnipresence or His ability to be everywhere at the same time, God can occupy every nook and cranny. That means you are never alone. God dwells in you by virtue of His Spirit if you know Him.

We celebrate God's exaltation, for He alone is above the heavens. He created the heavens and earth and everything that is in them.

The whole world will recognize God's sovereignty. Those who are not willing to acknowledge Him now will eventually do so in the end. Sadly, it will be too late for them.

God's glory permeates all the earth, and every creature is under His control. While Satan has limited power on the earth to carry out his evil deeds, his dominion has been significantly reduced by the death and resurrection of Christ.

Lord, I exalt you above all else because there is no one like you. No one can overcome your sovereignty.

Thank you so much for being there for me, no matter where I am.

Lord, I pray for the dismantlement of the power of darkness around me.

Be glorified in my life. Through the anointing of the Holy Spirit, allow me to make you known everywhere I go so that more people may come to experience your love and your glory in their lives.

JUNE 17

"Help me, LORD my God; save me according to your unfailing love." – Psalm 109:26 NIV

Lord, I am so happy for the opportunity to call on you for help. I do not know what I would do if you were not available. I call on you because you are my God. I want to serve only you, Lord. I close my eyes on other gods because they are useless.

Lord, give me strength to continue my journey without giving up serving you. My request to you, LORD, is to be faithful until the end. I do not want to disappoint you in life.

Lord, give me wisdom so that I can discern right from wrong. I know Satan is trying his best to tempt me. Please protect me from all harm.

Lord, thank you so much for your unfailing love. You have demonstrated your love to me when I was still living in darkness. I am glad you have chosen to send Jesus to die in my place. Thank you, LORD, for saving me.

Lord, I pray for my family and friends. I also pray for my church. Grant the leaders of my church wisdom so they can continue to make a difference in the community and around the world.

Moreover, I pray for my country and its leaders. Grant them wisdom to carry out your duties in righteousness. I pray in the name of Jesus. Amen!

JUNE 18

"The LORD has sworn and will not change his mind: "You are a priest forever, in the order of Melchizedek." – Psalm 110:4 NIV

The priesthood of Jesus Christ, the Messiah, is unique because He was both the priest and the sacrifice. Unlike the Levitical priesthood that was temporary, Jesus' priesthood needs no renewal because it has been established forever in the order of Melchizedek. Melchizedek's priesthood came directly from God, not from Judah.

Jesus is real. You can put your complete trust in Him as your Lord and Savior. He is not a temporary Messiah, who is here today and will not be around in the future. When you put your faith in Jesus, you are tied to Him both on earth and in heaven. Jesus will accompany you on your journey through life and will be with you long after your physical death.

If you are looking for something that has substance, look no further. Your faith in Jesus is enough. Jesus is your eternal security.

Do not allow people to make you doubt your faith in Jesus. God has sworn on this deal and will not change His mind. Satan, by his persistence, will not be able to break through the security blood line.

Your life in Christ is sealed and protected by the Holy Spirit. Your High Priest is Jesus Christ, and God has bet on Him forever.

JUNE 19

"The fear of the LORD is the beginning of wisdom; all who follow his precepts have good understanding. To him belongs eternal praise." – Psalm 111:10 NIV

A genuine quest for wisdom begins with love and respect for God. The fear of the Lord is different from the fear of man. It is not designed to turn you into a nervous wreck. It is an awe-inspiring reverence that comes from your knowledge of the Almighty.

God is not only your source of knowledge; He can also provide you with discernment so that you will be able to know what to do in complex situations.

Divine wisdom is far superior to conventional wisdom, which comes from your experience and your knowledge of things. Wisdom from God is a divine endowment. You can only get it if you are willing to love and respect God. Have you ever seen people who are supposed to know better doing horrible things? Those folks have a lot of knowledge, but they have no divine wisdom.

In addition to wisdom, good understanding comes from following God's precepts, which is the general rule you need to guide your Christian experience. Those precepts can be found in the Holy Bible.

The Holy Spirit also guides your thoughts in different circumstances. Continue to love and respect God and ask Him to grant you wisdom from above.

JUNE 20

"Praise the LORD. Blessed are those who fear the LORD, who find great delight in his commands." – Psalm 112:1 NIV

Blessings are reserved for you if you make loving and respecting the LORD your life's commitment. There is peace in loving God. There is also victory in praising the LORD.

Satan would like you to keep your mind on your problems so that you lose sight of God's blessings. When you praise the LORD, the chains that have kept you bound for so long get undone. Suddenly, the burden of this life gets lifted, a new sense of freedom gets released, and you have a new source of energy to confront the foe.

When you walk in obedience with the LORD, you do not find God's commands burdensome. It is the same when you abide by the law of the land. You do not worry when you see a police officer, if you are not breaking the law. People who are not following the law, they tend to be afraid of the police.

In the New Testament, the emphasis is not much on the Ten Commandments. However, we still need to abide by the general precepts found in the word of God.

As Christ's followers, we keep God's commands by loving God and others as we love ourselves. For salvation, we depend on God's grace through faith in Jesus Christ, not on our own performance. Praise the LORD for His mercy and grace.

JUNE 21

"From the rising of the sun to the place where it sets, the name of the LORD is to be praised." – Psalm 113:3 NIV

This verse does not mean that you need to stay up 24/7 to praise and worship the LORD. You need to find time to work and sleep. This simply means that God is always worthy to be praised, no matter the circumstances. It also shows that our God is unchangeable. He is very consistent in every way.

There are times that you may not feel that you should praise God. However, the Scripture encourages us to do so in all circumstances. "Rejoice always, pray continually, give thanks in all circumstances; for this is God's will for you in Christ Jesus" (1 Thessalonians 5:16-18 NIV).

Your praise to the LORD is not based on how things are in your life. God cares about your situations, but you should not allow your problems to dictate how you view God.

God wants you to be spiritually stable. He does not want you to drift like a boat whose anchor is broken. Your daily attitude toward God must be based on your faith in God through Jesus Christ, your Savior, and it is through Christ's righteousness that the Heavenly Father accepts you as righteous.

Continue to remain firm in the LORD. Be ready to offer up praises to God consistently. Acknowledge God in your life, even though things around you make no sense. This is God's will for you in Christ.

JUNE 22

"Tremble, earth, at the presence of the Lord, at the presence of the God of Jacob, who turned the rock into a pool, the hard rock into springs of water." – Psalm 114:7 and 8 NIV

Yahweh, the God of Jacob, has complete authority over the earth. He also has authority over you and your circumstances. Moses experienced God's dominion over nature when he was in a bind with the Israelites. They were thirsty, and Moses did not have water to quench their thirst. God ordered Moses to use the same staff he had used to strike the Red Sea earlier. "I will stand there before you by the rock at Horeb. Strike the rock, and water will come out of it for the people to drink" (Exodus 17: 6a NIV).

Is there an area in your life over which you want the God of Jacob, your God, to have dominion? God can alter your circumstances for His glory. Surrender your situation to God and trust Him to deal with it.

In this hour, I come to you, the God of Jacob, my God. I know you have a plan for my life.

I pray that your will be done in my life. I surrender my situation to you, LORD. Come to my rescue so that I can tell others about your wonderful deeds.

Thank you so much, LORD, for your favor. May your name be exalted above all the earth.

May your name be exalted in my life. I pray in the name of Jesus Christ, my Savior. Amen.

JUNE 23

"May you be blessed by the LORD, the Maker of heaven and earth." – Psalm 115:15 NIV

*T*oday receive God's blessings upon your life, your household, your friends, your church, and everything you touch. May God, the Maker of heaven and earth, bless the country where you live as well.

As God showers His blessings upon you beyond imagination, make yourself available to be a blessing to others. Do not be stingy.

As God was blessing Abraham, He declared that Abraham would be a blessing. "I will make you into a great nation, and I will bless you; I will make your name great, and you will be a blessing" (Genesis 12:2 NIV).

When you pray with the attitude of being a blessing to others, you are ready for all kinds of breakthroughs in this life because God wants you to help others.

God's blessings upon Abraham encompassed Abraham as an individual, his nation, and others.

Therefore, dream big when you pray for God's blessing. Do not pray just for enough to satisfy your own needs. Pray for enough to help many for the glory of God.

JUNE 24

"The LORD is gracious and righteous; our God is full of compassion." – Psalm 116:5 NIV

Yahweh, the God of Israel, is gracious. As a gracious God, you can count on His unmerited favor. It is by grace you can have a relationship with God despite your human frailties.

God has shown His grace toward us when He sent Jesus Christ, His Son, to die on the cross so that we could obtain mercy. We were totally separated from God due to the fall of Adam and Eve. The only thing we deserved was eternal punishment. God's grace has leveled the ground so that we can stand with confidence before God, for His righteousness would not allow sinners to associate with God.

Yahweh, the God of Israel, is righteous. As a righteous God, He does not tolerate sin in His presence. By His grace, He has provided a way out for us.

Jesus Christ's death and resurrection paid the necessary price for us. Now when God looks at us, He sees Jesus Christ. When He sees Jesus Christ, He sees perfection. Without this solution, no one would be able to see the face of God.

If you have made Jesus Christ your Savior, God has a perfect reason to let you in heaven. You are riding on Christ's righteousness, not your own performance. Yahweh has shown His compassion through Jesus Christ, His Son.

JUNE 25

"Praise the LORD, all you nations; extol him, all you peoples. For great is his love toward us, and the faithfulness of the LORD endures forever. Praise the LORD." – Psalm 117:1 and 2 NIV

As you read Psalm 117, the shortest Psalm, a total of two verses, think of the worldwide invitation to acclaim or rave about the LORD. This mandate extends to all nations, irrespective of their languages and cultures. We are serving a universal God. He is not confined to one nation or culture.

Scripture ascribes praise to the LORD. Yes, there are many entities and images that nations revere as gods with the lower case "g." They do not deserve our praises. According to the Christian Bible, those gods are idols, and they are simply useless.

It is to be noted that God hates idols. Yahweh, the God of Israel, said this: "I am the LORD your God, who brought you out of the land of slavery. "You shall have no other gods before me" (Exodus 20:2 and 3). Here, God had recognized the possibility of having other gods, so He warned the Israelites not to associate with any of them.

Yahweh, the God of Jacob, is the only true God. All other gods are false. They are useless in that they are not able to save anyone. Only Yahweh can save, and He does it through His Son, Jesus. God's love toward us is awesome, and His faithfulness endures forever. Let us continue to praise Him!

JUNE 26

"The LORD is with me; I will not be afraid. What can mere mortals do to me!" – Psalm 118:6 NIV

When I was a little boy, I used to be afraid of the dark. One night, my dad and I traveled about fifty miles from the southeast border of Haiti to the Dominican Republic on foot. It took us the whole night to make the crossing. There was no electricity along the way. That means we had to walk in utter darkness the whole time. As I walked, I tried to stay close to my dad. And so long as I could see my dad in front of me, I had no fear. My dad was with me.

Similarly, you have no reason to be afraid when you walk with God. God is with you, even though you may not feel His presence. Depend on God's protection, for He is faithful. No mortals can touch you if God does not grant them access to you. And if He does grant them access to you, the outcome will be in your favor. Somehow, something positive will come out of it.

Yes, we are living in a fallen world, where people are constantly trying to harm us. However, with God on our side, we do not have to be paralyzed by fear. Mortals do not have the last word. Remember our help comes from the LORD, the Maker of heaven and earth.

JUNE 27

"Your word is a lamp for my feet, a light on my path." – Psalm 119:105 NIV

As you navigate this world of darkness, you need God's word to help you keep your feet on the path of righteousness.

Today it is very difficult to live a life of integrity. Given the ubiquity of social media, sin is very accessible, for distance is no longer an issue.

Allow God's word to guide you as you make decisions on many situations. The world is full of all kinds of enticements, so it is important that you evaluate your options so that you do not get involved in things that dishonor the name of the Lord. Remember you are the light of the world.

God can use you to bring glory to His name. Be willing to be an instrument in God's hands, and let your light shine brightly for all the world to see.

Do not sacrifice your godly values for financial benefits or to please people. It is okay to wait for a few years to be promoted instead of selling your soul to get rich or get an important gig.

Keep in mind, nothing is more important than your relationship with God. God will continue to take care of you if you put your trust in Him. Remember you may have to suffer for a little while to maintain your integrity for the glory of God.

As you journey through life, your path may not be easy, but continue to use God's word as your life's compass.

JUNE 28

"I call on the LORD in my distress, and he answers me." – Psalm 120:1 NIV

*N*o matter what you are going through today, God has your back. You are never alone when you walk with the Almighty. He is with you now and will be with you forever.

Going through distress is not easy. Those moments of great anxiety can cause you to lose your mental balance. It is important that you do not dwell on those moments too long without seeking help from God.

Sometimes, God can use others to answer your prayers. Be flexible as you seek God for answers. Humans are instruments in God's hands. He can use them however He sees fit. What is important is to give thanks to God for answering your prayers.

In your distress, do not let your faith be weakened. The deeper your sorrow the stronger your faith should be. Do not abandon God to seek help from people who do not believe in God.

Keep in mind that Satan will try to tempt you so you can doubt God's power to help you. Keep the faith, even though you are going through great difficulties. God knows the hour of your deliverance.

JUNE 29

"My help comes from the LORD, the Maker of heaven and earth." – Psalm 121:2 NIV

Don't hesitate to call on God for help. He can really help you. God has the solution for your problem, so He can help you discover it. I say "discover it" because God wants you to participate in the solution. If you need money, you may not necessarily find it on the ground, but God can help you find a job. God can send someone your way to bless you tremendously as well.

It does not matter the medium God uses. What is important is that God has the capacity to help you if you are willing to approach Him for help. When seeking medical treatment, trust God to use your physicians in their effort to find a cure for your illness.

God knows about the universe because He made the heavens and the earth and everything that is in them. Despite your academic accomplishments, you can believe in God because you don't know everything there is to know. Do not allow skepticism to prevent you from putting your faith in God. You have nothing to lose and everything to gain.

When you acknowledge that your help comes from God, you tend to be less frustrated. People may try to keep you down, but they cannot do it forever.

God will intervene on your behalf so you can have your breakthrough. Therefore, continue to rely on God as you pursue your career goals or continue to develop your skills at work. God loves you, and He has your best interest at heart. Don't give up!

JUNE 30

"I rejoiced with those who said to me, "Let us go to the house of the LORD." – Psalm 122:1 NIV

When you have a chance, invite people who are not churchgoers to go to church with you. This is a great place to introduce them to the Almighty.

The house of Yahweh is a place of worship. Since God created us to praise and worship Him, it is a good thing to dedicate an hour or so to worship with God's people.

Going to church is not a requirement for salvation, but people who have received salvation should see the relevance of going to church. Worshiping together is a good habit to have. It is a good place of fellowship with other believers.

Going to church gives you the opportunity to contribute to projects aimed at reaching out to your community, your city, and the world.

You may not have the opportunity to travel abroad to preach the gospel, but if you belong to a local church, you will have many opportunities to invest in worthy causes. You may also have a chance to participate in short-term mission trips or support world missions. All those activities are made possible by contributions from members of a local church.

Another important reason to go to church is to be with God's people. When you get to heaven, you will be with God's people, so you should get used to being with them while you are here. Furthermore, it is a lot of fun to worship God together. Satan does not like that.

JULY 1

"I lift up my eyes to you, to you who sit enthroned in heaven." – Psalm 123:1 NIV

*T*his song reminds you where to go when you need help in your life. It is important that you turn to God and worship Him with all your mind. It takes wisdom for a person to acknowledge God.

By ignorance people tend to turn to the force of darkness when they need help. If you open yourself up to evil spirits, they will come to inhabit you. That's why there are so many people who can communicate with demonic spirits. They are mediums. Demonic spirits are not dedicated to serving the true God. They follow Satan and are available to carry out his devilish bidding.

It is important that we stay in harmony with Yahweh, who is the God of Israel, the God of light. Anything else belongs to the force of darkness. God is jealous and does not want us to serve other gods.

In the Old Testament, God was among His people, but He did not choose to live in them. In the New Testament, God decided to live in those who have put their trust in Him through the Spirit (Romans 8:9b).

While God sits enthroned in heaven, He also lives in you if you have accepted Jesus Christ as your Savior.

Knowing that God lives in you through the Spirit, you can call on Him anytime. You do not need to address demonic spirits or visit a medium. God is available to listen to your prayers.

JULY 2

"Our help is the name of the LORD, the Maker of heaven and earth." – Psalm 124:8 NIV

*I*f our help is in the name of the LORD, it is important that we know His name. Having fled to Egypt, Moses went to Midian to find refuge. While in Midian, He had a chance to integrate the household of Reuel, also known as Jethro, a priest with seven daughters. Zipporah, one of the seven daughters, was given to Moses in marriage. They had a son; whose name was Gershom.

While Moses was in Midian, he had a special encounter with God in Horeb, the mountain of God, according to Genesis 3. While he was tending sheep, he saw a burning bush. "Do not come any closer," God said. "Take off your sandals, for the place where you are standing is holy ground" Then He said," I am the God of your father, the God of Abraham, the God of Isaac and the God of Jacob" (Exodus 3:5 and 6).

In the Hebrew language, the official name of God is Yahweh. Initially, there were no vowels in God's name (YHWH), so biblical linguists inserted the vowels A and E to make it easier to pronounce.

In this devotional book, when you see the word "LORD" written in all caps, it refers to Yahweh, the God of Abraham, Jacob, and Isaac.

Our help is in Yahweh, the God of Abraham, Isaac, and Jacob. And by virtue of Jesus, the God of Jacob is our God as well. Don't hesitate to call on Him any time for help.

JULY 3

"Those who trust in the LORD are like Mount Zion, which cannot be shaken but endures forever." – Psalm 125:1 NIV

*K*ing David had a stronghold in Mount Zion in the City of David. A stronghold is a place used for protection from enemies. Mount Zion is sometimes used to refer to the entire land of Israel or Jerusalem.

In a biblical sense, Jerusalem is God's "Holy City, which will be coming down out of heaven from God" (Revelation 21:10b). After the judgment of the Great White Throne, God will establish the New Jerusalem, where we will live forever with Him. In this connection, Mount Zion cannot be shaken.

If you trust in the LORD, He is your stronghold. You can rely on Him for protection. Just like Mount Zion, your stronghold in God is solid and cannot be shaken.

God's protection is not limited to an earthly experience; you can also count on it beyond the grave.

It is good to know that we are not going to make the final journey alone. We can take comfort in the fact that God will be with us both here and in eternity. Like Mount Zion, God's protection will endure forever.

Lord, thank you for the opportunity to trust in you for protection. I know I can count on you, no matter what. Help me to continue to rely on you forever. Amen.

JULY 4

"Those who sow with tears will reap with songs of joy. Those who go out weeping, carrying seed to sow, will return with songs of joy, carrying sheaves with them." – Psalm 126:5 and 6 NIV

Whatever you are sowing right now, don't be discouraged. The time will come when you will be able to reap a harvest if you do not give up. There is no prayer that does not have an amen. The day of your independence is near!

If you are working hard to pay off your debts, keep making those payments regularly. Someday you will be delivered from your creditors. You will be able to enjoy the freedom of being debt-free. Similarly, if you are working on your difficult marriage, ask God for patience and wisdom. God will make a way out for you.

If you are working on your college degree, keep on studying and turning in those research papers. You will be excited when you are walking across the stage to receive your diploma.

If you lost a loved one, do not give up hope. Someday you will have a chance to see him or her in heaven.

Finally, continue to serve the LORD faithfully. I know it is hard to say no to temptation, but do not succumb. Continue to pursue holiness.

Submit yourself to God and resist the devil. During your earthly journey, keep sharing the love of Jesus with others. Keep sowing the seed of salvation when you have a chance. You will be happy to reap a spiritual harvest in heaven.

JULY 5

"Unless the LORD builds the house, the builders labor in vain."
– Psalm 127:1 NIV

Although God has given you autonomy to be at the helm of your life, that does not preclude God totally from being involved in your life. Therefore, it is important that you acknowledge God as you embark on conquering the world.

There is nothing wrong if you plan your life; nevertheless, try to invite God in the planning process. God is the Chief Architect in the building process. The builders are to follow closely the blueprint that God has designed for the house.

Whether you know it or not, God is in control of your life. When the dust has settled, you will have to give God an account of your journey through life. Your best approach is to surrender your future to God and ask Him to guide your steps. No matter what you are doing in life, always invite God to be your co-pilot. God knows everything about you, and He will be in control of you long after you say goodbye to this world.

If your life is built on your own understanding without God's involvement, all your efforts are vain. Try not to spend your time on earth ignoring God. Be wise and ask God to reveal Himself to you. Find time to seek the LORD with all your heart. Furthermore, live your life honoring God. Trust the Chief Architect so that your labor is not in vain.

JULY 6

"Blessed are all who fear the LORD, who walk in obedience to him." – Psalm 128:1 NIV

*I*t is not enough to revere God or stand in awe of God. You also need to walk in obedience to Him. If you have not done so, your first act of obedience should consist in surrendering your life to Jesus as your Lord and Savior.

In the New Testament, Jesus does not emphasize the Mosaic Law or the Ten Commandments. We are called to obey God. Jesus said, "If you love me, keep my commands" (John 14:15 NIV). The emphasis is on loving God. Jesus' commands require that we love God with all our hearts and love others as we love ourselves.

By virtue of the cross, we have now the opportunity to receive salvation by faith and through grace. That means that we are no longer depending on our own works of righteousness to make it to heaven. At the same time, we are called to represent Jesus on earth after salvation. We cannot represent God if we walk in disobedience to God.

On one hand, we are saved by grace; on the other hand, we are called to be witnesses. In order to represent Jesus in this fallen world, we are to walk in obedience.

If you revere God and walk in obedience to Him, you will eat the fruit of your labor. Above all, you will have the opportunity to bestow those blessings upon your immediate family and many generations to come.

JULY 7

"Plowmen have plowed my back and made their furrows long. But the Lord is righteous; he has cut me free from the cords of the wicked." – Psalm 129:3 and 4 NIV

You do not need to consult a voodoo priest if you feel that you have been attacked by someone or your enemy. You can go straight to God. You have full protection in the LORD, the God of Abraham, Jacob, and Isaac. If you have made Jesus your Savior, have no fear!

Ask God to cut the chains that have kept you in bondage. Run to God and ask Him to deliver you from all harm. Do not be deceived in thinking that someone else can deliver you from the wicked. There is no deliverance in no one else. In fact, if you surrender your will to Satan by thinking that he can deliver you, you will become his servant. Satan does not deserve your worship. Only God is worthy of worship.

Those who purport to have power to deliver you know who is in control. As a matter of fact, voodoo priests often use psalms and other verses from the Holy Bible to try to deliver people from bondage. Satan is an imposter and knows that God is fully in control of the universe with everything that is in it.

It does not matter what people have plotted against you. You can overcome the power of darkness by putting your trust in God. God will cut the cords of the wicked and set you free.

JULY 8

"If you, LORD, kept a record of sins, Lord, who could stand?"
– Psalm 130:3 NIV

God is righteous and cannot condone your sins. And you will not be able to count on your performance to get to heaven. Is there a way out for you? Yes, there is a way out for you.

The solution is in Jesus, the Savior. God had examined humans and realized that we are all doomed without His own intervention. Consequently, He decided to deploy a new plan of redemption. Without that redemptive plan, no one would be able to stand before God.

By virtue of His holiness, God cannot tolerate sins. In order to stand before God, we must be perfect. How can we be perfect in a sinful world? We cannot be perfect on our own; we need Christ's righteousness to cover us when we stand before God. God will let us in if we are covered by Christ's righteousness. By His blood, Christ has cleansed us from all sins and presented us before the Heavenly Father as saints. What a glorious victory! We are now fully ready to stand before God with confidence.

LORD, thank you for the opportunity to stand before you with the knowledge that my sins are forgiven by the blood of Jesus, your Son. I am grateful to know that you have not kept a record of my sins, for they have been washed away by the blood of the Lamb. Thank you, LORD, for your amazing grace!

JULY 9

"My heart is not proud, LORD, my eyes are not haughty; I do not concern myself with great matters or things too wonderful for me." – Psalm 131:1 NIV

Be willing to surrender yourself to the LORD like a child. As a child, you are putting yourself in a position that you must depend on God for your destiny. Such an exercise requires your absolute humility.

As you humble yourself before God, your biggest obstacle is your pride. Your pride would want you to be in control of your life all the time, but you must allow God to take the helm of it spiritually. This does not mean a complete abdication from your social responsibilities. You still need to get yourself a good education if possible. Keeping a job is also part of this equation. However, you can still trust God to fight your battle for you by inviting Him to be involved in your daily dealing with society.

Additionally, you need God's help not to succumb to temptation. Your eyes will constantly afford you with ample opportunity to exercise your ego. You will be tempted to set God aside from time to time as you journey through life, but do not hesitate to bring all godless thoughts under control through your submission to God.

Know that God is your concern and eternity is your focus in life. Be engaged with your environment, but do not lose sight of your divine purpose.

Pray and ask God to keep you from having a proud heart!

JULY 10

"LORD, remember David and all his self-denial." – Psalm 132:1 NIV

*D*avid had a burning desire to build a dwelling place for the LORD, so he sought the LORD with all his heart denying himself physical rest.

Sometimes, if we want to have a breakthrough, we must be willing to deny ourselves certain comforts in life. Keep in mind that you are not working for your salvation. Self-denial is to be viewed as part of your overall Christian walk after salvation.

If you want to have fun all the time, you will not be able to reach your full potential. You need time to go school, keep a job, and carry out certain societal responsibilities. That does not mean that you should not relax at all. Approach life responsibly by making necessary sacrifices to get where you need to be.

Although David was not able to build the LORD a temple himself, he was able to obtain God's guarantee that his son, Solomon, would build a dwelling place for the Mighty One of Jacob.

As you seek the LORD with all your heart and present your requests to Him, He will not ignore your cry for help. God will remember your efforts and your self-denial.

JULY 11

"How good and pleasant it is when God's people live together in unity!" – Psalm 133:1 NIV

As Christ's followers, we are to practice brotherly fellowship. We should try our best to avoid infighting among us because we are witnesses for the LORD.

Regarding the body of Christ, which is the Church, Apostle Paul encouraged unity in diversity. "For we were all baptized by one Spirit so as to form one body- whether Jews or Gentiles, slave or free – and we were all given the Spirit to drink" (1 Corinthians 12:13 NIV). Apostle Paul continued to say, "There should be no division in the body, but that its parts should have equal concern for each other" (verse 25).

When God's people live in unity, they can attract nonbelievers to Christ. Nothing is more dissuasive than believers who act like they belong to the devil. When that happens, they make it more difficult to persuade people to accept Jesus as their Lord and Savior. Ask God to give you wisdom so you can use the love of Christ and the anointing that is in you to bring more people to God.

Practice unity among believers. If there are disputes among you, try your best to resolve the issues amiably. Do not involve unbelievers in resolving problems with your brothers and sisters unless it is necessary. Caveat: Do not hide criminal activities behind the walls of the local church. Report crimes to the respective authority. Seek advice from the elders of the local church if you cannot resolve the matters among you. Ask God to grant you wisdom to preserve the brotherly unity with your brothers and sisters.

JULY 12

"Lift up your hands in the sanctuary and praise the LORD." – Psalm 134:2 NIV

We go to the local church to worship and praise the LORD. Of course, we also listen to sermons among other things. When we praise God, we express our respect and gratitude toward Him.

We must respect God because He is the Ultimate Authority in our lives. No one is higher than God. He is the Almighty, the Alpha and the Omega, and the Maker of the heavens and earth. Most importantly, He is our God.

We show gratitude toward God for all He has done for us. God has provided us with salvation free of charge. All we need to do is to repent and turn to Him for forgiveness.

When we consider Jesus' ultimate sacrifice on the cross, no amount of praise is adequate. We will never be able to pay God back with our praise and worship.

When we go to the sanctuary, we are to lift our hands and praise God. We need to practice praising God because in heaven we will continue praising Him.

While there will be no need to preach the gospel in heaven, praise and worship will continue to be relevant.

Don't be ashamed to lift your hands and praise God in the local church. Ask God to embolden you today so that you can enjoy the freedom of praise in the sanctuary.

JULY 13

"I know that the LORD is great, that our Lord is greater than all gods." – Psalm 135:5 NIV

One of the major reasons that we should serve God is because He is above all gods. Throughout the world, people bow down before images, sacrifice animals to idols, and worship natural objects. They go through all those rituals because it is impossible for them not to worship.

The truth is that you were created to worship the true God, who is Yahweh, the God of Abraham, Isaac, and Jacob. Anyone who fails to surrender to the true God will end up finding a substitute.

You cannot live without worshipping, for it is in you to do so. If you have not surrendered yourselves to Yahweh, and you have not bowed down before some natural objects, you can be sure that you are worshiping yourself. You become your own god.

If you have surrendered your heart to the LORD, rejoice that your name is written in the Lamb's book of life. Your God is greater than all gods! Praise the LORD that you are counted among the wise, for wisdom is to know whose you are and where you will spend eternity.

If you have not encountered the true God, please make an honest effort to meet Him. The Bible says, "Seek the LORD while he may be found; call on him while he is near" (Isaiah 55:6 NIV).

JULY 14

"Give thanks to the LORD, for he is good. His love endures forever." – Psalm 136:1 NIV

*T*wenty-six times in this Psalm, the sentence "his love endures forever" is repeated. Each mention is for a specific reason, or something that God has done to merit such praise.

Some of the things in this Psalm are focused on God's prowess in the book of Exodus, especially how God was able to dismantle the Egyptian army and delivered the Israelites from slavery. For the Israelites, God's intervention was simply spectacular! Imagine what would have happened if God had not shown up just in time to open the Red Sea in order to provide an escape route for the Israelites.

In the New Testament, God did something extraordinary for the entire human race. He sent His Son, Jesus Christ, to save us from the bondage of sins.

The Israelites were dealing with physical bondage. Today we are dealing with spiritual bondage.

Take a few minutes to think about your own life and write down a list of things for which God deserves to be praised. Whatever is the nature of your situation, you can count on God to save you.

Give thanks to the LORD for He is good. His love endures forever.

JULY 15

"By the rivers of Babylon we sat and wept when we remembered Zion." – Psalm 137:1 NIV

*I*t pays to listen to God's warnings. For years, God had used the Prophets to warn the Israelites about their infidelity. They refused to listen to reason. They continued to prostitute themselves with other gods instead. They were keen on listening to false prophets, who were telling them what they wanted to hear. Consequently, God allowed the Babylonians to uproot them from their homeland and took them to Babylon. While in Babylon, they had time to reminisce about how good they had it in Jerusalem.

It is important that we continue to walk in the light. Satan's goal is to convince you that life on the other side of the fence is more enjoyable. Little do you know that danger is waiting for you on the other side. One way to overcome darkness is to continue to walk in the light.

In this fallen world, please pay attention to wisdom and do not allow Satan to invade your space. You are in the world, but you are not of the world.

God has a special purpose for your life. Allow God to mold you and train you in the way of righteousness so that you do not fall in the trap of the enemy.

JULY 16

"Though I walk in the midst of trouble, you preserve my life." – Psalm 138:7 NIV

When you are surrounded by difficulties, know that God has not abandoned you. Satan is there to convince you, during your moments of weakness, that your God is not able to deliver you.

The Sovereign God is never short of solutions. He is always on the throne and never abdicates His responsibilities as the Creator of the universe.

As a believer, you are not exempt from trouble. What you need to know, however, is that through your trouble, God will determine your way of escape. Instead of throwing in the towel, you need to continue to focus your eyes on the LORD.

Do not be discouraged when you are in trouble, because the LORD, your God is with you. He is there to figure out a way out for you.

Do not listen to the voice of the ungodly that tend to question the effectiveness of your faith in God. They are quick to ask, "Where was your God when you got sick? Where was your God when your marriage was on the rock? They only have questions, but they have no viable solutions for your dilemma.

Continue to put your trust in God, even when you do not understand all the ins and outs of your situation.

Your God is able and is fully capable of handling your trouble. Surely, He is in control of your destiny.

JULY 17

"You have searched me, LORD, and you know me. You know when I sit and when I rise; you perceive my thoughts from afar." – Psalm 139:1 and 2 NIV

God does not need a lie detector to find out what you are thinking about. He knows everything you are thinking about as you are reading this sentence. He also knows what you will think about in the future.

Knowing that God knows everything about you, you do not have to feel embarrassed to share your deepest feelings with Him.

When you come to God in prayer, you are not revealing anything to God. God is already aware of your situation. Your prayer to God enables you to unload your burden on God. It is therapeutic to have a conversation with the Highest Being in the universe.

God has examined you thoroughly, and He knows what your aspirations are. Most importantly, He is in control of your life today and forevermore.

You do not have to be anxious about anything. You can simply come and share your heart with God. Ask Him to continue to search your heart.

Ask Him to cleanse you from all sins. If there is anything in you that is not pleasing to God, ask Him to remove it from you. God can grant you your heart's desires if you are willing to use those desires to please Him.

Have no fear. God is watching over you.

JULY 18

"Do not grant the wicked their desires, LORD; do not let their plans succeed." – Psalm 140:8 NIV

While it is important to display God's love in every circumstance, you are not required to sit quietly and let your enemies clobber you. There are times the righteous must stand up to their enemies and call on God to fight them with fire and fury.

James 4 verse 7 reads, "Submit yourselves, then, to God. Resist the devil, and he will flee from you." After your submission to God, you are required to apply fierce resistance to the devil. Do not sit around and allow the enemy to destroy your family, your finances, and your marriage. Call on God and ask Him to intervene on your behalf. Come against sickness and diseases in your body. Do not be a sitting duck.

Satan's plan is to destroy you. He does not want you to succeed. He wants you to spin around in doubt so that you never reach your full potential. It does not matter if you have been very successful; the devil still wants you to think that you have wasted your life. If he could get you to spend your time worrying about earthly things, he would manage to confuse you, and ultimately, he will plunge you into depression, and even despair.

Always ask God to grant you victory over your enemies. Ask Him to dismantle all the plans that Satan has forged against you and your family. Exercise your faith in the Sovereign God and rebuke your enemies in the name of Jesus.

JULY 19

"Set a guard over my mouth, Lord; keep watch over the door of my lips." – Psalm 141:3 NIV

Commit yourself to speaking less and listening more. While your mouth is an important tool of communications, you must measure each word. Your lips can cause many to suffer. With your lips, you can change the world positively or negatively. If you want to be a change agent, you must learn to use your lips wisely. Otherwise the enemy will capitalize on your words to perpetuate his evil plans.

Ask God to guide your thoughts so that you can speak with precision and clarity. Pray God for wisdom and discernment so that you can speak words of healing. The Holy Spirit can use your mouth to bless others tremendously if you are a willing instrument in God's hands. Take advantage of God's anointing in you to edify many people for God's glory.

Keep in mind that your words have the power to build people up. Conversely, your words have the power to destroy people. That's why it is important that you pray that God sets a guard over your mouth.

Do not allow Satan to use your mouth to curse people. Do not succumb to temptation by using your mouth to speak filthy words, because you need your mouth to praise the LORD. Furthermore, ask God to help you control your tongue. As James points out, "Those who consider themselves religious and yet do not keep a tight rein on their tongues deceive themselves, and their religion is worthless" (Chapter 1:26 NIV).

JULY 20

"Set me free from my prison, that I may praise your name. Then the righteous will gather about me because of your goodness to me." – Psalm 142:7 NIV

While unbelievers need to see God's miraculous works so they can believe in Him, people of faith want to see God's sovereign power at work as well. From time to time, Christ's followers need a faith-booster to get them excited about God.

For that reason, it is important that you get together with people of faith to share testimonies about God's goodness. People need to hear about what God has been doing in your life over the years. Don't keep those wonderful testimonies to yourself. Be willing to share God's goodness with others.

David asked God for a reason to praise Him. Keep in mind that we were created to worship God for Who He is, but we also praise God because of what He has done for us. In other words, we do not need a reason to worship God, but we need a reason to brag on Him.

What reason do you need to praise God? David's prison was a cave. He was in hiding. You may be in hiding for something that no one knows about except God.

Regardless of your circumstances, cry out to the LORD for His mercy and favor. He can set you free from your prison so that you can praise Him and tell many people about His saving grace.

JULY 21

"Teach me to do your will, for you are my God; may your good Spirit lead me on level ground." – Psalm 143:10 NIV

When you are confused, throw yourself in God's hands and ask Him for guidance. You need God's help to do His will. There are so many distractions around you; it is not uncommon to get drifted away. In order to stay anchored in God, you need to remain connected with God. Try to meditate upon His words daily.

If God is your God, you would want to follow His will. On that ground, you have all the right to ask God to teach you.

In the Old Testament, David wanted God's good Spirit to lead him. Today you need the Holy Spirit, what the King James Bible calls the Holy Ghost, to lead you. The Holy Spirit is your Comforter. He can draw you closer to the Heavenly Father. Through Him, you are always close to God. You are never alone.

When your feet start going in the wrong direction, the Holy Spirit is there to put you back on track. Be sensitive to the voice of the Holy Spirit. God speaks to you through the reading of His words. He also speaks to you through the Holy Spirit. Today pray that the Holy Spirit leads you on level ground.

JULY 22

"Praise be to the LORD my Rock, who trains my hands for war, my fingers for battle." – Psalm 144: 1 NIV

Although your battle may not be physical like in the case of David, you are still involved in spiritual wars against demonic forces. "Finally, be strong in the Lord and in his mighty power. Put on the full armor of God so that you can take your stand against the devil's schemes" (Ephesians 6:10 NIV).

Satan is doing everything in his power to diminish the full impact of God's kingdom. We must use God's full armor to withstand his onslaught against the Church. And this battle is spiritual in nature.

As we engage in battles for the kingdom of God, we must depend on God, our Commander in-Chief, to train our hands for war. We are not able to win without God's full armor. David, a great warrior, understood the importance of trusting in God as his Rock.

Today God is still our Rock. He has reinforced us by sending Jesus Christ to be our Rock of salvation. Now we can depend on Him for eternal life.

Through the power of the Holy Spirit, we can do even more to destroy the power of darkness.

Ask God to give you strength to overcome the powers of this dark world as well as spiritual forces in the heavenly realms. With God on your side, victory is yours.

JULY 23

"Your kingdom is an everlasting kingdom, and your dominion endures through all generations. The LORD is trustworthy in all he promises and faithful in all he does." – Psalm 145:13 NIV

*T*he kingdom of God is fully established in heaven, and it is governed by divine principles. God's kingdom is an everlasting kingdom and is unshakable. Satan has no dominion over God's kingdom. God has complete dominion over His kingdom.

Jesus prayed for God's kingdom to come on earth. When we make Jesus Christ our LORD, we become children of God's kingdom. And this entrance to the kingdom has bestowed upon us tremendous privileges and opportunities. In the eyes of God, we are princes and princesses because we belong to the King of kings. If we behave like paupers, it is because we do not understand our role as children of the King.

After the judgement of the Great White Throne, God's kingdom will be moved from heaven to the new earth, where God will dwell among His people. "I saw the Holy City, the New Jerusalem, coming down out of heaven from God, prepared as a bride beautifully dressed for her husband" (Revelation 21:2 NIV).

God is trustworthy and faithful. Surely, He will accomplish all He promises. Pray for God's kingdom and everyone who is part of this everlasting kingdom through Jesus Christ, our Savior.

JULY 24

"Do not put your trust in princes, in human beings, who cannot save." – Psalm 146:3 NIV

*F*or society to function, a modicum of trust in people is a necessity. When you walk to a bank to deposit your paycheck, you put your trust in that financial institution to protect your money. When you visit your primary care doctor for a checkup, you trust him or her with your very life. Most of you do not worry too much about your order when you go to your favorite restaurant. You trust the restaurant cooks and servers to do a good job with your order. I can give you hundreds of examples in which you need to exercise some trust in order to survive. It is obvious that this verse is not talking about earthly trust.

In spiritual matter, however, you cannot trust in human beings to save your spirit. Metaphysically speaking, only Yahweh, the God of Abraham, the God of Isaac, and the God of Jacob can save your spirit through Yahshua, His son. Yahshua, Yahushua, and Yeshua are varied spellings of Joshua's and Jesus' name in the Hebrew language. In Hebrew, Jesus means Yahweh saves. Jesus is the Savior of the world.

Princes and human beings have no dominion over your future. When princes and human beings die, their earthly dreams are finished. They do not have any power to take you to eternity. You need God to secure your passage to eternity.

Therefore, put your trust in Jesus Christ, the Savior of the world. He alone can save your spirit and grant you eternal life.

JULY 25

"Great is our LORD and mighty in power; his understanding has no limit." – Psalm 147:5 NIV

God, I come before you today because I know that you are great! Your qualities are matchless, LORD. Your attributes elevate you above all humans. There is no one like you, LORD.

Loving Father, I pray for your compassion and mercy today. Renew my mind so I can understand the time.

Show me your glory so I can triumph over the powers of darkness. Help me to be an effective witness for you. Keep me humble so that I can glorify you instead of myself.

I exalt you above all principalities, governors, kings, and presidents of this world. Let every human being acknowledge you as God. May your name be praised in every corner of the world. May the pride and haughty recognize you as the Almighty.

You are mighty and powerful. When you exercise your will, no one can stop you. In your name, I speak confusion in the kingdom of darkness.

May the forces of darkness be defeated every time they come against the Church of Jesus Christ.

I am glad to know that you understand everything. I open my heart to you, LORD.

I pray that you will open my mind so I can understand you even more.

Grant me wisdom and understanding so that I can do your will. I pray in the name of Jesus. Amen.

JULY 26

"Praise the Lord. Praise the LORD from the heavens; praise him in the heights above." – Psalm 148:1 NIV

The name of the LORD is to be praised everywhere. His name is to be praised in every nook and cranny. There is no place on earth where the name of the LORD should not be praised.

The name of the LORD is to be praised over the oceans of the world. His name is to be praised under the sea. The name of the LORD is to be praised on board of every ocean liner that navigates over the oceans of the world.

The name of the LORD is to be praised on board of every aircraft and space shuttle.

May the name of the LORD be pronounced by kings, presidents, governors, mayors, senators, representatives, and everyone who holds office everywhere in the world.

The name of the LORD is to be praised by angels in heaven. May the name of the LORD be respected by all, even by Satan and all his demonic spirits.

LORD, I stand in awe of your holy name. I thank you for the opportunity to have access to your name through Jesus Christ, my Savior.

May the world marvel every time your name is invoked. May the powers of darkness be shrunk at the mention of your name. I pray in the name of Jesus. Amen.

JULY 27

"Praise the LORD. Sing to the LORD a new song, his praise in the assembly of his faithful people." – Psalm 149:1 NIV

While it is suitable to praise the LORD when everything is going well, it is also good to praise the LORD on every occasion, especially during times of great confusion.

When you praise the LORD, Satan is furious! If there is anything that ticks Satan off is praise that is directed to the LORD, our God. Praise is a powerful weapon against the onslaught of the evil spirits. Put Satan to flight through your praise and worship to the LORD. Exalt the mighty name of the LORD. He is most worthy of your praise.

When you praise the LORD, your problems become insignificant. When you can, sing to the LORD a new song. The Holy Spirit can inspire your spirit and put songs in your mouth. Allow the Holy Spirit to sing to the LORD through you.

Join in with God's people throughout the week to sing praise to the LORD in the local assembly. Do not abandon the local church. Commit yourself to attending a local church on a regular basis so that you can have fellowship with your fellow believers.

Enjoy raising your hands and dancing before the LORD. Do not allow fear and human traditions to handicap your praise and worship. God created you to glorify Him with your life. Praise the LORD!

JULY 28

"Let everything that has breath praise the Lord." – Psalm 150:6 NIV

*I*f you are reading this passage, you are one of those who need to praise the LORD. Just in case you are wondering why you should praise the Lord right now; the reason is clear. You are breathing. Isn't that a good reason to praise God?

In addition to your breath of life, I am sure you can find many reasons for which to praise the LORD. You may find it interesting to make a list of some of the wonderful things God has done for you over the years. Your age does not matter; you can look back on your life and find something that God did for you.

It is a good habit to praise God for your family, your friends, your church family, your job, your retirement check, and any other benefits you have for the moment.

If you are praying for something important in your life, you may start praising the LORD for it. You don't have to wait for the answer to your prayer. When you praise God for something you have prayed for, you are telling God by faith, you have received it.

When praying for something, this is the attitude you should have. "Now faith is confidence in what we hope for and assurance about what we do not see" Hebrew 11:1 NIV). You do not have to wait until you see it to start praising God for it. Have faith.

JULY 29

"For since the creation of the world God's invisible qualities – his eternal power and divine nature – have been clearly seen, being understood from what has been made, so that people are without excuse." – Romans 1:20 NIV

You do not have to be a scientist to marvel at creation. Through simple curiosity, everyone should question the origin of all these marvelous things in creation. What we have seen, however, is a scientific enthusiasm to explain away creation without acknowledging the Creator.

While it is imperative that we pursue scientific research about the origin of the universe, we must take into consideration the metaphysical aspects of creation. Scientific discoveries will not be able to prove the existence of the Creator, because spiritual understanding requires a leap of faith, not a quantum leap.

Scientific discoveries will continue to show the complexity of the universe and the limitations of scientific studies. The human mind is limited to the four known dimensions of the universe. To understand concepts beyond those known dimensions, a divine revelation is necessary, and that revelation is based on faith in the Creator of the universe. For that reason, the universe will continue to baffle the human mind. With that said, if you choose to deny God, you have no excuse. Creation has shown God's eternal power and divine nature.

JULY 30

"There will be trouble and distress for every human being who does evil: first for the Jew, then for the Gentile; but glory, honor and peace for everyone who does good: first for the Jew, then for the Gentile." – Romans 2:9 and 10 NIV

When it comes to God's judgment, He has no favoritism. He will use the same measure to administer judgment to everyone. Because God is righteous, He cannot treat Jews one way and Gentiles another way.

Although we are not in the Old Testament, if we refuse to accept God's plan for salvation, we will still face God's judgement in the end. The only way we can escape God's judgment is to turn from our evil ways and turn to Jesus Christ, the Savior. There is no other way to escape God's judgement, because He is a righteous God. He cannot condone our sins.

If God does not spare the Jew of His judgment, He will not spare the Gentile either. God provides the same way out for both Jews and Gentiles. They are on an equal footing. No one is going to have a good excuse for continuing to do evil.

Under the dispensation of grace, we do not have to offer animal sacrifice for our sins, because Jesus Christ shed His own blood to save us. However, we need to accept Jesus Christ as our Savior. This is good and acceptable in the eyes of God. By accepting God's plan of salvation, we will escape God's judgement and receive glory, honor, and peace.

JULY 31

"But now apart from the law the righteousness of God has been made known, to which the Law and the Prophets testify. This righteousness is given through faith in Jesus Christ to all who believe." – Romans 3:21 and 22b NIV

These two verses hold the key to understanding salvation through faith. It is important that we understand the role of the Mosaic Law in the New Testament.

The purpose of the Mosaic Law is to convict us. The law diagnoses our human conditions and we are found guilty. Since the law has no remedy for our sinful conditions, our remedy is only found in Jesus Christ.

Jesus Christ came to do something that the law could not do. He can provide a cure for sin. In the Old Testament, the Prophets testified about this cure, but they did not have a chance to receive it.

The cure Jesus Christ can provide is called "righteousness by faith." What does that really mean for the sinner? It means the sinner can now count on Jesus Christ's righteousness to satisfy the righteous God, who cannot tolerate sin.

By way of substitution, Jesus Christ took our bullet when He died on the cross. Had Jesus Christ not died on the cross for us, we would not be able to count on God's mercy. In the end, we would have to face God's wrath. Thanks to Christ's righteousness, all of us who choose to believe will be able to stand before God with confidence.

AUGUST 1

"He was delivered over to death for our sins and was raised to life for our justification." – Romans 4:25 NIV

*I*n the Old Testament, it was customary for the Israelites to offer a burnt offering for their sins. Those who could afford it were required to offer a lamb. The priest was responsible to offer the burnt offering to God as an aroma pleasing to God. Those who could not afford a lamb could offer two doves or two young pigeons for a sin offering (Leviticus 12).

Jesus was our sin offering. "He was delivered over to death for our sins. Jesus' death stopped God's wrath from destroying us forever. His blood on the cross was an aroma pleasing to God. It was so pleasing that God does not need another sacrifice for our sins. The price for our sins was paid once and for all.

"He was raised to life for our justification." Following Jesus' death was His resurrection. His resurrection went one step further. He presented us as just or righteous before His Father through His resurrection. Now when God looks at us, He sees Jesus. He does not see our sins. This is what the death and resurrection of Christ did for us.

Today you can come before the Father boldly in the name of Jesus. You have been justified by the resurrection of Jesus Christ.

If you have surrendered your life to Jesus Christ as your Savior, you are no longer guilty of your sins. You have been forgiven and are now alive in Christ. Praise the LORD for His compassion and love.

AUGUST 2

"But God demonstrates his own love for us in this: While we were still sinners, Christ died for us." – Romans 5:8 NIV

Jesus' death was God's demonstration of love for us. Considering the immense suffering of Jesus on the cross, God's love for us is very profound. Can you imagine giving your only son for a bunch of sinners? This is exactly what God did for us. We were rebellious toward God. We turned our back on Him and followed the advice of Satan. But God chose to bestow His grace upon us.

Grace is unmerited favor. We did not do anything right to deserve God's grace. He did it because He loves us.

Because we were sinners, we could not meet God's standards. Keep in mind that God is righteous, and sinners cannot stand before Him. God did not wait for us to clean up. God sent Jesus to die for us while were still living in sins. God's grace was necessary.

As mentioned on the August 1 devotion, Jesus' death paid for our sins, and we got justified through His resurrection. God did not want any of us to perish in sins. He wanted to set us free from bondage by giving us the opportunity to be reunited with Him.

Today salvation is available to all through the death and resurrection of Christ. Christ came down to our level when we could not get up to Him. Please share this good news about salvation every time an opportunity presents itself. God wants everyone to know the truth about salvation.

AUGUST 3

"For if, by the trespass of the one man, death reigned through that one man, how much more will those who receive God's abundant provision of grace and of the gift of righteousness reign in life through the one man, Jesus Christ!" – Romans 5:17 NIV

The way the Heavenly Father had orchestrated the plan of salvation for the entire humanity is truly awesome! This verse, in a nutshell, explains how the whole mystery has unfolded by revealing the main characters and their key role in the whole process.

Upon completion of the works of creation, God witnessed something cataclysmic that forever altered the beautiful universe that He put into motion. Through Satan's craftiness and Adam's and Eve's subsequent disobedience, death has entered the scene. That one act of disobedience ended up putting a complete stop to eternal life for humans and destroying their relationship with the Creator of the universe.

In order to repair the damage caused by that catastrophe, God sent Jesus Christ to take the place of Adam, who messed up so badly.

Per Jesus Christ's own connection with His Father, He can accomplish something far greater than what God intended to do through Adam. Jesus Christ has established a new way for human beings to receive eternal life. And now by faith in Jesus Christ, we can receive God's abundant provision of grace and the gift of righteousness. How wonderful it is to know that God is now at peace with us!

AUGUST 4

"Do not offer any part of yourself to sin as an instrument of wickedness, but rather offer yourselves to God as those who have been brought from death to life; and offer every part of yourself to him as an instrument of righteousness." – Romans 6:13 NIV

Upon accepting the gift of eternal life by faith through Jesus Christ, something supernatural occurred in you. The Holy Spirit has transformed you from death to life. Before that intervention, you were dead spiritually, which means you did not have a personal relationship with God.

Before your encounter with God, you were a slave to sin. You did not have any control over your behavior. Sin, as your master, was dragging you to wherever it wanted. Now with the new birth in Christ, you are no longer a slave to sin. You have a new master, who is Jesus Christ.

You are now an instrument of righteousness in Christ and have received God's abundant grace. Given your new commitment to God, you should not continue to satisfy the desires of the flesh. That means those things you used to do with your friends before your encounter with God have no place in your life. This new change requires that you reprioritize your life's agenda.

Your body may still have those desires, but you need to remind yourself that you are the temple of the Holy Spirit, and you cannot afford to succumb to them. God wants you to devote yourself to serving Him as an instrument of righteousness.

AUGUST 5

"I do not understand what I do. For what I want to do I do not do, but what I hate I do." – Romans 7:15 NIV

*I*n this verse, Apostle Paul explained how difficult it is for us to please God through our own efforts. While we may desire to perform in such a way to bring glory to God, we do not have the capacity to do so successfully. As human beings, we have proven repeatedly that we are incapable of walking in the way of righteousness without God's intervention.

Apostle Paul further emphasized this point in this quote: "There is no one righteous, not even one; there is no one who understands; there is no one who seeks God" (Romans 2:10 and 11 NIV). How can we resolve this issue?

According to Apostle Paul's conclusion, the solution is found in Jesus Christ. Referring to his own personal dilemma, he said, "Thanks be to God, who delivers me through Jesus Christ our Lord! Only Jesus can rescue you from the dominion of sin.

Today if you are struggling with sins in your life, I want you to know that you are not able to set yourself free. Despite your burning desire to please God, you will continue to fail miserably until you have decided to rely on God totally for your righteousness.

You need God's help to live the Christian life. Trust God to give you strength to withstand the power of Satan. Trust God to help you overcome temptation. You simply cannot do it alone.

AUGUST 6

"Therefore, there is now no condemnation for those who are in Christ Jesus, because through Christ Jesus the law of the Spirit who gives life has set you free from the law of sin and death." – Romans 8:1 and 2 NIV

*I*n the previous devotion, you read about your incapacity to overcome sin alone. These verses showcase your freedom in Christ Jesus. Before your full reliance on Christ, you were trying to do it alone. Now Jesus came to your rescue.

While the law of sin and death does not cease to magnify your sins, Jesus Christ, by His blood on the cross, has set you free from all the charges that the law has piled on your head.

The law of the Spirit can override everything of which the law of sin and death has accused you. Yes, you were guilty on every count, but you have a new advocate who has successfully defended you with His own blood. If you had not been guilty, Jesus Christ would not have had to die for you. Because God is fair and just, He could not tolerate impunity. Someone had to pay for your transgressions, hence the necessity of the death of Christ on the cross.

Considering this absolute truth, if you have accepted Jesus as your Savior, there is now no condemnation for you. However, if you refuse to accept Jesus' payment for your sins, you remain guilty, your sins are not forgiven, and you stand condemned in the eyes of God.

If you have not accepted Jesus yet, please open your heart to Him and allow the Holy Spirit in. If you know Jesus as your personal Lord and Savior, tell others about this wonderful news.

AUGUST 7

"And if anyone does not have the Spirit of Christ, they do not belong to Christ." – Romans 8:8b NIV

As you meditate on this verse, keep in mind that it is not referring to the gifts of the Holy Spirit. It is about being born again.

Here is what you need to know about the born-gain experience. The death of Christ has provided the means for your salvation, but it is the Spirit of God who does the work of transformation. In other words, it is impossible for you to be born again without the intervention of the Spirit. As you repent and turn to God, He comes in you and changes you for eternity.

Through the transformation process, the Spirit of God comes to live in you permanently. "Now it is God who makes both us and you stand firm in Christ. He anointed us, set his seal of ownership on us, and put his Spirit in our hearts as a deposit, guaranteeing what is to come" (2 Corinthians 1:21 and 22 NIV).

Apostle Paul is basically saying, if you do not have God's seal of ownership on you, you simply do not belong to Christ.

As a born-again individual, you have God's seal of ownership on you, who is the Spirit of God. By virtue of this redemptive transformation, you now have God's anointing in you. Remember you are now a priest of God and of Christ (Revelation 20: 6).

This is one way of saying that you belong to God forever. Whether you feel God's Spirit or not, He lives in you. You are never alone if you have accepted Christ as your Savior. This is an awesome experience!

AUGUST 8

"I consider that our present sufferings are not worth comparing with the glory that will be revealed in us." – Romans 8:18 NIV

While we are living in this fallen world, we are subject to physical and emotional sufferings. We are not exempt from adversity. However, we know the day will come, when we will receive a glorified body, one that is not subject to decay. Sickness and death will have no dominion over us, because death will be no more.

The earth is also waiting for a spectacular transformation. There will be a new earth and a new heaven. God will dwell among His people forever. Satan and all his followers will be destroyed forever. He will never be able to torment us any longer.

Knowing what is waiting for us in heaven, let us continue to serve the Heavenly Father faithfully. Let us cast aside all those things that want to keep us from being totally committed to praising and worshiping the LORD, our God.

When God is fully revealed in us, when we see God face to face, and when we are no longer limited to the four known dimensions of the universe, we will marvel at the unlimited opportunities that eternity will afford us.

There will be nothing like it. It is beyond comparison. Let us rejoice in the hope of being in the presence of God forever. May God help you not to succumb to your present sufferings. And may He give you wisdom and strength to persevere until the end.

AUGUST 9

"We do not know what we ought to pray for, but the Spirit himself intercedes for us through wordless groans." – Romans 8:26b NIV

Even when we have good intentions, we do not always come before God with the correct motive. Sometimes, we allow our fleshly desires to guide our prayers. When that happens, we end up deviating from God's will in order to gratify our egotistic plans.

Would you like to be sure that you pray according to God's will? God's Spirit who lives in you can help you achieve such a goal. If you want your prayer to be effective, rely on God's Spirit to intercede for you.

The Spirit of God knows exactly what God is thinking, and He serves as an arbitrator for God's people. God's Spirit will not tell God anything that is contrary to His will on your behalf. You can count on Him to help you convey your genuine desires to God every time.

God is fully aware of your needs, so you do not need to beg Him. The essential is to come before God with confidence in the name of Jesus.

Jesus commands us to pray in His name for a good reason. Jesus said, "I am the way and the truth and the life. No one comes to the Father except through me" (John 14:6 NIV).

Finally, when you are not sure what to pray for, you can groan. God's Spirit can interpret your groaning because He can read your mind.

AUGUST 10

"And we know that in all things God works for the good of those who love him, who have been called according to his purpose." – Romans 8:28 NIV

God is in the business of taking care of His children. Regardless of your circumstances, if you are one of God's children, you have no reason to doubt God's involvement in your life. Even when things are not going well in your life, God can alter your situations just like He changed Joseph's life trajectory.

Joseph was sold into slavery, falsely accused by Potiphar's wife, and thrown into jail, and yet God was able to restore him to honor. This guarantee is made to "those who love God and have called according to his purpose."

God's children live and move to glorify God. Among all the priorities in the world, God's purpose is the highest one. When you commit yourself to loving God and pursuing His will for your life, you embark on achieving the most valuable goal in life. As a result, your life's circumstances are under divine control.

Your life's pursuit should include God's will because a future without God's involvement is a road to nowhere. That does not mean that you should not pursue other goals. Be sure God is included in your plans.

In order to secure your passage to eternity, you must ensure that you are equipped with a divine passport and visa. Your divine visa is the blood of Jesus Christ and His righteousness. If you are washed by the blood of the Lamb, you are ready for your trip to eternity.

AUGUST 11

"For I am convinced that neither death nor life, neither angels nor demons, neither the present nor the future, nor any powers, neither height nor depth, nor anything else in all creation, will be able to separate us from the love of God that is in Christ Jesus our Lord." – Romans 8:38 and 39 NIV

When you enter a covenant relationship with God, you become part of God's design. God's design is cemented in Christ Jesus. And given the magnitude of God's sacrifice, the divine impact Christ's death and resurrection have on humanity, when you say yes to Jesus Christ in all sincerity; you enter an eternal covenant with God.

Death has no impact on your relationship with God, because it only serves as a transitional mechanism for you. If you know God, death can only catapult you to eternity.

Beyond the grave, death is totally powerless if you are in Christ. Those who are not in Christ on earth will be without Christ in eternity. As a result, they will end up experiencing the real death, which is also known as the second death.

You are so secured in Christ that divine beings, like angels, cannot impact your relationship with the Heavenly Father. Similarly, no demonic powers under the aegis of Satan can alter God's love for your life. It is in this context the theological notion of eternal security makes sense.

When all the above factors are considered, you can clearly say that your life is eternally secured in Christ Jesus.

AUGUST 12

"As it is written: "See, I lay in Zion a stone that causes people to stumble and a rock that makes them fall, and the one who believes in him will never be put to shame." – Romans 9:33 NIV

*T*his verse is a summary about the people of Israel. It speaks of the Israelites' unbelief and stubbornness. It is to be noted that God has not rejected His people. Israel will be saved. However, they failed to embrace the Messiah when He came as the sacrificial Lamb.

The Israelites' loss became the gain of the Gentiles. Those of us who were not part of God's original people found an unusual opportunity to become God's people by faith.

If we are not careful, we can turn Christ into a stumbling block by trying to invent our own way to heaven outside of Christ's righteousness.

We have obtained righteousness by faith, not by works. That does not mean that we should not do good works, because God created us to do so. However, we should not use our good works as a passport to heaven.

The Israelites stumbled because they wanted to obtain righteousness by their zeal and efforts. They had a hard time understanding the concept of receiving righteousness by faith.

The lesson here is that you cannot gain God's favor by your good works. Instead of stumbling over the stumbling stone as the Israelites did, you need to believe in Jesus so that you will not be put to shame when you stand before God.

AUGUST 13

"If you declare with your mouth, "Jesus is Lord," and believe in your heart that God raised him from the dead, you will be saved." – Romans 10:9 NIV

This verse explains, in a nutshell, how one receives salvation. One day I was reading a small pamphlet about how Jesus died on the cross for my sins. There were some bloody pictures that showed how Jesus was crucified on the cross and how excruciating the pain must have been for Him to endure. Upon reading the pamphlet, I accepted the fact that Jesus died for me. Subsequently, I kneeled and asked Jesus to be my Lord and Savior.

Salvation is a gift, but you must accept it by faith. That means you must understand that you cannot save yourself. "There is no difference between Jew and Gentile, for all have sinned and fall short of the glory of God, and all are justified freely by his grace through the redemption that came by Christ Jesus" (Romans 3:22b and 23).

Salvation happens when you accept Christ as your Lord. This is a process of submission. You are no longer in control of your life. You are telling God that you belong to Him forever.

With your mouth, you confess Jesus as your Lord and believe with all your heart that He died on the cross for you. And you also believe with all your heart that He is no longer in the tomb. He is alive forevermore. In the spiritual realm, God's Spirit comes to dwell in you upon your confession. You are now saved.

AUGUST 14

"Oh, the depth of the riches of the wisdom and knowledge of God! How unsearchable his judgments, and his paths beyond tracing out!" – Romans 11:33 NIV

*I*f you find yourself questioning everything about God, it is not because you are foolish. Not at all. In fact, questioning things is a sign of intelligence. What you need to grasp, however, is that your intelligence will always be found wanting. You will never be able to fathom the depth of the riches of the wisdom and knowledge of God.

After your meticulous analysis, you have two options: accept God for Who He is or reject Him outright. Be sure you are aware of the eternal impact your decision will have on your destiny.

Apostle Paul came to the above conclusion after he had explained the intricacies of God's covenant relationship with the Israelites. He took time to expound on the ramifications of the Israelites' rejection and how their stubbornness had opened a door for Gentiles to experience God's mercy and grace. He also revealed that God has not rejected His people in that all Israel will be saved. In the end, Israelites' stumbling will enable them to taste God's mercy and grace.

Unraveling such a mystery of God's grace and mercy is indeed mind-blowing. All things considered; I have a single reaction. To God be the glory for all He has done for us. Glory to the Lord God Almighty forever! Amen.

AUGUST 15

"Therefore, I urge you, brothers and sisters, in view of God's mercy, to offer your bodies as a living sacrifice, holy and pleasing to God – this is your true and proper worship." – Romans 12:1 NIV

*I*n the past few days, you had a chance to meditate upon deep, spiritual things. If you did not have a chance to read the past fourteen devotions, try to go back and catch up. Those are foundational topics that are essential for proper understanding of salvation by grace and through faith. They are designed to help you understand God and His plan of salvation. Without a good understanding of God's plan for salvation, you might attempt to gain God's favor by works, a challenge you will not be able to beat on your own.

Turning the page from the process of salvation, now your new focus is on the practical aspects of Christianity. Christianity is not a mere ritual; it is a practical approach to cultivating an active relationship with God. Christianity helps you serve God with your whole being. It is a lifestyle that is governed by divine principles.

Worshiping God with your body is one way of telling God that you belong to Him. Your body is the last thing that wants to worship God. Your spirit is always willing to worship God because it has been subject to God through salvation. Your body and soul always try to lag. It requires a lot of efforts to get them to follow your spirit.

AUGUST 16

"If it is possible, as far as it depends on you, live at peace with everyone." – Romans 12:18 NIV

This verse is especially true in a relationship. Sometimes, fights break out because one of the interlocutors is so bent on winning the argument. There is nothing wrong with being competitive or trying to make a point. However, it is important that you try to keep the peace in the household.

Winning at all costs may cost you your marriage, your friendship, your job, or even your life. Be willing to compromise if it means keeping the peace. Allow yourself to lose every once and a while. Losing an argument will put you in touch with your own humanity.

It takes a huge dose of humility to agree to disagree. "Before a downfall the heart is haughty, but humility comes before honor" (Proverbs 18:12 NIV).

Keep in mind that there are things that cannot be compromised. You should never compromise your integrity.

If your partner decides to abuse you or cheat on you, it no longer depends on you to keep the relationship going. It depends on both of you to preserve the wedding vows.

Above all, use your discretion and common sense as you determine what your options should be. Furthermore, seek professional counseling to help you and your mate resolve your marital conflict. Keep the peace if it is possible.

AUGUST 17

"Let everyone be subject to the governing authorities, for there is no authority except that which God has established. The authorities that exist have been established by God." – Romans 13:1 NIV

As Christ's followers, we should be willing to submit to authorities because we belong to God, the Highest Authority. Earthly authorities are temporary symbols of God's eternal authority.

Eventually, theocracy will be the only form of government. God's kingdom will be established upon the new earth, and God will reign over it forever.

What should our attitude be toward earthly authorities? We should strive to be good examples for others to follow because we are God's witnesses in the world. Even though earthly authorities may not always be fair to us, we should not be disrespectful toward them. When having an encounter with a law enforcement officer, we should comply according to the law of the land. Being aggressive is not the way to deal with law enforcement authorities.

Jesus has supreme authority over all the earth. However, when he was confronted by the guards who came to arrest him, He did not use His divine power to destroy them. Jesus is a very good role model.

Because God oversees all authorities, when we obey earthly authorities, we acknowledge God's sovereignty over all governing powers on earth as well as in heaven.

AUGUST 18

"The commandments, "You shall not commit adultery," "You shall not murder," "You shall not steal," "You shall not covet," and whatever other command there may be, are summed up in this one command: "Love your neighbor as yourself." – Romans 13:9 NIV

*I*n the Old Testament, God introduced the Ten Commandments to the Israelites. They were required to live according to those rules established by God (Exodus 20). In the New Testament, Jesus has put emphasis on "love." He said, "If you love me, keep my commands" (John 14:15 NIV).

If you are governed by love, you do not have to worry about the Ten Commandments, because love enables you to keep all the other rules. If you love, you will not want to hurt your spouse by sleeping with another person. It is very selfish to commit such an act. Your spouse will be emotionally devastated when he or she finds out that you have been unfaithful.

In the same token, if you love, you will not kill someone. We were made in God's image. Love enables us to appreciate people, even though we may be different from one another. Similarly, love will keep us from stealing people's stuff. Love causes us to have empathy for others. Would you like others to steal your stuff? Why would you conspire to do such a thing?

When we are motivated by love, we rejoice when we see others' blessings. We do not covet their stuff. If you are happy when your friends are blessed, God will bless you in return.

AUGUST 19

"The night is nearly over; the day is almost here. So, let us put aside the deeds of darkness and put on the armor of light." – Romans 13:12 NIV

This world is temporary, and the time will come when God will put an end to this world as we know it. Being aware of this reality, we need to spend our time glorifying God instead of gratifying the desires of the flesh.

While we understand that our performance will not get us to heaven, we need to produce fruit that will enable us to receive an eternal reward. What do you mean?

I mean your good works will not get you to heaven, but they will be counted toward your eternal reward.

God will reward us for our good works during the Judgment Seat of Christ (2 Corinthians 5:10; Revelation 22:12). The Judgment Seat of Christ is for Christians, not for nonbelievers. Nonbelievers will be judged during the Judgment of the Great White Throne, which is a judgment reserved for those who died without Christ (Revelation 20:11-15).

While you may not go to Hell for the things that you have done after salvation, God will deal with you for your failure to live according to His precepts.

Instead of living your life like a person who does not know Christ, try to devote yourself to exemplifying Christ wherever you are so that many people may come to know your God by your lifestyle.

AUGUST 20

"It is written: "As surely as I live, says the Lord, every knee will bow before me; every tongue will acknowledge God." So then, each of us will give an account of ourselves to God." – Romans 14:11 and 12 NIV

According to the Scripture, everyone will acknowledge God, even those who do not believe in Him. That means all atheists will acknowledge that God exists. Not only will they recognize God, they will bow down before Him and worship Him as God. They will have no choice. God will fully demonstrate His power over every human being.

God created us for a very special purpose. He expects us to reach our full potential spiritually. That does not mean that we should not pursue earthly goals. It simply means that we must leave room for God's purpose to be fulfilled in our lives as we pursue those earthly goals.

We will have to give God an account of ourselves. Knowing this truth, we know we must live for God while we are on earth. We have an eternity before us, so we need all our time here to prepare for it. This is not something we should take lightly.

The way you spend your temporary life will determine how you will spend your eternal life. For that reason, do not allow the desires of the flesh to clutter your life in such a way that you do not have time to plan for life beyond the grave. One thing is certain: people's denial of God is all but temporary.

AUGUST 21

"If your brother or sister is distressed because of what you eat, you are no longer acting in love. Do not by your eating destroy someone for whom Christ died." – Romans 14:15 NIV

As Christ's followers, we do not have the same level of spiritual maturity. Our biblical understanding may vary to some extent without significantly affecting our relationship with God. Consequently, we must be very careful so that we do not cause our brothers and sisters to stumble spiritually.

Whatever you are doing, do it with an eternal purpose. Always strive to place God first in all you do. Do not give Satan any opportunity to declare victory over you. For instance, going to a bar does not have any impact on your salvation, but someone who is not as mature as you may not see it that way.

Apostle Paul knew very well that eating certain foods did not have any impact on salvation, but he did not want such action to become a stumbling block for some Christians. He knew people's tendency to emphasize outward appearance in lieu of righteousness by faith.

The important thing to remember is that we do not live for ourselves in this life. We live with the knowledge that God has an eternal purpose for our lives. Whether we are in the body or out of the body, we are under God's control, and our destiny makes sense only when it is viewed through the lens of God's eternal plan for humanity.

AUGUST 22

"May the God of hope fill you with all joy and peace as you trust in him, so that you may overflow with hope by the power of the Holy Spirit." – Romans 15:13 NIV

*I*n a world that is full of distress, you need the God of hope to maintain your spiritual balance. God is the only stability you have in this life. God will remain unchanging no matter how shaky life becomes.

The real joy and peace come from God. If your joy is based on your material possessions, when they are destroyed, your joy will be dashed. You need to be sure that your joy is anchored in your trust in Christ Jesus, the Author and Finisher of your faith.

As a believer, you need peace that surpasses all understanding daily to remain sane. There are enough life's uncertainties to drive you crazy if your peace is not from God.

The Holy Spirit is there to guide and support you every step of the way. When things get tough, He is there to see you through. In fact, without the power of the Holy Spirit, it is impossible for you to live a triumphant Christian life.

Satan will use everything in his power to shatter your hope, but you must not give up. The Holy Spirit is your Comforter, and you are never alone in this life.

With the help of the Holy Spirit, you can overcome your personal obstacles and experience victory.

AUGUST 23

"I urge you, brothers and sisters, to watch out for those who cause divisions and put obstacles in your way that are contrary to the teaching you have learned." – Romans 16:17 NIV

As you meditate on this Scripture today, I encourage you to think about God's grace and mercy. Think about what Jesus did on the cross so that you can have the hope of eternal life. In this book, Apostle Paul made it very clear that God demonstrates His love toward us in that while we were still sinners Christ died for us (Romans 5:8).

Don't rely on your good works to get you to heaven. It is not possible for anyone to stand before God without the righteousness that comes from Christ Jesus. The only thing you can do is to surrender your life to the Lord. When you do that, God's Spirit justifies you by declaring you righteous in the eyes of the Heavenly Father. This is purely an act of God's grace through faith.

In the end, God will reward you for all good works you perform while you are on earth. Your performance makes sense when it is a product of salvation- fruit produced after salvation.

To put it simply: what you do cannot save you. You are saved by God's grace, and then you go out there and do something good for God's kingdom.

Considering Apostle Paul's exhortation, I urge you to watch out for false doctrine. Don't base your salvation on your performance. Rely totally on God's grace and the blood of Jesus.

AUGUST 24

"The God of peace will soon crush Satan under your feet. The grace of our Lord Jesus be with you." – Romans 16:20 NIV

I want you to know that your day of deliverance will soon be here. Satan does not have absolute power. As a matter of fact, his power is very limited. Since he is a deceiver, he would like you to know that he holds the key to your destiny, but he does not. The Sovereign God has the key to your destiny.

The God of peace knows that Satan's day will come. Jesus started the demolition operation of Satan's kingdom. When Jesus came out of the grave, He dealt a devastating blow to everything that Satan has represented, including his hopes of reigning on this earth as well as his lies about God's design for humanity.

For this purpose, Jesus humbled Himself and came down to earth in the form of a man to take over where Adam had failed. Jesus came to restore hope in our hearts by making it possible to receive eternal life through His sacrifice on the cross.

Just in case you were not sure about Satan's position, he belongs under your feet. He has no power over you. The power he has is what you, by your own volition, give him.

If you humble yourself before God and resist Satan, he has no choice but to flee from you.

Don't be timid when you are faced with temptation. Be bold and stand up to Satan. Tell him where he belongs. You are truly an overcomer through Christ.

AUGUST 25

"I appeal to you, brothers and sisters, in the name of our Lord Jesus Christ, that all of you agree with one another in what you say and that there be no divisions among you, but that you be perfectly united in mind and thought." – 1 Corinthians 1:10 NIV

*D*espite our different opinions, we are called upon to be united in mind and thought. As Christ's followers, what unites us is more important than what divides us.

We often focus on issues that have very little weight in the eternal balance. If an issue has nothing to do with salvation, we should not allow it to destroy the spiritual harmony that comes from our common beliefs in the Lord Jesus Christ.

Our minds should focus on what Jesus did on the cross for us, especially, the ultimate sacrifice He made for us. We should not set our minds on different styles of worship, or denominational practices. Some Christians even have time to argue about certain versions of the Holy Bible. The essential issue is to know that salvation is found in Jesus Christ, the Son of the Living God.

We should focus on the things of God. We should not allow the worries of this world to keep us from meditating on God's words daily. Furthermore, we should focus our energy on making Jesus known.

The worries of this world will pass. The only thing that will remain is our trust in the finished work of Jesus on the cross. For that reason, let us center our minds and thoughts on those things that have eternal values. Those are things that can unite us.

AUGUST 26

"For the message of the cross is foolishness to those who are perishing, but to us who are being saved it is the power of God." – 1 Corinthians 1:18 NIV

People whose minds are on the things of this world do not understand the message of the cross. The idea that God would send His Son, Jesus Christ, to die on a wooden cross for our sins simply does not make much sense. For them, such a message is nonsensical. That's why atheists tend to say that they do not believe in the Holy Bible.

It takes the power of the Holy Spirit to open our eyes in order to catch a glimpse of the things that are unseen. The message of the cross does not concern life on earth. It deals with the issues of eternity. When we think of reality, we may think of life on earth. However, in the spiritual realm, reality is what has the potential to live forever. Life on earth will pass, but those whose hope is in the Almighty will live forever.

The phrase "being saved" explains the two distinct aspects of salvation: the present and the future aspects. The present aspect of salvation deals with the work of the Holy Spirit that has transformed us and presented us as righteous or just in the sight of God when we repent of our sin and turn to God by faith. The future aspect of salvation will deal with the glorification of the human body (1 Corinthians 15:35-58). While we are in the physical body, we are subject to pain and temptation. The glorification aspect of our salvation will put an end to all our sufferings. Death will cease forever, and our salvation process will be complete. Of course, this only makes sense to you if you are being saved.

AUGUST 27

"We do, however, speak a message of wisdom among the mature, but not the wisdom of this age or of the rulers of this age, who are coming to nothing. No, we declare God's wisdom, a mystery that has been hidden and that God destined for our glory before time began." – 1 Corinthians 2:6 and 7 NIV

These two verses define the type of wisdom this devotional book is about. The wisdom in question is not human wisdom or what is often referred to as conventional wisdom. I am talking about a mystery that God has reserved for those who love Him. It is something marvelous that God had set aside for us, even before He created the universe.

God's mystery of salvation has been revealed through Jesus Christ. It is no longer a mystery for those who have made an encounter with God. This is what the born-again experience is all about. When you become a new creation through the work of God's Spirit, you become part of God's family – a member of God's kingdom.

God's mystery cannot be understood by human wisdom. That's why it is necessary to have a spiritual encounter with God. The message of wisdom to which Apostle Paul is referring in this passage is something that has been hidden to the wise of this world. May God's wisdom be imparted to you today. May the deep things of God be revealed to you by the Spirit as you search for divine wisdom.

AUGUST 28

"The person without the Spirit does not accept the things that come from the Spirit of God but considers them foolishness, and cannot understand them because they are discerned only through the Spirit." – 1 Corinthians 2:14 NIV

By examining this verse, you may begin to understand why so many people have failed to understand the good news about Jesus Christ. Many of those people are extremely educated. Some of them are gifted and talented. And some of them are geniuses. Nonetheless, they have a hard time grasping the truth about God's gift of salvation.

If you were in doubt, you now know why. They do not have God's Spirit. In order to accept and understand God's things, one must surrender to God's Spirit first. This calls for obedience and humility.

First, one must obey the voice of God's Spirit. It is through the Spirit; God brings us into conviction. We can choose to ignore God's Spirit or accept to listen to Him and obey.

Second, one must be willing to accept God's wisdom over human wisdom, and this requires humility as well.

Through the lens of human wisdom, spiritual things do not make sense. That's why Solomon said, "Trust in the Lord with all your heart and lean not on your own understanding; in all your ways submit to him, and he will make your paths straight" (Proverb 3:5 and 6 NIV).

When you trust in the Lord with all your heart, He will illuminate your mind so that you will be able to understand spiritual things.

AUGUST 29

"Don't you know that you yourselves are God's temple and that God's Spirit dwells in your midst? If anyone destroys God's temple, God will destroy that person; for God's temple is sacred, and you together are that temple." – 1 Corinthians 3:16 and 17 NIV

These verses refer to the Church of Jesus Christ, not the local church building. Apostle Paul is talking about those who have accepted Jesus as their Lord and Savior. God's Spirit dwells among us, but He also dwells in you as an individual – a member of the Church of Jesus Christ.

When we think of the sacredness of the temple of God, we begin to understand the kind of attitude we should have toward the body of Christ – the Church. Moreover, everyone should see himself or herself as the temple of the Spirit of God. During salvation, God's Spirit comes to dwell in the individual in order to claim that person for God. Without this initial intervention, there can be no spiritual transformation. And if there is no spiritual transformation, the redemptive process does not occur.

God's temple belongs to God. The Church belongs to God, and Satan cannot destroy her. Jesus said, "I will build my church, and the gates of Hades (Hell) will not overcome it" (Matthew 16:18b NIV). As God's temple, handle yourself with utmost respect. Allow God's Spirit to show God's love to others through you. Do not willingly use your body to satisfy the desires of the flesh.

AUGUST 30

"For the kingdom of God is not a matter of talk but of power."
– 1 Corinthians 4:20 NIV

By nature, a kingdom is a power structure. At the helm of a kingdom is a king that has full control over everything in his sphere. He can impact all the people who live within the parameter of the kingdom. He exercises his kingship in every imaginable area of life. Those who choose to oppose him are bound to meet fierce resistance as well as punishment. A queen possesses similar power and authority as well.

When a king speaks, people obey. No one can say no to a king without facing the consequences. In God's kingdom, everything is controlled by God, even the wicked for the Day of Judgment.

Those who work for the King of kings are given the authority to operate in His name. They become kingdom minded. When you surrender yourself to become a child of God, you are a prince or a princess. You are endowed with significant amount of power because of your relationship with the King and your position in the kingdom.

When you speak in God's name by faith, you can expect things to happen. Do not just talk about God. You also need to demonstrate God's power in this world.

Be ready to speak things into existence by faith in the power of the Almighty God. Use the anointing that God deposited in you when you received God's Spirit at the time of salvation. The Holy Spirit may give you certain gifts as well. Trust God to bring to pass His promises as you proclaim His word because "the kingdom of God is not a matter of talk but power."

AUGUST 31

"What business is it of mine to judge those outside the church? Are you not to judge those inside?" – 1 Corinthians 5:12 NIV
Apostle Paul was dealing with a case of incest in the local church. He advised the people in the church to deal with the sin.

Even though you are a follower of Christ, you may still have tendencies to engage in behaviors that are considered immoral in the eyes of God. You do not become a mature believer in a twinkling of an eye. And even with maturity, you are still vulnerable. However, in the spiritual realm, you are righteous by virtue of what Jesus did on the cross for you.

Keep in mind that it can be very confusing for a young Christian to have physical feelings he or she had before salvation. Such experiences may cause the individual to doubt the impact of salvation altogether. It takes time for the born-again person to get used to living for God in the flesh. This is what the Christian walk is all about. It is a walk toward spiritual maturity.

As believers, we must be careful not to become too cozy with sin that we do not lift a finger to help our immature brothers and sisters to deal with it. We must take steps to assisting them in living according to the precepts of God by encouraging them to pursue holiness and purity.

If we condone sinful behaviors, immature Christians may take it to mean that there is nothing wrong in continuing in sin. It is our duty to help one another in Christ. It is not an outsider's job if it is not a crime. All crimes must be reported to the established authorities.

SEPTEMBER 1

"I have the right to do anything," you say – but not everything is beneficial. "I have the right to do anything" – but I will not be mastered by anything." – 1 Corinthians 6:12 NIV

While our salvation is not based on our performance, we should not use our freedom in Christ to indulge in sinful behaviors. What we do in the flesh has eternal impact because God will reward our performance during the Judgment Seat of Christ (2 Corinthians 5:10).

The extent of our freedom in Christ is determined by our ability to refrain from doing things that we have freedom to do. As Christians, we should practice integrity in everything we do. We may have the freedom to engage in sexual immorality, but that does not mean that we must do it. Similarly, we may have the freedom to embezzle our company's funds, but that does not mean that we should succumb to such temptation.

As we journey through life, we will have many opportunities to sin from time to time, but our true freedom will be tested by our resolve not to defile ourselves that way.

Daniel was assigned a daily amount of food and wine from the king's table, but "he resolved not to defile himself with the royal food and wine, and he asked the chief official for permission not to defile himself this way" (Daniel 1:8 NIV). We should also resolve to be faithful to the Lord.

As you pray today, ask God to give you wisdom and strength so you can be a faithful witness for Jesus.

SEPTEMBER 2

"The husband should fulfill his marital duty to his wife, and likewise the wife to her husband." – 1 Corinthians 7:3 NIV

If you are married, this verse reminds you of your responsibility as husband or wife. If you are not married or planning to get married in the future, keep this advice in mind. If you don't fit any of these two categories, share this information with people who might need it.

Being married is a huge responsibility. Once you are married, you are no longer living for yourself. You have entered into an agreement to take care of your spouse, come what may. It is important that you live a selfless life. A successful marriage requires many sacrifices. If you don't have anything to give, you should wait until you are ready to get married.

Marriage works best when two independent people get married. If you are not ready to stand on your own two feet, you are not ready to contribute to the success of the marriage. Your spouse is not there to babysit you. He or she is there to contribute to a partnership. You have your part to play, and she has hers to play.

While sexual intercourse is an essential part of a marriage, your duty goes beyond that. You both should work toward financial independence. You both should work to create an environment that is conducive to a prosperous household. Furthermore, you both must ensure that God is the ultimate head of the family.

Ask God to grant you wisdom to fulfill your duty as a mate. This is a mutual responsibility that is essential for harmony in the relationship.

SEPTEMBER 3

"Those who think they know something do not yet know as they ought to know." – 1 Corinthians 8:2 NIV

One of the characteristics of wisdom is humility. Wise people tend to measure their words, examine their thought pattern and the depth of their knowledge. Wise people do not talk too much, because they spend more time thinking about what they are going to say.

If you know as you ought to know, then you know how much you do not know. It does not matter if you have a doctorate; you still have a lot to learn in your discipline. Knowledge is not static. Every year new discoveries are being made. If you do not keep abreast of new scientific discoveries in your field, you will soon find out that you are out of the loop.

The context of this quote is food sacrificed to idols. One of the pagans' practices was to offer food to images, the dead, and fetishes. And those practices are still being practiced today. Those who know about the sovereignty of God know full well that there is one true God. Yes, people have deified objects and even people, but those actions do not necessarily negate the fact that the Almighty is the only true God.

Although we know that those idols mean nothing and that they are not gods, Apostle Paul pointed out that we should be careful so that our actions do not cause the weak to fall. If people who have limited understanding of Christianity see us eating food that was offered to idols, they may conclude that it is okay to worship idols as well.

SEPTEMBER 4

"To the weak I became weak, to win the weak. I have become all things to all people so that by all possible means I might save some." – 1 Corinthians 9:22 NIV

To be an effective witness for God, you must be very tactful. While you should be careful not to compromise your integrity, you have to be flexible. As you strive to win the lost for Christ, you will find that it is necessary to make frequent cultural as well as linguistic adjustments to your evangelistic methods. Jesus Christ was the epitome of flexibility. Although He is the Son of God, He did not take advantage of His divine nature. He was willing to be humiliated for our sake. He accepted to endure excruciating, physical pain in order to become our righteousness before the Heavenly Father.

Know your priority. Your priority determines your motive in life. If your priority is to build for eternity, you are not going to allow material possessions to get the best of you. Instead, you will use material possessions to advance God's kingdom.

Be willing to change your strategies from time to time. Evangelistic methods cannot be a one-size fits-all approach. The key objective is to fulfill the mission God has entrusted you. Different situations require different strategies.

Ask God to give you wisdom for each life's experience. God will give you the necessary strength to carry on.

SEPTEMBER 5

"No temptation has overtaken you except what is common to mankind. And God is faithful; he will not let you be tempted beyond what you can bear. But when you are tempted, he will also provide a way out so that you can endure it." – 1 Corinthians 10:13 NIV

Jesus was tempted by Satan when He was on earth fulfilling the mission that the Father gave Him. As a Christian, you are subject to temptation as well, but do not lose heart. God, in His sovereignty, is aware of your frailties.

While you are not exempt from temptation, it is very encouraging to know that God is faithful. Through His faithfulness and mercy, God will not allow you to be tempted beyond your human strength. According to this verse, your temptation will be limited to what you are able to endure. Having said that, when you are tempted, ask God to show you a way out.

Ask God for wisdom so that you can see the trap the enemy has put on your path. Exercise self-control and avoid being in places that are conducive to sinful activities.

Remember you are not a superhuman. Know your vulnerability and your weaknesses. God is willing to forgive you, but you should not take advantage of God's grace to keep sinning. Be willing to use your body to honor God.

As you pray today, ask God to protect your mind from evil thoughts and imaginations. Surrender everything to God. He can take care of you.

SEPTEMBER 6

"Everyone ought to examine themselves before they eat of the bread and drink from the cup. For those who eat and drink without discerning the body of Christ eat and drink judgment on themselves." — 1 Corinthians 11:28 and 29 NIV

When you sit in church partaking the Lord's Supper, it is important that you understand the significance of such a symbol. There is nothing magic about the Lord's Supper, but it has a special meaning for the body of Christ, which is the Church.

If you have not decided to follow Jesus Christ with all your heart, you should not participate in the Lord's Supper. If you do that, you are making a mockery of God's precious Son.

The Lord's Supper signifies that God has paid for our sins with the blood of His Son. The bread symbolizes the body of Christ that was nailed on the cross for our iniquity. And the drink symbolizes the blood of Jesus Christ that was shed on the cross to wash our sins away.

Every time you participate in the Lord's Supper, you should remember what Jesus did for you. You must never forget the ultimate sacrifice God made to make it possible for you to have eternal life.

If you take part in the Lord's Supper without making a genuine decision to follow the Lord, you will not receive its intended benefits. As a result, you will not be able to escape God's wrath. Be sure you approach the Lord's Supper with the right motive. Be honest with yourself.

SEPTEMBER 7

"For we were all baptized by one Spirit so as to form one body – whether Jews or Gentiles, slave or free – and we were all given the one Spirit to drink." – 1 Corinthians 12:13 NIV

The Corinthian church was having problems understanding the gifts of the Spirit, so Apostle Paul took time to explain the different kinds of gifts that the same Spirit gives to different people. Apostle Paul wanted us to know that while we were all baptized by the same Spirit, we are not entitled to the same gift. And I think this is something we all need to understand in the local church today.

First, if you are born again, you are deemed baptized with the Spirit. Be sure you understand the difference between baptism in the Spirit and the gifts of Spirit. Baptism refers to the initial intervention of God's Spirit in your life, and this is part of the salvation process. Keep in mind salvation is not possible without that first supernatural act. This transformational act takes place in your spirit, not in your body proper.

In addition to baptism in the Spirit, there are gifts of the Spirit, including, but not limited to, apostles, prophets, teachers, the gift of healing, of helping, of guidance, of different kinds of tongues, etc. (1 Corinthians 12:28). Now those gifts are given to believers as the Spirit sees fit.

If God wants you to be just a helper at church, rejoice as you help. You are as valuable in the eyes of God as those who are called to be apostles. You are contributing toward building God's Church.

SEPTEMBER 8

"If I speak in the tongues of men or of angels, but do not have love, I am only a resounding gong or a clanging cymbal." – 1 Corinthians 13:1 NIV

*L*ove is the strongest force there is in the whole universe. As a matter of fact, the universe continues to exist because of love. After the fall of Adam and Eve, God in His righteousness could have eliminated the whole world, but love impelled Him to show mercy and grace by sending Jesus Christ to die in our place. "For God so loved the world that he gave his one and only Son, that whoever believes in him shall not perish but have eternal life" (John 3:16 NIV).

Life without love is nothing but an empty shell. When you commit yourself to loving others, you begin to live. The world's number one problem is love. War is the absence of love. All the hatred we are experiencing in this world has been caused by a lack of genuine love. When you commit to loving people, you do not judge people based on their race, color or origin. You just see God's people.

If you want to revolutionize your environment, make love the motive of everything you do. This includes your service to God. When you worship, do it because you love God.

Ask God to fill you with genuine love so that you can be a source of blessing to those around you. Make love your number one priority in life.

SEPTEMBER 9

"The spirits of prophets are subject to the control of prophets."
— 1 Corinthians 14:32 NIV

The context of this verse is order in worship. Apostle Paul seemed to have had an issue in the Corinthian church regarding speaking in tongues.

Yes, speaking in tongues is one of many gifts of the Holy Spirit. There are other gifts as well. Apostle Paul was not saying that it was wrong to speak in tongues, but he wanted the people in the congregation to do it in an orderly fashion. He wanted to be sure people were not just speaking in tongues just because they could.

Apostle Paul emphasized the gift of prophecy because of its potential to edify or build the congregation. By that, Apostle Paul meant that people were more likely to be encouraged by hearing a prophetic word than hearing many people speaking in tongues all at once. He encouraged them to do it one at a time and with the help of an interpreter.

If you are a prophet, you cannot use it as a pretense to disrupt a worship service. As a prophet, your spirit is under your control. And this is applicable for any position. If you are the boss of a company or department, you have authority. Your authority is under your control as a human being. Do not use your managerial power as an excuse to abuse others. You can control your authority.

Apostle Paul concluded by saying, "But everything should be done in a fitting and orderly way" (1 Corinthians. 14:40 NIV). God does not operate in confusion. In God, everything has its place.

SEPTEMBER 10

"If only for this life we have hope in Christ, we are of all people most to be pitied." – 1 Corinthians 15:19 NIV

*E*veryone who truly believes in Jesus Christ has one thing in common. They all believe that life on this planet is just a transitional experience. The real life is what we hope for after physical death.

Because God raised Jesus from the dead on the third day after his burial and is alive forevermore, we too hope to defeat death in the end. Yes, we are not exempt from physical death, but death has no power over our spirits. Death only serves to introduce us to eternity.

According to the Scripture, we will have a spiritual body. And the new body will not be vulnerable to decay. If you believe in Christ, you will only experience death just once. The second death will have no power over you.

The second death is eternal. Those who have refused to accept Jesus Christ as their Savior will face the second death, which is the lake of fire, according to Revelation 20:14b.

Life on this earth is not all there is. You will have to face eternity someday. You had better be sure that you face eternity with Jesus Christ as your Lord and Savior. Jesus conquered death. And with His help, you will conquer death as well.

SEPTEMBER 11

"Be on your guard; stand firm in the faith; be courageous; be strong. Do everything in love." – 1 Corinthians 16:13 and 14 NIV

*I*t does not matter how spiritual you are. If you are not paying attention, you may fall before you know it. Satan is very crafty, and he often has an element of surprise. Satan is always lurking around looking for an opportunity to torpedo your life's boat. The secret to victory is to always be on your guard. In your prayer, ask God to grant you wisdom so that you can detect the subtlest attack of the enemy.

A lack of faith exercise can be an area of vulnerability. If your faith is not solidly placed in the Lord, when the storm of life comes, you will not be able to withstand the waves. When everything begins to shake around you, do not lose faith in the Sovereign God. He has everything under control. Nothing can happen to you without His permission.

Knowing that your God is stronger than your enemy, you have a good reason to be courageous. Do not lose your confidence in the Lord. He is there to help you fight the battle. You are never alone when you walk with the Lord. Your strength is from the Almighty. Satan will not be able to defeat God in the final battle of life. If you walk with God, victory will be yours.

Above all, be motivated by love, for God is love. "And now these three remain: faith, hope and love. But the greatest of these is love" (1 Corinthians 13:13 NIV).

SEPTEMBER 12

"Now it is God who makes both us and you stand firm in Christ. He anointed us, set his seal of ownership on us, and put his Spirit in our hearts as a deposit, guaranteeing what is to come." – 2 Corinthians 1:21 and 22 NIV

*I*f you are interested in buying a house in the United States, you are required to pay an earnest payment as a guarantee that you mean business. God is interested in our eternal value, so He put His Spirit in us as a guarantee.

If you were not sure about your true value, I want you to know that your owner is the Almighty. He risked the life of His Son to redeem you. No wonder He decided to put His seal of ownership on you. You are precious in God's eyes.

What you will be has not fully been revealed. God is still working in you toward the goal. The result of salvation through faith is glorification. Until you are glorified, you are subject to temptation and sufferings. That's why Apostle Paul declared, "I consider that our present sufferings are not worth comparing with the glory that will be revealed in us." (Romans 8:18 NIV).

There is nothing that can compare with what God has in store for those who love Him. Yes, it is tough to be a believer nowadays. You should be willing to be called a fool for Jesus. With the exponential growth of technology, people are becoming more and more self-reliant. They don't think they need God. Despite those challenges, stand firm in Christ.

SEPTEMBER 13

"For we are to God the pleasing aroma of Christ among those who are being saved and those who are perishing." – 2 Corinthians 2:15 NIV

As Christ's followers, wherever we are, we represent Christ. Among fellow believers, we must be a source of encouragement. Believers have ups and downs as well. Remember that we are still in the flesh. While waiting to be clothed with a glorified body, we need a spiritual boost from time to time so that we do not despair like the unbelievers. That is why it is important for us to encourage believers in the Lord.

Christ is our Redeemer. Every time God sees Jesus Christ, He remembers the price that was paid for our transgressions. He remembers that we are no longer condemned and that we are free from guilt. Since Christ was both the High Priest and the sacrifice, Christ's aroma is constantly before God. That pleasant smell of the blood of Jesus has been permanently placed before God, and it is a pleasing smell that brings complete satisfaction to God.

In addition to being helpful to believers, we are to be helpful to the nonbelievers as well. Those who are perishing need to hear that there is hope in Jesus. If we fail to let them know about the goodness of God and the way to salvation, they will indeed perish. While they are in the flesh, there is hope for salvation. We need not be ashamed about the gospel.

SEPTEMBER 14

"Now the Lord is the Spirit, and where the Spirit of the Lord is, there is freedom." – 2 Corinthians 3:17 NIV

Considering what we have in Christ, we have something that is far better than what Moses and all his contemporaries were able to experience. In Moses' time, the people were not allowed to approach God. Moses had to serve as the people's representative because they were not worthy to appear before God.

Now with the resurrection of Christ, we have so much freedom. Through Jesus Christ, we can approach God's throne when we pray in the name of Jesus. This is something unheard of in the Old Testament.

The fact that God dwells in us through the Spirit is truly awesome. We are God's temple. In the Old Testament, only the high priest was permitted to enter God's temple. Today Jesus is both the High Priest and the sacrifice for our sins. And He paid for all our sins once and for all.

We are free because God's Spirit lives in us. How can we be in bondage when God's Spirit dwells in us? No way! Where God's Spirit is there is liberty.

Lord, I rejoice in the freedom that I have in you. Thank you so much for making it possible for me to break the chains of sin and guilt. I have been set free by your blood. Help me to continue to walk on the path of freedom. Amen.

SEPTEMBER 15

"And even if our gospel is veiled, it is veiled to those who are perishing. The god of this age has blinded the minds of unbelievers, so that they cannot see the light of the gospel that displays the glory of Christ, who is the image of God." – 2 Corinthians 4:3 and 4 NIV

If you are among those who are being saved, I thank God for you. Join in with me to give thanks to God for His mercy. Today you can see the light of the gospel that shows the glory of Christ.

The gospel is hiding in plain sight. Those who are perishing cannot see it. Why? The god of this age has blinded their minds. If you are having a hard time believing in the saving power of Jesus, please stop reading for a few minutes. Take a few moments to ask God to reveal Himself to you. Be honest with yourself and ask God to show you His glory. Please do it with all your heart. God is real and can speak to you in the Spirit. Listen to the voice of the Holy Spirit. God is drawing you closer to Him. Please allow Him to win you over.

Christ is the image of the invisible God. When Christ was on earth, He displayed the glory of God. You can see God in the works that Christ accomplished on the cross. Today if you believe in the sacrifice Jesus made on the cross, you are saved. The god of this age has no power over your mind. Praise the Lord for His love and grace!

SEPTEMBER 16

"So we fix our eyes not on what is seen, but on what is unseen, since what is seen is temporary, but what is unseen is eternal." – 2 Corinthians 4:18 NIV

As believers, we must be very careful about the mirage around us. Otherwise we may end up spending too much time focusing on the mirage.

Everything we see before us is temporary, including, but not limited to, immorality, sufferings, and the increasing desires for fleshly desires, diseases, and death. They will all disappear in the end.

Temporary realities will be replaced with eternal ones. The time will come when you will not have to put up with all the sufferings of this world. If you feel disoriented right now, please do not give up hope. Before you know it, you will be in a better situation, where joy and peace will be the norm forever and ever.

If you are being persecuted because of your faith in Jesus Christ, stand firm and be courageous. God will give you the strength to withstand your current sufferings. Do not surrender to the enemy.

Continue to focus your eyes on those things that are eternal. Be willing to share your faith with those who are perishing. Ask God for favor to carry on in the face of great resistance. Even though you cannot see God, He is with you.

SEPTEMBER 17

"For we must all appear before the judgement seat of Christ, so that each of us may receive what is due us for the things done while in the body, whether good or bad." – 2 Corinthians 5:10 NIV

*I*f you have been wondering about the importance of your hard work after salvation, this verse clarifies things for you. This is the gist of what you should expect when you stand before God during the Judgement Seat of Christ.

It is important that you understand that the Judgment Seat of Christ is a special evaluation of your performance after salvation. The goal of this judgement is not to determine whether you are going to live in the New Jerusalem with God. In other words, the outcome of this judgement will not keep you out of heaven. The Judgment Seat of Christ is for believers, people who are already eligible for eternal life. For pre-tribulation believers, this judgement will take place during the Tribulation period.

The Judgment Seat of Christ is designed to determine whether you will receive a reward. If you did not do much after salvation, you will not receive much at the conclusion of this judgement.

Some people will make it to heaven, but they will not receive a reward, because they did not do jack after salvation. In addition, some people will be rebuked in heaven because they did many shameful things after salvation. Since salvation is not based on performance, they will still make it to heaven.

SEPTEMBER 18

"Therefore, if anyone is in Christ, the new creation has come: The old has gone, the new is here!" – 2 Corinthians 5:17 NIV

For this purpose, Christ came. He came to give us a new life. What Adam did in the Garden of Eden had basically killed us spiritually.

When people are separated from God, they are considered dead spiritually, though they seem to be alive in the natural. To use an oxymoron, they are living dead. And if they do not decide to accept Christ, they will remain dead.

Jesus, through His sacrifice on the cross, made it possible for those who are dead spiritually to become born-again – new creation. Jesus took upon Himself the punishment that was reserved for the transgressors. This was an extraordinary act of love orchestrated by the Heavenly Father. Surely, we did not deserve it. What we deserved was eternal death, but God is merciful and full of compassion. He showed His love toward us while we were still sinners.

Life in Christ has changed everything for us. Before Christ's intervention, we were condemned and were Hell-bound. We did not have any hope beyond the grave. Life, as we know it, was only limited to a lifespan on earth.

When Christ came, He has changed eternal damnation into eternal life. He has transformed darkness into light. We are no longer bound to the old way of life. We are now a new creation in Christ and are full of hope and life.

SEPTEMBER 19

"Do not be yoked together with unbelievers. For what do righteousness and wickedness have in common? Or what fellowship can light have with darkness?" – 2 Corinthians 6:14 NIV

*I*f you set out to have a fruitful relationship, it is important to pray for someone who has the same spiritual experience as you do. Now if you are already in a committed relationship and your spouse is not a believer, Apostle Paul said that you should not try to get out of that relationship.

This spiritual principle is applicable to business partnerships as well. It is much better when there is harmony in a business. You may decide to contribute a percentage of your business earnings to the Lord's work. If your business partners have no respect for God, you may find it difficult to agree on what you want to give.

When two believers are married or have a business together, there is spiritual unity in the marriage or the business deal.

Righteousness and wickedness have nothing in common. God reigns in righteousness and Satan reigns over the darkness. You can never reach any lasting, meaningful consensus if God is not Lord over you both. Similarly, light and darkness cannot coexist. You can save yourself a great deal of trouble by keeping these principles in mind as you pray for a mate or a business partner.

Don't think you will be able to change your partner after marriage or after the business deal is signed. It is not impossible, but it is a hard thing to do.

SEPTEMBER 20

"Godly sorrow brings repentance that leads to salvation and leaves no regret, but worldly sorrow brings death." – 2 Corinthians 7:10 NIV

On one hand, sorrow does not cause salvation, but it can lead us to salvation if it is godly. Godly sorrow helps us to realize our spiritual state. And since we cannot save ourselves, the Holy Spirit draws us to God for salvation through Jesus Christ.

On the other hand, worldly sorrow is fatal. It brings despair. Despair makes you think that there is no hope. It is a very difficult state of mind to be in, for you cannot live without hope for long. Satan is there to exploit you in every way. He wants to steal your joy and peace, but do not allow him to get the best of you. Cling to hope in the Lord Jesus Christ.

Being the Comforter in-Chief, the Holy Spirit is always in the business of comforting you in times of distress and discouragement. He is there to draw you closer to God through godly sorrow.

Do not allow worldly sorrow to invade your mind. Welcome the sweet voice of the Holy Spirit, who wants to win you over for God. It does not matter how deep you are in the mess; God is able to pull you out and clean you up.

Remember if you are on God's side, He's got your back. He will never abandon you nor will He forsake you.

SEPTEMBER 21

"But since you excel in everything – in faith, in speech, in knowledge, in complete earnestness and in the love we have kindled in you – see that you also excel in this grace of giving."
– 2 Corinthians 8:7 NIV

Although Apostle Paul noted many excellent qualities in the church of Corinth, he wanted to ensure that there was spiritual balance also. He urged the members of the church to excel in giving.

It is good to excel in faith because living for God requires believing in the unseen. It is impossible to connect with God without faith. If we could see God with our naked eyes, faith would not be necessary. The day will come when we will be able to see God just as He is. This will happen when we are clothed with our glorified body.

Being an eloquent speaker is a great gift, especially if you are called to be a preacher. God needs folks who can speak the word of truth with absolute clarity. When coupled with knowledge and anointing, eloquence can draw a crowd for the glory of God. In this case, there is nothing wrong in having those qualities. What else is important?

For the advancement of God's kingdom, we also need generous givers. God does not need your wealth, but He wants you to know that everything you are and everything you have belong to Him. When you give, you acknowledge the source of your blessings. Be all you can be, but do not miss out on the opportunity to give as well.

SEPTEMBER 22

"Remember this: Whoever sows sparingly will also reap sparingly, and whoever sows generously will also reap generously." – 2 Corinthians 9:6 NIV

Although you may not be a farmer, you can conceptualize the idea of sowing and reaping. Farmers, who want to reap a lot of beans, see to it that they work hard to sow a lot of beans.

When it comes to farming, it is all about volume. When I was growing up, my parents were very poor, so they did not have enough resources to have a big farmland. They were quite content to sow just enough to feed the family. And from time to time they would harvest enough food to store some for later use.

Conversely, not far from my parents' little farm was a farmer with a lot of means. He used to contract poor farmers to help till his land. My dad was one of those men who would spend hours preparing the rich farmer's land. During harvest time, not only did the rich farmer have enough to eat, but he had many truckloads of beans left to sell.

Apostle Paul used a farmer's analogy to explain the importance of generous giving. If you are willing to give generously, God will bless you so that you can always have something to give. However, you should give with joy, not under pressure. God looks at your heart and your giving attitude.

SEPTEMBER 23

"We do not dare to classify or compare ourselves with some who commend themselves. When they measure themselves by themselves and compare themselves with themselves, they are not wise." – 2 Corinthians 10:12 NIV

Avoid the game of comparing yourself with others because it always leads to disappointment. No matter where you are on your journey through life, you are bound to find someone who can outperform you. Apostle Paul defended his ministry by letting those who were trying to judge him by human standards know that he did not want to be involved in the game of comparing himself with others, and he made it clear that those who were doing so were not wise.

You cannot maximize your calling or your God-given potential if you always compare yourself with someone else. If there is a race, the race is with yourself. With God's help, you must strive to improve yourself daily.

Greatness can only be found in Jesus. If you want to find a gauge for your life, use Jesus as your role model. Your identity is found in Jesus Christ.

The game of comparison does not work, because God created you as a unique individual. Your standard is Jesus.

The truth is that you will never win the race if Jesus is not your target. Your true value is determined by God's eternal precepts. You are what God's words say you are. Just in case you wonder, if you have submitted your will to God, you are perfect in God's eyes through Christ's righteousness.

SEPTEMBER 24

"I am jealous for you with a godly jealousy. I promised you to one husband, to Christ, so that I might present you as a pure virgin to him." – 2 Corinthians 11:2 NIV

Apostle Paul was jealous because false apostles were trying to deceive the Christians. As a Christian, you must be careful not to allow people who say that they are the Lord's servants to deceive you. Read your Bible regularly. At the local church, take advantage of equipping classes to deepen your understanding of Christianity, for many false teachers are trying to come up with false interpretations of Scriptures. Those teachers are interested in advancing their own agenda. They are not preaching the true gospel.

Do not be naïve. Because people are talking about Jesus, that does not mean they are telling the truth. You must be careful about the way they explain salvation. Salvation is a very difficult topic to grasp because the common tendency is to replace God's grace with human efforts and Christ's righteousness with self-righteousness.

Apostle Paul wanted the church of Corinth to be more careful about false teachers. His understanding was that they were being too nice.

If people are preaching a different Jesus, we are not to allow such pernicious ideas to continue in the congregation. We are to be jealous for God's people because Christ paid a very high price to redeem them. Accepting false doctrine is a type of spiritual infidelity to Christ. We must show godly jealousy and categorically reject false teachings.

SEPTEMBER 25

"Therefore, in order to keep me from becoming conceited, I was given a thorn in my flesh, a messenger of Satan, to torment me. Three times, I pleaded with the Lord to take it away from me." – 2 Corinthians 12:7 and 8 NIV

*E*veryone has a thorn to put up with. If you don't have one, you are not living. To tell the truth, not all thorns are the same. There are small thorns, medium thorns, and large thorns. The fact is that everyone has a thorn to keep them humble.

The way you choose to deal with your thorn will determine the degree of your success on your journey through life. The important thing is that you must find a way to deal with it so that it does not get the best of you.

In the case of Apostle Paul, he went to the Lord with his thorn. He wanted God to get rid of it, but the response was quite surprising. "But God said to me, "my grace is enough for you, for my power is made perfect in weakness" (2 Corinthians 12: 9a NIV).

The Bible does not say exactly what Apostle Paul's thorn was. However, one can bet that it was an issue that really bothered him, and he would have loved to put it to rest.

Do not give up hope when you have a thorn in your flesh. Do consult the Lord about it but be ready to endure it through God's grace if nothing can be done to get rid of it.

The reason for Apostle Paul's thorn was to prevent him from being conceited. You may have a different reason for your thorn. Ask God to reveal it to you so you can have peace about it.

SEPTEMBER 26

"Examine yourselves to see whether you are in the faith; test yourselves. Do you not realize that Christ Jesus is in you – unless, of course, you fail the test?" – 2 Corinthians 13:5 NIV

*T*his constitutes Apostle Paul's powerful advice to those who would not stop sinning in the Corinthian churches. This advice is also suitable for individual application.

When was the last time you conducted self-examination? As a child of God, have you been behaving in a manner that brings glory to God? Or have you let your guard down? Have you been a good witness wherever you go so that more people can come to know your God?

Answers to those questions are important because they will help you reexamine your conscience as a born-again person. These questions are not designed to make you doubt your salvation –not at all. After all, I presume you are a child of God and that you are ready to stand before God through Christ's righteousness. The issue here is your testimony in the community.

As believers, we are free in Christ, but we must ensure that we are not abusing our freedom. Upon accepting Christ as our Lord and Savior, we become ambassadors for Christ. As ambassadors, we duly represent God's kingdom on earth. This is not a small matter. This is serious stuff.

Our lifestyle can do serious damage to the local church. Therefore, self-examination is important.

SEPTEMBER 27

"I am astonished that you are so quickly deserting the one who called you to live in the grace of Christ and are turning to a different gospel– which is really no gospel at all. Evidently some people are throwing you into confusion and are trying to pervert the gospel of Christ." – Galatians 1:6 and 7 NIV

$\mathcal{T}$he churches in Galatia were experiencing the same doctrinal problems as the Corinthian churches. Apostle Paul was very concerned for apparent perversion of the gospel of Christ. Apostle Paul of all people had a good grasp of heresy because he was involved in destroying the Church through implementation of Judaic traditions. Now having seen the light, he was not about to allow heresy to creep in and pervert the truth about Christ.

Living in grace is always a problem for people who want to work for their salvation instead of relying on Christ's righteousness. It is okay to want to do something to please God, but you cannot depend on what you do for your salvation. This is the type of perversion you need to avoid when it comes to the gospel of Jesus Christ. If you are not careful, people will reduce the gospel to a short list of dos and don'ts.

It is a misunderstanding if you think you can earn your salvation by doing good works. Doing good works will enable you to receive a reward at the Judgement Seat of Christ. Good works make sense after salvation, not before. Get saved and go out there and do some good works for the kingdom of God.

SEPTEMBER 28

"I do not set aside the grace of God, for if righteousness could be gained through the law, Christ died for nothing."– Galatians 2:21 NIV

This verse emphasizes the idea of being saved through grace, and not by the works of the law. The fact that God sent Jesus Christ to die on the cross for us is proof that it was not possible for us to gain God's favor by obeying the Mosaic Law.

The law itself is not a problem. It is there to gauge your performance and let you know about your failure. Unfortunately, God was not able to find anyone who could abide by the law one hundred percent. Jesus Christ was the only One who could meet the requirements of the law one hundred percent. As far as the law is concerned, it is all or zilch.

According to Apostle Paul, God's grace is a must. There are no other options for salvation. When it comes to meeting God's requirements for heaven, the key issue is righteousness. And you cannot get that by obeying the law or good works. These are the nuts and bolts of salvation. If you fail to understand this salient point, your Christian experience will be like a roller-coaster – up and down. You will be happy when you think you did something good that merits God's favor, and you will be miserable when you mess up.

The solution for your struggle is to depend completely on Christ's righteousness for your salvation, and trust in Him to help you meet the requirements for eternal life. Therefore, Christ died for something; He died for us.

SEPTEMBER 29

"Clearly no one who relies on the law is justified before God, because the righteous will live by faith." – Galatians 3:11 NIV

*F*aith and grace are two key words that set the New Testament theology apart from that of the Old Testament. And justification by faith is Apostle Paul's mantra. Without those two words, it is impossible to understand fully the theology of the New Testament. In this verse, Apostle Paul pointed out that the law has no role to play in justification.

While the law was an important element in the lives of God's people in that they were governed by it, the law takes a backseat in the New Testament. In fact, the New Testament represents God's new covenant with His people.

In the new covenant, God introduces a new circumcision that is not based on external performance. It is done in the hearts of the believers through faith in the Lord Jesus Christ. It is that faith Apostle Paul was talking about in this verse.

By faith, when you accept Jesus Christ as your Savior, God justifies you through the Spirit –meaning that you are now free from condemnation. In other words, you are no longer guilty of sin, because Christ's precious blood has redeemed you once and for all. This is not something that the law was able to do. All this was made possible by God's grace and through faith in the shed blood of Jesus Christ. Know that you are duly justified by faith in the Lord Jesus Christ, not by the law.

SEPTEMBER 30

"But when the set time had fully come, God sent his Son, born of a woman, born under the law, to redeem those under the law, that we might receive adoption to sonship." – Galatians 4:4 and 5 NIV

Salvation by faith did not happen by chance. It was orchestrated by God and carried out by the birth, death, and resurrection of Jesus Christ. And all that was done when the set time had fully come. God used Virgin Mary to facilitate the incarnation of Jesus, who came as the sacrificial Lamb to redeem us from the yoke of the law. We are now sons and daughters of God through a spiritual adoption. This is the mystery the gospel sets out to unveil to everyone who is willing to believe.

Here, Apostle Paul continued to explain why the law is not a major focus of the New Testament's theology. The Galatian churches did not fully grasp the idea of being justified by faith outside the observance of the law. Apostle Paul's concern was that those Christians were trying to embrace the new covenant, but they were reluctant to let go of the old one. In other words, they were trying to have their cake and eat it too.

The same principle is true for believers today. Be careful not to hold on to your old sinful habits while enjoying your new freedom in Christ. You cannot have it both ways. Either you live for God or you live for the devil. Ask God to give you strength to withstand worldly temptation.

OCTOBER 1

"But the fruit of the Spirit is love, joy, peace, forbearance, kindness, goodness, faithfulness, gentleness and self-control." – Galatians 5:22 and 23 NIV

*I*n order to produce the fruit of the Spirit, you must live and walk by the Spirit. Apostle Paul said, "So I say, walk by the Spirit, and you will not gratify the desires of the flesh" (Galatians 5:16 NIV). The first fruit of the Spirit is essential because it fulfills all the requirements of the Mosaic Law. When an expert of the law questioned Jesus about the greatest commandment, He replied: "Love the Lord your God with all your heart and with all your soul and with all your mind. This is first and greatest commandment. And the second is like it: 'Love your neighbor as yourself.' All the Law and the Prophets hang on these two commandments" (Matthew 22:37-40 NIV).

When love begins to flow from your heart, joy follows naturally, and what comes after is peace within. Love takes care of all your worries so that you can rest in peace.

When you are full of love, it is much easier for you to be patient and tolerant toward others, which is what forbearance is all about. If you are patient and tolerant, you have no problem being kind to people. Kindness and goodness become your way of life.

Because love is your pillar, faithfulness is your steadfast goal in life, and self-control creates the spiritual balance you need to continue to walk by the Spirit. Without the fruit of the Spirit, you will not know how to utilize your freedom in Christ. Apostle Paul said," Do not use your freedom to indulge the flesh" (verse 13). Therefore, pray and ask God to give you wisdom so you can live by the Spirit.

OCTOBER 2

"Let us not become weary in doing good, for at the proper time we will reap a harvest if we do not give up." – Galatians 6:9 NIV

After Apostle Paul had taken the time to explain grace and justification by faith, he saw fit to mention the importance of doing good. Doing good is part of the mission of the Church. Apostle Paul did not belittle good works. He simply wanted to ensure that the Galatian churches did not go backward by placing their reliance on the Mosaic Law, which is a thing of the past.

The law had its role in the Old Testament. It was a good thing for that epoch, not now. When Jesus came, He did not abolish the law. He simply fulfilled it by meeting all the requirements that were impossible for us to meet. Now we are led by the Spirit. "But if you are led by the Spirit, you are not under the law" (Galatians 5:18 NIV).

Since Jesus fulfilled the law, we can now close this chapter and move forward toward a righteousness that is by faith. We are no longer relying on the law or on a circumcision that is based on the flesh. We now have a new covenant that is based on the precious blood of Jesus Christ.

Being justified by faith, we can now do good works in order to advance God's kingdom on earth. As we continue to work hard, we know we will reap a wonderful harvest if we do not give up. Let us continue to make a difference for God through good works but let us make sure that our salvation is not hinged on them.

OCTOBER 3

"Praise be to the God and Father of our Lord Jesus Christ, who has blessed us in the heavenly realms with every spiritual blessing in Christ." – Ephesians 1:3 NIV

*A*s a believer in the Lord Jesus Christ, you are the recipient, first and foremost, of every spiritual blessing that Apostle Paul mentioned here. God had orchestrated your blessings before the creation of the world, so it was not by accident that you are now a member of God's family.

What you will be in heaven, in terms of righteousness, is part of your spiritual blessings. God wants you to be righteous. Keep in mind that your righteousness is made possible by the blood of Jesus. Your own effort cannot make you righteous. You are righteous because God has declared you so by His grace through His Son Jesus Christ.

Your ultimate blessing is to know that your sins are forgiven. Forgiveness is the greatest gift you can ever receive from God because without it, there is no salvation. Salvation guarantees your gift of eternal life until your eventual glorification. Praise be to God for many spiritual blessings He has bestowed upon you.

Your opportunity to be a child of God is made possible through adoption. An adopted child enjoys the same privilege as a biological child in terms of rights. God miraculously adopted you by accepting you as one of His children. "Yet to all who did receive him, to those who believed in his name, he gave the right to become children of God" (John 1:12 NIV).

OCTOBER 4

"For it is by grace you have been saved, through faith –and this is not from yourselves, it is the gift of God–not by works, so that no one can boast. For we are God's handiwork, created in Christ Jesus to do good works, which God prepared in advance for us to do." – Ephesians 2:8-10 NIV

These three verses are key to understanding salvation.

Salvation is a very salient aspect of Christianity. It is the center of God's plan for humanity. As a matter of fact, the purpose of Christ's mission on earth is to redeem us. Redemption means to buy back. God had to find a way to purchase us back so that we could be admitted to God's kingdom.

The key issue is that you are not able to save yourself. It does not matter how good you are, you need God's favor. You can never do enough good works to deserve salvation. Salvation is only possible through God's grace, and that's it.

Now you understand how salvation is obtained, it is time to understand the role of your good works. For your information, God created you in Christ Jesus to do good works. However, you must be saved before your good works can be counted toward your reward. God only accepts good works after salvation. If you are not in Christ Jesus, your good works are futile. To put it simply, you do not do good works in order to be saved. It is just the other way around. You are saved to do good works.

OCTOBER 5

"This mystery is that through the gospel the Gentiles are heirs together with Israel, members together of one body, and sharers together in the promise in Christ Jesus." – Ephesians 3:6 NIV

One of the amazing things that happened with the birth, death, and resurrection of Jesus Christ is the opportunity for non-Jewish people to get united with God. Before that, the children of Israel were the only people entitled to be called God's people.

Now through Christ, Gentiles are also called God's children. We now have the same hope of spending eternity in the Holy City with God forever and ever, according Revelation 21. Christ will be the King of kings and Lord of lords.

God's marvelous gesture of bringing Jews and Gentiles together shows that He is interested in uniting people of different races and backgrounds. As God's children, there should be no racial divisions among us. We all depend on God's grace for salvation. We are the Church, the body of Christ. We are one people with one hope in Christ.

God's kingdom is the epitome of diversity. If you are a believer, pray that God will give you the desire to love all kinds of people. We are members of God's family.

When you get to heaven, you will be among God's people. The issue of class and race will be a thing of the past. All the racial differences that are causing so much suffering in the world today will be no more. God will bring complete peace and unity among His people.

OCTOBER 6

"In your anger do not sin. "Do not let the sun go down while you are still angry, and do not give the devil a foothold." – Ephesians 4:26 and 27 NIV

$\mathcal{A}$s believers, we are not exempt from adversity. We are still exposed to all types of persecutions in this fallen world. For this reason, it is important that we are watchful so that we do not allow the enemy to invade our camp.

Satan is very crafty and is waiting for our feet to slip to get involved in our business. In fact, as Christians, nonbelievers are eager to speak out against us because they are seeking for occasions to point out that we are not what we say we are. They want to find any trace of hypocrisy in us.

Keep in mind when you are not happy, you are emotionally vulnerable. You are more likely to say and/or do irrational things in your anger. Be sure you maintain your self-control so that you don't fall in Satan's trap. It is advisable that you have a strategy for dealing with your anger, so you don't have to improvise when something bad happens.

Try to resolve all the negative issues before you go to bed, especially if you are married. When you go to bed with anger, your spouse suffers tremendously. You too suffer a great deal because your spirit is not at peace.

It is important that you both find a way to get together in prayer. Often, the Holy Spirit can unite you as you pray together. If your spouse refuses to pray with you, go to God alone and ask for wisdom to deal with the situation. Be willing to forgive. Prayer is key to forgiveness and reconciliation.

OCTOBER 7

"Be very careful, then, how you live – not as unwise but as wise, making the most of every opportunity, because the days are evil." – Ephesians 5:15 and 16 NIV

Satan's continuous efforts are to diminish the impact of the gospel around the world. Some people think that they do not need God. There is an increasing push for self-sufficiency, which is good to a certain extent. However, we should feel the need to depend on God for our spiritual needs.

In 1 Chronicles 12:32, the Bible says that "from Issachar, men who understood the times and knew what Israel should do – 200 chiefs, with all their relatives under their command" joined David as king at Hebron.

These men were wise and knew those moments were crucial in that it was time to turn their back on Saul and throw their full support behind David. God was ready to do something new. He was ready to provide His people with a new leader who would honor him with all his heart.

Today we ought to be wise and understand that it is time for us to stand up for godly principles amid increasing pressure to accept godlessness. It is also time to proclaim the gospel of Jesus Christ so that those who do not know Him may have eternal life.

The time is right to get involved in building for eternity. Make the most of every opportunity because Jesus is coming back for His Church.

OCTOBER 8

"Put on the full armor of God, so that you can take your stand against the devil's schemes." – Ephesians 6:11 NIV

The devil is a spirit, so you cannot rely on flesh and blood to overcome a spirit. For that reason, you need to depend on spiritual means to fight the devil.

According to Apostle Paul, God's full armor consists of the belt of truth, the breastplate of righteousness, readiness that comes from the gospel of peace, the shield of faith, the helmet of salvation, and the sword of the Spirit, which is the word of God (verses 14-17).

It is important that you do not undermine any parts of the armor. You need a complete armor to ensure full protection. With the truth, you have freedom. You need it as your belt to hold everything together. Satan cannot scare your heart out when you stand before God if you depend on Christ's righteousness for your salvation.

In addition, you need the gospel of peace. The gospel is the truth about Jesus Christ. It has what you need to know so that the devil does not deceive you.

Faith sustains you so you can fix your eyes on God, even though you cannot see Him. With salvation, you are now saved by faith through God's grace.

And finally, with God's word you can debunk all the lies of the devil. You know God loves you, so you do not have to feel insecure when you are under attacks. You have all you need to overcome anything that the devil may throw at you. Take your stand against the devil.

OCTOBER 9

"For to me, to live is Christ and to die is gain." – Philippians 1:21 NIV

Before Apostle Paul made this statement, he had been through unimaginable physical traumas and emotional sufferings. This statement was based on tried and true Christian experiences. Apostle Paul was eager to transition to eternity, but he knew that God still had something for him to do on earth.

When it comes to life, Apostle Paul concluded that life only has real meaning through Christ. If you live in Christ, you are connected to the source of life. Death will not be able to disrupt your eternal existence. In fact, death is a blessing in disguise for Christians because it will serve as a transitional mechanism to unite them with God. That's why Apostle Paul said, "To die is gain."

When you die, you will lose your physical body, but you will gain a glorified one in return. Death is only a loss for those who are perishing because death will transition them to eternal death. Eternal life is reserved for those who are in Christ.

Eternal death will be the most traumatic punishment that anyone would ever experience. This is not something I would wish on my worst enemy. Rejoice if you are counted among the saved. You do not have to suffer eternal death, for through Christ's righteousness, you will not have to face God's wrath.

OCTOBER 10

"Whatever happens, conduct yourselves in a manner worthy of the gospel of Christ." – Philippians 1:27 NIV

*T*he gospel does not promise you a problem-free life. As a born-again person, you have a lot to endure because you must be a witness for Christ. People who do not know God tend to let their emotions run wild. They do whatever pleases them without any compunction whatsoever.

Even in difficult times, you are called to exemplify Christ. Your lifestyle is what draws people to Jesus. You need to live your life in such a way that people can see Jesus in you. That does not mean that you are not allowed to show emotional reactions. Of course, you can.

While you are not exempt from adversity, in adversity you should be able to maintain your peace. As a believer, your peace does not depend on your daily circumstances. You should not behave like someone who has no faith. The Almighty is also your God. For that reason, you are to continue to hold firm in the faith.

Nonbelievers should wonder how you are able to show so much joy during extreme challenges and personal adversities. Keep them guessing until they come to experience the same joy that you have in Jesus. Your hope is anchored in the gospel of Christ, the rock-solid truth that cannot be shaken by the storms of life. Yes, you can overcome by the precious blood of Jesus Christ.

OCTOBER 11

"Do nothing out of selfish ambition or vain conceit. Rather, in humility value others above yourselves, not looking to your own interests but each of you to the interests of the others." – Philippians 2:3 and 4 NIV

As a follower of Christ, God's word is designed to provide you with the necessary guidance you need to live for Christ. Keep in mind that this passage is not talking about salvation. Here, the focus is on your daily living in Christ. Upon salvation, you have the responsibility for walking in the light as Christ is in the light. You should shine your light so that those who are living in the darkness can come to know the fullness of Christ.

Apostle Paul encouraged the church in Philippi to imitate Christ's humility. Christ willingly accepted to become human so that He could forgive our sins. Being humble requires a lot of sacrifice and determination in order to deal with selfishness.

Christ's decision to die for us shows the greatest level of selflessness. He was not looking after His own interests. He had our best interests at heart.

You should show a similar level of commitment to others in your relationships with them. Often, you will be tempted to go after selfish ambitions. Ask God to give you strength and wisdom to endure temptation without giving up.

OCTOBER 12

"I press on toward the goal to win the prize for which God has called me heavenward in Christ Jesus." – Philippians 3:14 NIV

*I*n his quest for the knowledge of Christ and full participation in His sufferings, Apostle Paul was keenly aware that he was not there yet. He had a lot to accomplish before he could safely make such a claim. Consequently, he was determined to pursue his mission. His main goal was to win the prize.

God has a prize for you as well. Pressing toward the goal is not easy. You must ignore the distractions around you if you are going to win your prize. The enemy is determined to thwart your plan by discouraging you in every turn.

It does not matter where you are on your journey through life; God is interested in helping you to reach your full potential in Christ.

As an individual, you are unique in God's eyes, so you do not have to compare yourself with others. Pray and ask God to give you strength and wisdom to accomplish the mission for which He has called you.

Remember to keep your eyes on the prize ahead. Whether you are working on a special project, a college degree, your marriage, or your finances, you need to continue to focus on your goal. You cannot achieve your goal if you do not maintain your course. Be careful not to compromise along the way by taking a shortcut. Shortcuts will delay the process and slow your momentum.

OCTOBER 13

"Do not be anxious about anything, but in every situation, by prayer and petition, with thanksgiving, present your requests to God." – Philippians 4:6 NIV

Dealing with anxieties can take a toll on our health if we are not careful. That is why Jesus commanded us not to worry about our lives. He said, "Therefore I tell you, do not worry about your life, what you will eat or drink; or about your body, what you will wear. Is not life more than food and the body more than clothes?" (Matthew 6:25 NIV)

One of the reasons we are anxious is because we are not sure how things will pan out. We worry a great deal about life's uncertainties. Jesus is right in telling us not to worry about anything, because He knows everything about our future. He knows how things will turn out in the end, even though we have no clue.

In line with Jesus' command, Apostle Paul encourages us to take a different approach to problem solving. First, instead of being anxious, Apostle Paul wants us to go to God in prayer.

God knows what we need, even before we ask Him. Second, by faith, we need to thank God for what we ask Him for. By thanking God, we are telling Him that we know that He has heard our prayer and petition.

Because God is in control of our circumstances, we can have peace in the middle of them. It is exciting to know that God is in the business of taking care of us.

OCTOBER 14

"The Son is the image of the invisible God, the firstborn over all creation." – Colossians 1:15 NIV

As a believer, you may not know how the first particle was formed, but you should know who formed it. Let scientists continue to figure it out. For example, I do not have to have in-depth knowledge of the electric light bulb to appreciate the contributions of Thomas Edison and many other scientists who laid the foundations for electricity, including, but not limited to Benjamin Franklin and his fellow scientists.

The whole universe came about through Jesus Christ and for Jesus Christ. Jesus was in command during creation, and He is the glue that keeps all things together.

Although the Heavenly Father is invisible, Jesus Christ, through His incarnation, gave the people who were still alive during His earthly mission a glimpse of what the Almighty is.

If you need to know what God is like, examine Jesus Christ, the Son, by reading the story about His birth, death, and resurrection in the four gospels.

Jesus' life reveals the Father's heart, His love as well as His sovereignty. Furthermore, when you surrender your heart to Jesus Christ as your Lord and Savior, you get to experience the Father's love for you through the forgiveness of your sins and the hope of eternal life.

OCTOBER 15

"For in Christ all the fullness of the Deity lives in bodily form, and in Christ you have been brought to fullness. He is the head over every power and authority." – Colossians 2:9 and 10 NIV

Through the process of incarnation, Christ, the Son of God, became a man. And since Christ was one hundred percent God and one hundred percent man while He was in the flesh, He knows our needs.

As mentioned in Colossians 1, "The Son is the image of the invisible God, the firstborn over all creation." (Verse 15) In Christ, you have everything you need to qualify you for eternal life.

Because the Heavenly Father has given all authority to Christ, if you accept Christ as your personal Lord and Savior, you have the greatest spiritual encounter – you have been brought to the fullness of God. You are connected to the highest power.

Based on this spiritual knowledge, you no longer need to visit a medium, or a spiritualist, or a voodoo priest, for that matter. When you need spiritual assistance, you can go to Jesus Christ, the head of every power and authority.

In the name of Jesus Christ, all rulers, whether they are natural rulers or supernatural ones, must bow down. It does not matter if they are willing to submit to Christ now or not, they all will end up acknowledging that Christ is the King of kings and Lord of lords in the end.

OCTOBER 16

"Since, then, you have been raised with Christ, set your hearts on things above, where Christ is, seated at the right hand of God." – Colossians 3:1 NIV

*F*rom a spiritual standpoint, we, believers, died to the flesh and are now alive with Christ. We are no longer slaves to sin. For that reason, Apostle Paul reminds us to set our hearts and minds to things above. When we set our hearts and minds on things above, we become kingdom minded. We are less interested in gratifying the desires of the flesh, because we know that we died to the flesh, and our lives are hidden in Christ (verse 3).

The mystery of the gospel is that we are in the world, but we are not to conduct our business as those who are in the world. By the world, I mean the worldly system that has undermined the power of the gospel of Christ and has elevated the power of darkness and godlessness.

As Christ was about to return to His Father, He made us a special promise. He said, "My father's house has many rooms; if that were not so, would I have told you I am going there to prepare a place for you" (John 14:2 NIV)?

Based on this promise, we are not permanent residents of this world. We are just passing through. Our permanent home will be in the New Jerusalem, where God's throne will be established forever. Meanwhile, let us fix our eyes on Christ.

OCTOBER 17

"Be wise in the way you act toward outsiders; make the most of every opportunity. Let your conversation be always full of grace, seasoned with salt, so that you may know how to answer everyone." – Colossians 4:5 and 6 NIV

Since you belong to Christ, you have access to infinite wisdom. "In Christ are all the treasures of wisdom and knowledge" (Col.3:3 NIV).

You need to take advantage of every opportunity to share the love of Christ with people who do not know Jesus. You cannot behave like an unwise person and expect nonbelievers to want to come to Christ. Lifestyle evangelism is very powerful. Do not tell me how great your God is if you are not willing to demonstrate His love in the way you live.

In your conversation, show grace so you can draw people to Christ. If you are inconsiderate toward people who do not know the Lord, they are not coming to Christ – at least not because of you. Be gracious in your dealing with the unbelievers so they can see Jesus in your life.

As a Christian, you cannot respond to nonbelievers the same way they talk to you. When they are rude to you, you need to be kind enough to answer them with a loving tone of voice. Remember that you are a source of hope for the hopeless. When nonbelievers talk to you, they need to have a sense of wonder toward you. Ask God for wisdom so you may be His faithful witness.

OCTOBER 18

"Brothers and sisters, we do not want you to be uninformed about those who sleep in death, so that you do not grieve like the rest of mankind, who have no hope." – Thessalonians 4:13 NIV

After Apostle Paul had given thanks to God for the faith of the Thessalonian church, he encouraged them to continue to be strong in trials. He also urged them to live in a manner pleasing to God. Finally, he turned their attention to the importance of the afterlife and the eminent Rapture of the Church.

One of the key pillars of Christianity is life beyond the grave, which is eternal life. Without this unshaken hope, Christianity is meaningless. Christianity makes sense because it provides believers the opportunity to continue living. This means death does not pose a threat to those who believe in Jesus Christ as their Lord and Savior.

Our hope of eternal life is hinged on our firm conviction that Jesus died, and God raised Him from the dead. We know that we will live beyond death because Jesus overcame it.

Apostle Paul wanted to remind the church of Thessalonica that people who are alive when Jesus comes for the Church will have the opportunity to experience a sudden transformation. They will be transformed from a physical state to a spiritual one. Praise God for this glorious hope in Jesus!

OCTOBER 19

"Rejoice always, pray continually, give thanks in all circumstances; for this is God's will for you in Christ Jesus." – Thessalonians 5:16 and 17 NIV

*H*ow can you rejoice always when everything is so chaotic around you? Is it possible to maintain such a level of spiritual equilibrium in times of distress?

In order to remain steadfast in your faith, no matter your circumstances, you must focus your eyes on Jesus Christ. You must use your spiritual lens, not your natural assessment of your situation. When you focus on the unseen, you can see possibility in impossibility.

Praying without ceasing can keep your mind on the Lord instead of your problems. That does not mean it is useless to figure out possible solutions. Because if you need a job, you need to try to fill out some job applications. The important thing is that you need to rely on God's favor.

God's will for you in Christ Jesus is to maintain your spiritual balance by staying spiritually connected with Him during chaos. David said, "Even though I walk through the darkest valley, I will fear no evil, for you are with me" (Psalm 23:4 NIV).

This kind of spiritual stubbornness enables you to push through the darkest valley knowing that God is in control of your circumstances. That's why it is spiritually possible to rejoice always.

Rejoicing always does not mean ignoring the reality. It simply means knowing who is in control of your reality.

OCTOBER 20

"May the Lord direct your hearts into God's love and Christ's perseverance." – 2 Thessalonians 3:5 NIV

Amid an apparent surge of lawlessness and idleness in the church of Thessalonians, Apostle Paul saw fit to encourage his brothers and sisters to stand firm "through the sanctifying work of the Spirit and through belief in the truth" (Thessalonians 2:13b).

From time to time, we may become unsettled in our faith because of life's circumstances or apparent weaknesses in our daily walk with Christ. Satan always takes advantage of uncertainties among us to shake the foundations of our faith. We must stand firm in Christ's perseverance. Christ came and suffered the worse punishment for our sins, so He understands our daily trials.

In our prayer, we ought to ask God to direct our hearts. When our hearts try to take a detour, we need to rely on God to redirect our path so that we do not lose sight of our God-given purpose in life. God has plans for our lives, and the enemy is trying hard to confuse us with "all sorts of displays of power and wonders that serve the lie" (verse 9b).

It is important that we remain in God's love and Christ's perseverance. In so doing, we will be able to continue to shine for the kingdom of God.

We are waiting patiently for the Rapture of the Church and Christ's subsequent second coming to crush the power of darkness and rule as King of kings and Lord of lords.

OCTOBER 21

"Now to the King eternal, immortal, invisible, the only God, be honor and glory for ever and ever. Amen." – 1 Timothy 1:17 NIV

Apostle Paul turned to God in worship after he had charged Timothy to oppose false teachers. We should never forget the source of our strength and daily victory over the power darkness. Our victory comes from our King. Our King lives!

What makes Christianity unique is that our King is eternal. He is not a piece of wood that cannot speak, nor is He an image that cannot budge. He is alive forever. Our God is immortal; death has no power of over Him. He has conquered death when the Heavenly Father raised Him from the dead on the third day.

All the so-called gods that people worship around the world are not real. They are not immortal like Yahweh, the Almighty. Although our God is invisible, we know that He exists because He has demonstrated His power among us through Jesus. Jesus is the image of the invisible God (Colossians 1).

Our God is the only true God. There is no one like Him. For that reason, we honor Him and give Him glory forever and ever.

Thank you, Jesus, for shedding your precious blood to save us from eternal death. Today we have eternal hope through your resurrection. We are holding on to faith in you.

OCTOBER 22

"This is good, and pleases God our Savior, who wants all people to be saved and to come to a knowledge of the truth." –1 Timothy 2:3 and 4 NIV

Ultimately, if someone does not make it to heaven it is not because of God. God wants everyone to be saved. However, because God created us with certain autonomy, He is not willing to force us to serve Him.

Although God, in His infinite wisdom, had chosen not to force us to obey Him, He has provided everything we need so that we all could come to the full knowledge of Him. He had made that decision before the foundation of the world. For that very purpose, He sent Jesus, His Son, to die in our place. "For God so loved the world that he gave his one and only Son, that whoever believes in him shall not perish but have eternal life" (John 3:16 NIV).

Coming to the full knowledge of God is the most important decision a person could ever make. This is an encounter designed to be personal. This knowledge of the truth is essential for eternal life and freedom in Christ Jesus. "It was for freedom that Christ has set us free. Stand firm, then and do not let yourselves be burdened again by a yoke of slavery" (Galatians 5:1 NIV). Through the birth, death, and resurrection of Christ, God has given everyone the same access to forgiveness of sins and eternal life.

OCTOBER 23

"Beyond all question, the mystery from which true godliness springs is great: He appeared in the flesh, was vindicated by the Spirit, was seen by angels, was preached among the nations, was believed on in the world, was taken up in glory." – 1 Timothy 3:16 NIV

When we think about the way God had chosen to redeem us, we cannot but marvel at His wisdom as well as His sovereignty. Being the Creator of the universe, God could have found another way to save us without resorting to the incarnation of His Son, but He did it anyway. No one would have believed Christ's sacrifice on the cross if He had not lived in the flesh like humans. The incarnation has authenticated Jesus Christ's crucifixion.

God did not choose an easy way out. He gave us His best. Jesus appeared in the flesh to do His Father's will, and the Spirit of God was there to witness it. "Then Jesus was led by the Spirit into to the wilderness to be tempted by the devil" (Matthew 4:1 NIV). He was tested through and through and came out victoriously. After Jesus had passed the test in the wilderness, angels were at His service. "Then the devil left him, and angels came and attended Him" (Matthew 4:11 NIV).

The gospel has been preached around the world in the name of Jesus, and many people have come to know Him as their Lord and Savior. According to Mark 16:19, "Jesus was taken up into heaven and he sat at the right hand of God" (NIV).

OCTOBER 24

"The Spirit clearly says that in later times some will abandon the faith and follow deceiving spirits and things taught by demons."
– 1 Timothy 4:1 NIV

*I*f we are not careful, we may accept false interpretations from the messengers of Satan of those marvelous truths mentioned in 1 Timothy 3 verse 16 about Jesus. For that reason, it is imperative that we adhere to the principles found in the gospel of Jesus Christ. Otherwise we will be vulnerable to the lies of the devil.

Deceiving spirits are dispatched all over the world to confuse people about the truth regarding the incarnation of Jesus, His death, and His resurrection. If Satan could convince people that Jesus did not come in the flesh, then he would keep them from accepting Christ as their Lord and Savior.

The death of Christ is significant because it pays for our sins. Without Christ's death, there is no forgiveness of sins. His death was the price paid for our transgressions. Therefore, it is Satan's number one objective to persuade people that Jesus Christ's death did not happen as the Bible describes it.

In addition to Christ's death, His resurrection is of paramount importance. Christ's resurrection is the ultimate confirmation that we will defeat eternal death. Because Christ overcame death, we have hope that we will overcome it as well.

Death is not the end of your existence. With that said, be vigilant and keep on believing in the gospel of truth.

OCTOBER 25

"Anyone who does not provide for their relatives, and especially for their own household, has denied the faith and is worse than an unbeliever." – 1 Timothy 5:8 NIV

The Christian label comes with a sense of prestige. A Christian is a person who believes in Christ. If you believe in Christ, you accept the fact that Christ's Father is your Father as well. That automatically makes you a prince or a princess. Have you ever thought of this marvelous reality?

Now if the King of kings is your Heavenly Father, you must carry yourself accordingly. That means you should not live a life that is unbefitting of your identity in Christ. You would not want unbelievers to belittle the name of your God by saying that He is not able to take care of you. That is why Apostle Paul advised Christians to provide for their relatives and their household.

Some of us who are living in a developed country are blessed to have a decent welfare system. However, it is a shame that there are so many local churches around, and yet poor people are still living under bridges. If more local churches were willing to work together, they would be able to help homeless people to live in dignity. I know there are local churches that are making progress toward that goal, but more collaboration is still needed.

Be willing to support your relatives, especially your family members when they are in need. Do not abandon your parents when they get old. Be ready to step in and help them when they are no longer able to care for themselves. This is the Christian thing to do in this situation.

OCTOBER 26

"For the love of money is a root of all kinds of evil. Some people, eager for money, have wandered from the faith and pierced themselves with many griefs." – 1 Timothy 6:10 NIV

While money is necessary for the advancement of the mission of the Church and society at large, the love of money is a problem because it can cause people to hurt others just to get rich. When this type of excess occurs, money becomes an idol.

Anything that occupies your mind more than God is an idol, and God hates idols. God must be your priority in life. Apostle Paul said, "Godliness with contentment is great gain" (1 Timothy 6:7 NIV). The problem with the love of money is the absence of contentment. It is the tendency to amass more wealth just for the sake of having it. With that said, there is nothing wrong in being rich if you know how to handle your riches and wealth.

If the love of money becomes the focus of everything you do, you will lose your sense of purpose in life. Accumulation of wealth will be your number one objective. The important thing is to make the advancement of God's kingdom your focus and use wealth to get things done in God's kingdom.

Motive is everything. Be sure your motive is pure in everything you do. You should know that God is able to know your motive. Spare yourself some griefs by avoiding getting involved in corruption just to get rich, for you will not be able to take anything with you.

OCTOBER 27

"For the Spirit God gave us does not make us timid, but gives us power, love and self-discipline." – 2 Timothy 1:7 NIV

*T*imidity is the absence of confidence in ourselves or in God who has sent us. We know God has put His Spirit in us to make us bold so that we can stand firm in the faith and carry out the work of His kingdom. Since it was Apostle Paul who laid hands on Timothy to receive God's gift, he knew Timothy had God's anointing in him. Apostle Paul took it upon himself to mentor young Timothy. Apostle Paul encouraged Timothy to participate in the same sufferings in which he was involved for the glory of Christ.

The message of the gospel is a life changing experience that everyone needs to have. Timothy was charged with making sure that God's grace, which was revealed in Christ, was not remained hidden. Apostle Paul wanted Timothy to convey to everyone the message that "Christ has destroyed death and has brought life and immortality to light through the gospel" (2 Timothy 1:10b).

Those of us who have experienced God's grace have the same responsibility as Timothy for making the name of Jesus Christ known. We do not have to be afraid of people's judgment. God's Spirit who lives in us gives us the power, love, and self-discipline we need to carry out the work of the kingdom. We also have the responsibility for reaching out to everyone. The goal is to help them come to know the hope that is in Christ Jesus, especially the opportunity to live eternally in the Holy City, which is the New Jerusalem.

OCTOBER 28

"Do your best to present yourself to God as one approved, a worker who does not need to be ashamed and who correctly handles the word of truth." – 2 Timothy 2:15 NIV

As a follower of Christ, it is important that you try to educate yourself in the Holy Scripture so that you do not become a target for false teachers. Satan has used false teachers to argue with people about the gospel. Those teachers tend to pretend that they have the truth.

Don't let false teachers hoodwink you by their eloquence. Those folks enjoy discussing big theological terms. They are not interested in telling you about the importance of the precious blood of Jesus. Salvation is not their focus. Their goal is to confuse you so that you take your focus off the hope and faith you have placed in the Lord Jesus Christ.

Spend time reading God's precepts so that you know how God wants you to live. Live your life in such a way that others see God in you.

There are folks who are eager to talk about Jesus, but they are not interested in living for Jesus. Their lifestyle does not reflect God's principles.

Do not be ashamed to stand up for what you know about Jesus. Jesus did something extraordinary for you, so you don't need to walk with your head down. Lift your head and speak proudly about your spiritual blessings in Jesus. Be prepared to handle the word of truth.

OCTOBER 29

"All Scripture is God-breathed and is useful for teaching, rebuking, correcting and training in righteousness, so that the servant of God may be thoroughly equipped for every good work." – 2 Timothy 3:16 and 17 NIV

The Bible is God's word and is good to educate your mind in every good thing. If you make God's word your compass in life, you will reach your destination. You may struggle along the way, but do not give up hope. Being on God's side, you are headed in the right direction.

God's word is good for your spiritual education. It is also good to convict you of your sins. God's word will always show you the correct path when you fail to adhere to the truth about Jesus Christ.

Allow God's word to correct you when you are wrong. The Holy Spirit can show you your mistakes along the way. Value God's corrections because He corrects those He loves. Parents who love their children are quick to correct them so that they do not continue in their errors.

Training in righteousness prepares us to live according to the principles found in the gospel of Christ. Christ is the quintessential of righteousness. When we live for Christ, we emulate Christ's way of life. In brief, we live according to the gospel of Christ.

When we make living for Christ our aim in life, we are equipped for every good work. God had prepared us to do good works before the foundation of the world.

OCTOBER 30

"I have fought the good fight, I have finished the race, I have kept the faith." – 2 Timothy 4:7 NIV

*T*hese statements made by Apostle Paul should be included in every believer's final words on earth. It is not enough to fight; we must fight the good fight. Some fights are not worth fighting, because they do not help to advance the kingdom of God. For that reason, we need to choose our fights carefully so that we do not waste our energy in futile pursuits.

We need to fight the good fight, but we also need to finish the race that is before us. It is not enough to start the race; we also need to finish it for God's glory.

The race to win the lost souls for Christ is a worthy cause. Every day, people are dying without Christ. A person who dies without Christ is a person who dies without hope. We need to strive daily to ensure that many people come to know Jesus Christ as their Lord and Savior.

When all is said and done, we must keep the faith. Without faith, it is impossible to relate to God. Faith is the magnet that keeps us connected with the Almighty. Faith enables us to see the unseen. In fact, through our eyes of faith, we can place more value on what we cannot see than on what we can see.

When things get tough, keep the faith. When everything is collapsing around you, keep the faith. Keep the faith, even though it is the only thing you have left.

OCTOBER 31

"They claim to know God, but by their actions they deny him."
– Titus 1:16a NIV

*I*n his pastoral letter to Titus, Apostle Paul described the spiritual conditions of the people of Crete. Apostle Paul and Titus had a chance to take a missionary trip to the Island of Crete, and Titus was left behind to take care of business. As you may conclude in this verse, Apostle Paul did not have anything nice to say about those Cretans. Apostle Paul's description was a spiritual indictment.

As a Christian, you must be on the alert so that you do not allow false teachers to deceive you with their sweet talk. They tend to show their spiritual zeal by claiming that they know God. Be sure you have plenty of evidence through their actions to support their claims. If not, do not fall for it.

It is important that you examine people's lifestyle before you attach total credence to what they are saying in public. As it is often said, "actions speak louder than words." Basically, Apostle Paul was saying that those Cretans are a bunch of hypocrites. They say one thing and do another.

If you want to convince people of your faith in Christ, you had better pray that the Lord grant you wisdom to be able to exemplify Christ. Otherwise your lifestyle will push people away from Christ. Unbelievers will see you as a hypocrite. Living out the gospel is a good way for you to become a credible witness for Christ.

NOVEMBER 1

"For the grace of God has appeared that offers salvation to all people." – Titus 2:11 NIV

While Apostle Paul criticized the conduct of the Cretans, his goal was not to create a list of dos and don'ts for them to follow. Living for Christ requires God's grace. It is by grace we can overcome the power of darkness. We depend on God daily to grant us favor.

In addition to Titus' responsibility for cleaning up the mess in Crete, he was also charged with emphasizing the importance of God's grace. We must be careful not to limit salvation to a set of rules or good behaviors. Being good is not synonymous to being saved. We need God's grace through faith in Jesus to have access to eternal life, not our performance.

God, through His grace, has put salvation at everyone's disposal. Grace has appeared through Jesus Christ, the Son of God. He shed His blood on the cross so that we can receive forgiveness for our sins.

If someone is not saved, it is not God's fault. He has given everyone the same opportunity to receive salvation. Even in countries where the gospel is restricted, nature reveals "God's invisible qualities and His power" (Romans 1:20 NIV). Moreover, those of us who put our faith in Jesus, like Titus did, we are called upon to share the love of Jesus with others so that they may have the opportunity to know Jesus.

NOVEMBER 2

"But when the kindness and love of God our Savior appeared, he saved us, not because of righteous things we had done, but because of his mercy." – Titus 3:4 and 5a NIV

After the fall of Adam and Eve, God's mercy was the only thing that kept Him from destroying the world completely. God, through His love, kindness, and mercy, chose to save us by sending Jesus Christ, His Son, to die on the cross in our place. Jesus was the second Adam. Of course, that was God's plan before the foundation of the world. Everything is part of His eternal plan for humanity.

Like in his letter to the church of Ephesus, Apostle Paul made it clear that salvation is not the product of self-righteousness. Let it be reminded that you will never be able to do enough good works to merit God's favor. That means you will always depend on God's grace through faith to be saved (Ephesians 2:8).

Lord, thank you so much for your love and kindness. It was your mercy that compelled you to save me, even when I was still a sinner.

Thank you for sending Jesus Christ to die in my place. I pray that the Holy Spirit will continue to remind me of your love when my heart wants to deny you.

Lord, please give me strength to overcome temptation so that I can stand in faith. Grant me wisdom from above to understand the mystery of the gospel of Christ. Most importantly, help me to be a credible witness for you in this dark world. Amen.

NOVEMBER 3

"Formerly he was useless to you, but now he has become useful both to you and to me." – Philemon 1:11 NIV

This letter to Philemon, one of the leaders of the Colossian church and a slave owner, is absolutely uplifting. It reveals the liberating power of the gospel of Jesus Christ when expressed through love.

The gospel has the power to break all kinds of boundaries. Apostle Paul's encounter with Onesimus is a good example of that. The boundary that had existed between Apostle Paul and Onesimus disappeared as a result of Onesimus' conversion to Christianity.

In this letter, Apostle Paul made it clear to Philemon, Onesimus' master, that Onesimus was no longer the useless person he used to be. Suddenly, a guy who was a useless runaway slave became Philemon's equal. In Christ, there is no difference between Greeks and Jews or between Blacks and Whites. We are all God's people bought with the precious blood of Jesus Christ. This is what Apostle Paul wanted Philemon to understand.

Given the era, Apostle Paul was very tactful in his approach. Instead of asking Philemon to free Onesimus, he asked him to pardon and receive him. In Philemon 1 verse 8a, Apostle Paul said," Therefore, although in Christ I could be bold and order you to do what you ought to, yet I prefer to appeal to you on the basis of love."

Let love be the basis for everything you do. Love can make a useless individual useful for God's glory. Allow God to love the unlovable through you.

NOVEMBER 4

"The Son is the radiance of God's glory and the exact representation of his being, sustaining all things by his powerful word. After he had provided purification for sins, he sat down at the right hand of the Majesty in heaven." – Hebrews 1:3 NIV

Jesus, the Son, is highly exalted in this verse. He is exalted above angels. Jesus is being showcased as God, the exact representation of God. In other words, the Deity of Christ is clearly revealed in this verse.

If you have ever doubted the origin of the universe, this verse gives you a wonderful insight into who its sustainer is. Jesus, through His word, has sustained the universe and everything that is in it.

When God inspired about forty authors to write the Bible, the goal was not to explain how the universe functions. It is the job of scientists to probe the universe. The Bible simply tells us who created it.

Another powerful clue found in this verse is that Jesus can purify people. Jesus is the Purifier *par excellence*. He came, saved, and went back to heaven. He is now sitting at the right hand of the Father in heaven.

According to His promise in John 14 and in Revelation 22, someday Jesus will come back for His folks. If you are one of His faithful servants, your destiny is not questionable. You can rest assured that God will take care of your tomorrow.

NOVEMBER 5

"Because he himself suffered when he was tempted, he is able to help those who are being tempted." – Hebrews 2:18 NIV

*D*espite your perseverance and your sincere desire to please God, you will continue to face temptation everywhere you go. If Satan dared to tempt Jesus Christ, the Son of the Living God, you are not spared.

Per His incarnation, Jesus is keenly aware of your daily ups and downs. He knows your pain and sufferings. You do not have to be ashamed to come to Jesus in your weaknesses. For this very purpose, the Heavenly Father sent Jesus to participate in this human experience. Jesus' incarnation has qualified Him to become the second Adam.

When Jesus was on earth, He was not a half-human and a half-God. He was one hundred percent human and hundred percent God. As Hebrews 2:17 reads "For this reason he had to be made like them, fully human in every way, in order that he might become a merciful and faithful high priest in service of God, and that he might make atonement for the sins of the people" (NIV).

You should strive to live a holy life. Nevertheless, if you succumb in the process, Jesus can forgive your sins if you repent and ask Him for forgiveness.

Praise the Lord for His mercy and grace! Furthermore, praise Him for being the High Priest, who can atone your sins.

NOVEMBER 6

"Jesus has been found worthy of greater honor than Moses, just as the builder of a house has greater honor than the house itself." – Hebrews 3:3 NIV

Do not listen to false teachers who want you to believe that Jesus was just a prophet like Moses. While they may not openly oppose the teachings of Jesus, they may try their best to reduce Jesus to a mere prophet, thereby undermining His Messianic mission and Deity. Jesus is the Redeemer of humanity. He is the Messiah sent by Yahweh to save the world.

While Moses showed a lot of courage when he gave up a potential throne in Egypt in order to answer God's calling upon his life, he was not able to atone sins. Jesus did something that the previous high priests were not able to do. When He came, He presented Himself as the sacrificial Lamb and the High Priest. His own blood was shed for our sins.

Jesus was found worthy of greater honor than Moses because He fulfilled the mission His Father sent Him to do. Moses was not able to reach the Promised Land. He had to pass the relay to Joshua, who then was able to take the Children of Israel to Canaan.

Jesus was tempted in every way, but He was able to take it all the way to the cross. And finally, Jesus conquered death on the third day. He is now alive forevermore. Continue to place your hope in Jesus Christ, your Savior. He can see you through.

NOVEMBER 7

"For the word of God is alive and active. Sharper than any double-edged sword, it penetrates even to dividing soul and spirit, joints and marrow; it judges the thoughts and attitudes of the heart." – Hebrews 4:12 NIV

The word of God is always fresh, and you can count on it to satisfy your thirst every time you read it. For that reason, it would be good for you to get in the habit of reading God's word daily. I know you may have a hectic work schedule, but do not allow your busy life to take priority over your spiritual walk. Just like your body needs food daily to survive, you need to be spiritually fed as well.

If you choose to meditate on God's word regularly, your thoughts and attitude will be tremendously impacted by the principles of God's word. Generally, society is full of negative influences. If you are not equipped spiritually, you will become the product of your environment.

Arm yourself with God's word so that you can be a spiritual leader in your community. Allow God's word to renew your mind daily.

This devotional book was written so that you can have something to read every day of the year. It is not designed to replace the Bible. Its purpose is to give you something on which to meditate daily.

May the Lord continue to watch over you and bless you as you keep your eyes on Him. Ask God to grant you favor today.

NOVEMBER 8

"For we do not have a high priest who is unable to empathize with our weaknesses, but we have one who has been tempted in every way, just as we are —yet he did not sin." – Hebrews 4:15 NIV

Jesus knows exactly what you are going through right now. He knows about your ups and downs. He also knows about your desire to please Him with all your heart. Therefore, don't be ashamed to come to Jesus and tell Him all about your life's situations. He understands your daily struggle.

Today ask God to strengthen you so that you can continue to overcome the power of darkness over your life and your family. Whatever you are battling for the moment, pray and ask God to set you free from bondage. Satan would like to keep you bound, but God wants to break the chains. Declare your deliverance in Jesus today. It does not matter the source of your depression, ask God to clear your mind and fill you with joy from above. Jesus can turn your sadness into happiness. Be willing to lay it all at His feet. Don't continue to carry your own burden. Jesus said, "Come to me, all you who are weary and burdened, and I will give you rest" (Matthew 11:28 NIV).

Jesus feels what you are feeling this moment. Jesus did not succumb to temptation, so He knows how to overcome adversity victoriously. That is why He can help you. If you are suffering physically right now, Jesus understands the intensity of your pain because He himself suffered excruciating pain on the cross. Your present sufferings are temporary. You will soon forget all about them. Don't give up.

NOVEMBER 9

"Let us then approach God's throne of grace with confidence, so that we may receive mercy and find grace to help us in our time of need." – Hebrews 4:16 NIV

*B*ecause Jesus is our High Priest and is right there with the Father to intercede on our behalf, we never have to feel like we are unworthy to approach God. He came to break down all the boundaries that were keeping us from entering God's presence. In the Old Testament, the children of Israel were not permitted to enter the Holy Place. They had to depend on a high priest to offer their sin offering for them.

Today we are blessed to have Jesus Christ as our Savior. When we come to God in prayer, we are confident that He is there for us. Not only are we allowed to go to God boldly, we know He is able to forgive our sins. We are forgiven, not because of our own merit. We find grace in Jesus, our Savior.

Have you ever felt that you are not worthy to approach God? In your own strength you are not worthy, but in Jesus Christ, your High Priest, you have access to God. Do not hesitate to go to God any time. "For we do not have a high priest who is unable to empathize with our weaknesses, but we have one who has been tempted in every way, just as we are – yet he did not sin" (Hebrews 4:15 NIV). Yes, Jesus was in your shoes, and He lived on earth as a man. He knows what you need. He can feel what you are feeling right now. Trust God to provide for all your needs in Christ Jesus.

NOVEMBER 10

"Anyone who lives on milk, being still an infant, is not acquainted with the teaching about righteousness." – Hebrews 5:13 NIV

The teaching about righteousness is not simple. You need Christian maturity so you can distinguish between works and grace. This explains why inexperienced Christians tend to become the target of false teachers. When false teachers approach you with new interpretations of the gospel, you must be able to know whether they are trying to promote or undermine the authority of Christ. According to the author, infant in Christ is not ready to handle complex, biblical issues.

There is nothing wrong with being inexperienced for a while. Every life's stage has a beginning. However, there is something abnormal in wanting to maintain a baby stage. Personal growth should be based on a desire to learn continually. Similarly, Christians should strive to deepen their understanding of the gospel of Jesus Christ so that they will be able to distinguish truth from falsehood.

The teaching of righteousness helps us to understand that Christ is our High Priest in the order of Melchizedek (verse 10). Additionally, it helps us to know that we have access to the throne of God through Christ. It is through Him alone we can obtain forgiveness for our sins. Since Christ's priesthood is eternal, we no longer need to offer animal sacrifices to God.

NOVEMBER 11

"When God made his promise to Abraham, since there was no one greater for him to swear by, he swore by himself, saying, I will surely bless you and give you many descendants." – Hebrews 6:13 and 14 NIV

Christianity champions the God of Abraham as the true God and places Him above all other gods. He is sovereign in every aspect, and none is greater than He is. God does not need anyone's approval to act. The God of Abraham possesses unlimited power and abundant resources. There will never be a need for austerity in God's sphere.

If you put your trust in the God of Abraham, you can count on His promises. You can rely on Him to deliver you in times of distress. Things may not always come out the way you expect, but you will not be disappointed if God is at the helm of your life's circumstances.

Since there is no one higher than God, you do not have to waste your time contacting voodoo priests or spiritualists when you want spiritual insights into your destiny. God knows everything you need, and nothing in your future is a secret for the God of Abraham.

Knowing that God is trustworthy and stands by His own promises as a guarantee, you can come to Him in prayer with full confidence that He will hear your heart's desires. Don't hesitate to surrender your concerns to Him, for God is in control of your life. You do not have to be afraid of life's uncertainties. You will surely come out on top with God's help.

NOVEMBER 12

"Unlike the other high priests, he does not need to offer sacrifices day after day, first for his sins, and then for the sins of the people. He sacrificed for their sins once for all when he offered himself." – Hebrews 7:27 NIV

*B*ecause Jesus came to forgive the sins of humanity, He had to possess priestly qualifications. In the Old Testament, the high priests played important roles among the Israelites. They were responsible for representing the people before God. The people were required to go through them every time they want to offer sacrifices for their sins.

Jesus is superior to all the high priests who preceded Him. The Bible declared, "You are a priest forever, in the order of Melchizedek" (verse 17). Melchizedek represents a perfect priesthood, a type of Christ. Christ is the Great High Priest we all were waiting for.

With Jesus being our High Priest, He has given us access to the throne of God. Through His death and resurrection, Jesus eliminated all the boundaries that had existed in the Old Testament. The separation that existed between the Holy of Holies is gone forever. In the name of Jesus, we can now call upon God freely.

In the Old Testament, a priest had to offer a sacrifice on his own behalf, and sacrifices had to be offered repeatedly. With Jesus, repeated sacrifices are now unnecessary. He sacrificed Himself once for all our past, present, and future sins.

NOVEMBER 13

"No longer will they teach their neighbor, or say to one another, 'know the Lord, 'because they will all know me, from the least of them to the greatest." – Hebrews 8:11 NIV

I want to share a word of wisdom with you. Always pray for Israel, God's original people. As Christians, we are Israelites by faith. That means God has adopted us as His children by grace through Jesus Christ, His Son. When you honor God's people, God will honor you in return.

God made a promise to Israel by saying: "…I will forgive their wickedness and will remember their sins no more" (verse 17). When the dust has settled, the people of Israel will receive God's forgiveness despite their rebellion.

God's attitude toward Israel shows how merciful He is. We should not be jealous of God's compassion and mercy toward Israel. We too have tasted His mercy. "…God demonstrates his own love for us in this: While we were still sinners, Christ died for us" (Romans 5:8 NIV).

The time will come when God will put His words in the hearts of His people. At that time, there will be no need for preachers. The veil of disobedience will fall from the eyes of God's people. They will accept God for Who He is. This is God's promise to the children of Israel. They will begin to enjoy that promise during the first thousand years of the reign of Christ. They will continue to the New Jerusalem, the Holy City. Satan, the accusers of the brothers and sisters will be no more. He will be "thrown into the lake of fire" (Revelation.20:15 NIV).

NOVEMBER 14

"Just as people are destined to die once, and after that to face judgement, so Christ was sacrificed once to take away the sins of many; and he will appear a second time, not to bear sin, but to bring salvation to those who are waiting for him." – Hebrews 9:27 and 28 NIV

These verses reveal three important truths. First, as humans, we are expected to die once, as far as physical death is concerned. That means when you die everything is not over. You still must report to God, who created you. That is why it is important that you turn your heart to Jesus so you will not have to face eternity with uncertainties. You should know beyond a shadow of a doubt where you are going when you die. If you believe in Jesus as your Lord and Savior, you will appear before the Judgment Seat of Christ to receive your dues. This judgment is not designed to send you to Hell. It is a judgment designed to determine whether you will receive a reward (2 Corinthians 5:10).

Second, when Jesus came the first time, His mission was to die for our sins once and for all. He is now our High Priest.

Third, Christ is scheduled to come back. This time, He will not return as the sacrificial Lamb. He will come back as the King of kings and the Lord of lords.

We are waiting for Him to deliver us from the sufferings of this world. We are ready to participate in the great Supper of God and the wedding of the Lamb. It will be a glorious day indeed!

NOVEMBER 15

"And let us consider how we may spur one another on toward love and good deeds, not giving up meeting together, as some are in the habit of doing, but encouraging one another – and all the more as you see the Day approaching." – Hebrews 10:24 and 25 NIV

As Christ's followers, once we have come to the understanding that Jesus Christ died for our sins once and for all, and that we are no longer afraid of our tomorrow, we are encouraged to dedicate ourselves to doing the Lord's works.

This is a liberating place to be. We now know that we have eternal life. We are not working for our salvation. It is important that we come to grips with the fact that God expects us to be involved in His kingdom. We are not saved to sit around and do nothing. Those who don't see it that way seem to misunderstand their mission on earth.

Keep in mind that God created us to worship Him. If we are not worshiping God, we are not doing what we were created to do. In other words, we do not understand our purpose.

In these verses, we are advised to attend a local church. There are things that need to be done in God's kingdom, including, but not limited to worshiping, evangelizing, making disciples, and assisting those who are in need.

As we wait patiently for Christ's return, we need to carry out what God commissioned us to do. With the Holy Spirit's anointing, we can do those things for God's glory.

NOVEMBER 16

"It is a dreadful thing to fall into the hands of the living God." – Hebrews 10:31 NIV

God in His compassion has made it almost impossible for someone to fall into His hands unprepared. The only time one needs to be afraid of God is when he or she is not ready spiritually.

Being a loving God, He sent Jesus Christ, His Son, to die for us. There is no reason, whatsoever, for us to dread the eventual return of Christ, for His death and resurrection made it possible to have peace with the Heavenly Father once and for all.

Eternal life is available to all. People will have no excuses as to why they did not make it to paradise. By paradise, I mean the New Jerusalem. When the dust has settled, Christ will return for the faithful – those who have put their trust in the sacrifice Jesus made on the cross will not have to face the dreadful Day. The blood of Jesus is the only means of purification God has provided for sinners. People who decide to ignore such a huge sacrifice will not have an alternative solution. They will end up falling into the hands of the Living God when they die.

The toughest punishment a person could ever receive is to present before God without Christ. When you close your eyes for the last time, you want to be sure that you have Jesus Christ on your side. This is the only way you can avoid falling into the hands of the Living God. If you have already done that, way to go! If not, please consider doing so right now.

NOVEMBER 17

"Now faith is confidence in what we hope for and assurance about what we do not see." – Hebrews 11:1 NIV

The word faith comes from the Greek noun πίστις (pistis), which denotes trust, confidence as well as assurance.

I would like you to think of faith as a magnet that makes it possible for you to connect with God. If you could see God, you would not need faith to connect with Him. In heaven, you will not need to exercise your faith, because you will have the ability to see God just as He is. Now you need faith because you cannot connect with God in the flesh.

When asking God for something in your prayer, you must exercise your faith in order to receive it. God has given you the amount of faith you need to connect with Him. Paul said, "For by the grace given me I say to every one of you: Do not think of yourself more highly than you ought, but rather think of yourself with sober judgment, in accordance with the faith God has distributed to each of you" (Romans 12: 3 NIV).

It is through faith you can have confidence in God. Through that same faith, you can trust God to answer you when you pray. If you have confidence in God, you can then begin to thank Him for the answer to your prayer.

Faith is the absence of doubt. You cannot expect to receive anything from God if you doubt. Bishop James said, "But when you ask, you must believe and not doubt, because the one who doubts is like a wave of the sea, blown and tossed by the wind" (James 1:6 NIV). Today ask God to strengthen your faith in Him.

NOVEMBER 18

"And without faith it is impossible to please God, because anyone who comes to him must believe that he exists and that he rewards those who earnestly seek him." – Hebrews 11:6 NIV

We cannot please God if we do not trust Him, and we cannot trust God without a modicum of faith. It is through faith that we believe that God exists. People who refuse to acknowledge God's existence are unwilling to exercise their faith.

Faith cannot be tested by scientific methods. In other words, you cannot formulate a hypothesis to prove or reject God. You must come to God based on the information He has made available to you in the Bible and nature. Jesus Christ came to testify about God, and His testimonies were true. The Old Testament had announced Christ's mission, and the New Testament revealed His mission. Everything you need to know for your salvation is found in the Holy Scripture, but you must put your faith in it. That is why it is impossible to please God without faith.

Through faith people accept Jesus Christ as the Son of God and believe that His blood is powerful enough to cleanse their filthy hearts. It is through faith they know that Christ's righteousness is what they need to avoid God's wrath in that their own performance is not enough. Furthermore, it is through faith that Christians believe that Christ is coming back to take them to the great Supper of God. And finally, it is through faith that they believe that there will be a new heaven and a new earth, and God will dwell among them forevermore.

NOVEMBER 19

"Therefore, since we are surrounded by such a great cloud of witnesses, let us throw off everything that hinders and the sin that so easily entangles." – Hebrews 12:1a NIV

We are not alone in our faith pursuit. There are many witnesses who had come long before us, and they had chosen to put their faith in Yahweh, the God of Jacob and Abraham. They had come to the realization that Yahweh is the true God, for He had intervened victoriously on their behalf so many times.

In Hebrews 11 verses 4 - 40, the author enumerated our witnesses for us. They include, Abel, Enoch, Noah, Abraham, Isaac, Jacob, Sarah, Joseph, Moses' parents, Moses, the people who passed through the Red Sea, the army that walked around the walls of Jericho, Rahab, Gideon, Barak, Samson, Jephthah, David, Samuel, and the Prophets. Those witnesses had a chance to experience God in their own unique way. They all wanted to see the fulfillment of God's promises through Christ, the Messiah.

If those witnesses were able to suffer so much so that they could maintain their faith in God, we too should renew our faith in God daily by asking God to strengthen us so that we can get rid of those sinful behaviors that are not lined up with biblical precepts. We need to continue to focus on our spiritual journey as we wait patiently for the Lord to come for us. With God's help, we can do it.

NOVEMBER 20

"Through Jesus, therefore, let us continually offer to God a sacrifice of praise – the fruit of lips that openly profess his name." – Hebrews 13:15 NIV

Lord Jesus, I come to you today with my sacrifice of praise to you, which is the fruit of my lips. I do not care if my body feels like praising you or not. I praise you for the opportunity to know that you are my great Shepherd. You are the Author and the Finisher of my faith.

Thank you so much, Lord Jesus, for promising never to forsake me. Thank you, Lord, because of you I can call on the name of the Heavenly Father with confidence. I know He will not reject me. You have made it possible for me to have access to Him.

Lord, I praise you for teaching me how to love my brothers and sisters. Thank you for blessing me so that I can have enough to support my family, pay my tithe faithfully, and help those who are in need. Grant me wisdom so that I can be a good steward of the financial resources you have blessed me with.

Lord Jesus, I praise you for strengthening me spiritually so that I can be faithful. Please Lord Jesus, help me so that I do not succumb to temptation.

Help me, Lord, to continue to keep my faith in you as I journey through life. I pray that you will find me faithful.

Finally, Lord, I praise you for watching over me. I trust in you, Lord, my great Shepherd. May my lips continue to offer you sacrifice of praise. Amen!

NOVEMBER 21

"Let perseverance finish its work so that you may be mature and complete, not lacking anything." – James 1:4 NIV

There is a purpose for adversity in your life. Adversity is painful but useful. It is through adversity that your faith is tested. Think of it as labor pain. Although I am a man, I am keenly aware of the intensity of birth pain because I was in the room with my wife when she was giving birth to both of our sons. I could see the pain on her face. But one thing I did notice, however, was the joy she expressed when she saw those babies. It was something truly unspeakable!

Maturity does not come by easily. There is a process that you must go through to attain it. It is true for anything you would like to achieve in life. It is important that you do not allow your life's processes to overcome you. It is part of your destiny. That is why perseverance is essential. You need to stick to it, even though you do not feel like doing so. Do not allow your feelings to get in the way. Trust in the Lord and continue to press on.

Keep in mind that you are not alone as you go through those painful moments. God is with you. It does not matter what you are going through right now, you will experience victory if you continue to put your trust in God.

Those who trust in the Lord will never lose. That does not mean that you are exempt from temporary defeat. What this means is that you will win the final battle. Always try to find the positive side of your adversity. Do not give up hope. Persevere until the end.

NOVEMBER 22

"What good is it, my brothers and sisters, if someone claims to have faith but has no deeds? Can such faith save them?" James 2:14 NIV

These are two good questions. Allow me to ask my own questions so I can help you figure out why Bishop James, the brother of Jesus, questioned the validity of those folks' faith. What was Bishop James trying to convey to them? Were these rhetorical questions?

The crux of the matter is that there is no such thing as fake faith. You either exercise your measure of faith or you do not. And if you do exercise your measure of faith, it will certainly produce righteous deeds because faith is from God.

The faith that saves us can produce good works. "For we are God's handiwork, created in Christ Jesus to do good works, which God prepared in advance for us to do" (Ephesians 2:10 NIV). Salvation is not a product of good works, but it enables us to produce good works. Basically, Bishop James expected those folks that "claim" to have faith to produce good deeds.

It is important that you understand that you cannot obtain salvation through good works. This is a very important distinction you need to make. Bishop James wanted those believers to understand that people who are saved by faith are not exempt from doing good works, because God created them to do good works well before creation. As a believer, God dwells in you through the Spirit. And since God lives in you, you are equipped with amazing anointing and talents to reach out to others. Ask God to show you where you can serve.

NOVEMBER 23

"But the wisdom that comes from heaven is first of all pure; then peace loving, considerate, submissive, full of mercy and good fruit, impartial and sincere." – James 3:17 NIV

As you continue your quest for wisdom, keep in mind that there are two kinds of wisdom. In verse 15, Bishop James described a type of wisdom as "earthly, unspiritual, and demonic." This type of wisdom is characterized in verse 16 by "envy and selfish ambition." It is nothing like the wisdom that comes from Yahweh, the true God.

Wisdom from God is characterized by a sense of humility and selflessness. People who are endowed with wisdom from above are not likely to be involved in senseless activities. They tend be kind, considerate, and very measured as they interact with others. Furthermore, they are merciful, and peace-loving. They do things with a sense of divine purpose.

While wise people are not exempt from making mistakes, they tend to make fewer mistakes due to their use of discernment and good judgment.

Since God is the source of wisdom, ask God for wisdom. Solomon asked God for wisdom. "Give me wisdom and knowledge, that I may lead this people, for who is able to govern this great people of yours" (2 Chronicles 1:10 NIV).

Solomon could have asked God for other things, but he did not. He chose to ask God for wisdom instead. If you have wisdom from God, you will not lack anything. You will be able to capitalize on your wisdom to get what you need.

NOVEMBER 24

"Submit yourselves, then, to God. Resist the devil, and he will flee from you." – James 4:7 NIV

The key strategy for defeating Satan is to make sure you have a personal relationship with God. This is the approach that makes sense because it provides you with the necessary security to take your stand against God's greatest foe. Keep in mind that your battle is mainly a spiritual one. Satan is a spirit, so if you are going to overcome him, you must do it spiritually.

If you are not willing to submit yourself to God, you are living in rebellion. And if you are living in rebellion with God, you have no grounds for counting on Him to protect you from the enemy's attacks. It is that simple.

It is not enough for you to accept Jesus Christ as your Savior; you also must accept Him as your Lord. When you say that Jesus is your Savior, you are simply stating that He saved you from eternal punishment. As your Lord, you go a step further to recognize Him as your Master. If He is your Master, then you belong to Him.

Once you have submitted your will to God, you have His full protection. You do not have to sit around and allow Satan to destroy you and your family. You have authority, by virtue of your relationship with God, to ask Satan to stop messing with your life, your marriage, your family, your job, and your possessions. You are basically claiming those things that are yours. There are some of the things that you do not have to ask God for. For instance, you have authority to rebuke Satan in the name of Jesus Christ. You just must remember to do it consistently.

NOVEMBER 25

"Now listen, you rich people, weep and wail because of the misery that is coming on you." – James 5:1 NIV

*I*f you become wealthy because you use the wisdom that God has granted you to manage your time, resources, and business properly, should you be concerned about this verse? The answer is no. There is nothing inherently immoral about being wealthy. The problem with wealth is that some people tend to use it as a substitute for God. Jesus said, "No one can serve two masters. Either you will hate the one and love the other, or you will be devoted to the one and despise the other. You cannot serve both God and money" (Matthew 6:24 NIV).

In this passage of Scripture, Bishop James was talking about wealthy people who were in the habit of hoarding their wealth and failing to pay their workers. Those folks were murderers, who enjoyed living in luxury and self-indulgence. They were greedy in their approach to gaining wealth, and they did not care about helping the poor or investing toward the advancement of God's kingdom.

If you use your wealth to bless God's people and contribute toward the spreading of the gospel of Jesus Christ through your tithes and offerings, you will not have to dread misery. However, if you are bent on amassing wealth so that you can hoard it without any regard for God's people and His kingdom, if you are content in oppressing the poor, and if you are involved in killing people in the process, you should expect the same consequences Bishop James warned about in this verse.

NOVEMBER 26

"As obedient children, do not conform to the evil desires you had when you lived in ignorance." – 1 Peter 1:14 NIV

*I*n this passage of Scripture, Apostle Peter called upon us to live a life of holiness. Before salvation, we did not have God's Spirit in us, so it was normal for us to get carried away by all sorts of lustful behaviors. Once we had our encounter with God, His Spirit has taken residence in us – we became the temple of the Holy Spirit. We no longer have the same priorities we used to have, because our present focus is on Christ and His eventual return.

As born-again individuals, it does not make sense for us to continue living the same way we used to live before we knew Christ. Before our commitment to Christ, we did not know what we were doing. We thought it was okay to allow our minds to run wild. When we came to Christ, God set us apart, meaning He declared us holy. It is God who made us holy by sanctifying us. But we also try to live holy as part of our Christian walk.

While we are not striving to live holy so we can go to heaven, we are required to live holy because God is holy. Keep in mind that our holiness is a work in progress. We will not be completely holy until we have been glorified. We are to set ourselves apart for God's service.

Try to stay busy doing God's business. Do not pay attention to those things you used to do when you did not have any spiritual responsibilities. Ask God to give you strength to say no to the fleshly desires so that you can pursue holiness as you journey through life.

NOVEMBER 27

"But you are a chosen people, a royal priesthood, a holy nation, God's special possession, that you may declare the praises of him who called you out of darkness into his wonderful light." – 1 Peter 2:9 NIV

When you feel like your world is falling apart, think of who you are and whose you are. Can you imagine being God's special possession? Before Christ's crucifixion, only the Israelites had that special status. Through Christ, you are now God's special people. You have been set free by the blood of the Lamb.

The curtain that had separated you from God's presence was torn apart. It is finished! Jesus has provided a new path to the Heavenly Father. The pall of darkness that Satan had cast on the world has been lifted when God raised Jesus Christ from the dead. Christ's light has shone brightly in the darkness and brought hope to the whole world.

God has a special purpose for your life. You have been called by God to be part of the royal priesthood. Being the High Priest, Jesus can represent you before God. Through Him, you have access to God's throne daily.

In order to be called a holy nation, you must have been cleansed and set apart for God's service. These types of privileges have been bestowed upon you by God, and it is through grace and by faith in Jesus that God has sanctified you for eternal purposes. It does not matter what you are going through today, God has a plan for you. You have been called to declare His Praises.

NOVEMBER 28

"Do not repay evil with evil or insult with insult. On the contrary, repay evil with blessing, because to this you were called so that you may inherit a blessing." – 1 Peter 3:9 NIV

*B*ecause Jesus wants you to be a light in your community and the world, paying evil with evil will significantly diminish your brightness. In order to shine for the world to see Jesus in you, you must be different. Yes, it is difficult to turn the other cheek when most people tend to hit back harder.

When people hurl insults at you, allow Jesus to show you how to respond. Don't reciprocate with similar insults, because if you do, you will lose the opportunity to show Jesus to that person. When you show kindness to a person who was expecting to be treated badly by you, your kindness has the potential to unsettle him or her. Suddenly, the person will be asking himself or herself, "What is going on here? I deserve to be insulted, but this person is blessing me instead. Can you imagine the positive impact such a behavior can have on that person's psyche?

Keep in mind your sacrifice is not in vain. God will repay you for your kindness. Every time you go the extra mile, God sees you. Keep in mind that this is not something you are doing to gain God's favor for salvation. Throughout this devotional book, I have made it clear that salvation can only be obtained by grace through faith in the Lord Jesus Christ and that good works come after salvation. Your sacrifice is for the advancement of God's kingdom and your eternal reward, which you will receive from God during the Judgment Seat of Christ.

NOVEMBER 29

"If you are insulted because of the name of Christ, you are blessed, for the Spirit of glory and of God rests on you." – 1 Peter 4:14 NIV

Your Christian status does not exempt you from suffering. In fact, being a Christian can cause you to suffer if you live in a country where there is no religious freedom. Some of the First Century Christians were killed because they had believed in Christ.

The Christian journey is full of obstacles. While salvation is guaranteed by the blood of Jesus Christ, its full impact is still futuristic. In other words, we will not experience the full benefits of salvation until we are with God in eternity. In the meantime, we are exposed to all kinds of insults because of our commitment to God.

People who are perishing do not know the importance of serving God. For that reason, it is not unusual for them to make fun of believers out of ignorance. Christians are often treated as unintelligent because they are living by faith, not by sight.

If you want to be a witness for Christ, you will suffer from time to time. When people invite you to participate in something ungodly, you cannot join in with them, because you are Christ's ambassador in this world.

Ask God to help you become a role model. Let your lifestyle be guided by God's precepts established in the Holy Scripture.

Living for Christ can be painful, but you will be rewarded greatly by God if you do not give up along the way. Count it a blessing if you are being persecuted because of your faith in Jesus Christ.

NOVEMBER 30

"Humble yourselves, therefore, under God's mighty hand, that he may lift you up in due time." – 1 Peter 5:6 NIV

*I*f you want to be honored, you must be willing to stay humble until God decides your time of honor. It is not for you to decide. In due time, God will promote you if you remain faithful until your time. If you do something dishonest to get a promotion, eventually, you will be demoted. Wait for your time, though it may take a while. Here, I am not talking about things you can do naturally to receive a promotion at your job. Of course, I know you need to be diligent at work so your boss can notice you. However, if you do everything honestly to be promoted and you are still not promoted, do not be discouraged. God knows the time of your promotion.

Jesus is a good example for us to follow. Although He did not stop being God in the spiritual realm, as far as being part of the Godhead is concerned, He was willing to become flesh so that He could live among us just to save us from the power of sin.

Because Jesus was willing to humble Himself until death, God exalted Him above principalities and dominions. In the last day, Christ will come back in glory to establish His millennium kingdom on earth. He will reign as King of kings and Lord of lords.

You too will be rewarded when you get to heaven for your willingness to serve God despite of persecutions for the cause of Christ. Continue to humble yourself before God.

DECEMBER 1

"His divine power has given us everything we need for a godly life through our knowledge of him who called us by his own glory and goodness." – 2 Peter 1:3 NIV

*I*n the spiritual realm, when we say yes to Jesus Christ, everything God has for us becomes ours because we are His children. For instance, we have access to forgiveness through Jesus Christ because His blood was shed for us on the cross. God's divine power has made it possible for us to be united with Him through the Spirit who lives in us. We can maintain a personal relationship with God.

Although we still must suffer pain on this earth, we are full of joy when we think about eternal life and many spiritual blessings we have in Christ Jesus. God's divine power sustains us by enabling us to put our faith in the Lord as we journey through life.

While God can bless us financially, this verse is not referring to unlimited material possessions or wealth. It is about everything we need to live a godly life for God, including the anointing and all the spiritual gifts we need to fulfill God's calling upon our lives as we wait patiently for Christ's return.

In light of our understanding of God's divine power and what it represents for those who truly believe in Jesus Christ as their Lord and Savior, Apostle Peter encourages us "to add to our faith goodness; and to goodness, knowledge; and to knowledge, self-control; and to self-control, perseverance; and to perseverance, godliness; and to godliness, mutual affection; and to mutual affection, love" (2 Peter 1: 5-7 NIV).

DECEMBER 2

"Above all, you must understand that no prophecy of Scripture came about by the prophet's own interpretation of things." – 2 Peter 1:20 NIV

The key word here is no "prophecy of Scripture." God is behind the prophecies found in Scripture. Apostle Peter is not saying that you must attach credence to all prophecies, because there are false prophets who are masked behind the Bible to deceive people. If you are not careful, you will be deceived by those charlatans who try to distort the truth about Christ.

The fact that there are seventeen prophetic books in the Old Testament, we know that God is interested in communicating with His people through prophetic words. About 700 hundred years before the birth of Christ, Prophet Isaiah prophesied about Him. "Therefore the Lord himself will give you a sign: The virgin will conceive and give birth to a son, and will call him Immanuel" (Isaiah 7:14 NIV).

Why is it essential to know about this prophetic announcement about the birth of Christ? This fact is important because it confirms that Jesus Christ is real and that His birth did not happen by accident.

If you have any doubt whatsoever about the veracity of the gospel of Jesus Christ, the Son of the Living God, try to read the Holy Bible with an open mind. Ask God to reveal Himself to you.

If you seek God with all your heart, you will find Him. The Bible is the word of God and is written to convey God's love to you. God loves you so much! He is interested in living in you through the Spirit.

DECEMBER 3

"The Lord is not slow in keeping his promise, as some understand slowness. Instead he is patient with you, not wanting anyone to perish, but everyone to come to repentance." – 2 Peter 3:9 NIV

The concept of time does not exist in eternity. For God "a day is like a thousand years, and a thousand years are like a day (2 Peter 3:8 NIV). Additionally, God has delayed Christ's return in order to give everybody a chance to hear the gospel. Some of the First Century Christians had expected Christ to return shortly after His ascension to heaven, so they grew rather impatient when they did not see Him. You must be careful not to become impatient and lose hope. Christ will keep His promise, and someday He will come back for His Church.

As a Christian, you may not have the privilege of witnessing Christ's return in the flesh as you may transition to eternity before that awesome event. For that reason, be vigilant because you do not know when you are going to leave this world. Continue to put your trust in the Lord as you wait patiently.

Furthermore, take advantage of Christ's delay to spread the gospel about the kingdom of God as you journey through life. Many people need to know that there is hope in Jesus Christ and forgiveness is available to them in Christ. They need to know that Christ died on the cross so that they may have eternal life. The hope of living in God's presence forever is exciting! I know you must put up with a great deal of suffering on this earth, but do not lose sight of the fact that Christ is coming back when the time has fully come.

DECEMBER 4

"If we claim to have fellowship with him and yet walk in the darkness, we lie and do not live out the truth." – 1 John 1:6 NIV

Throughout this devotional book, you have come to understand what it really means to be a Christian and how God went about making it possible for you to be saved. You have learned that God demonstrated His love toward you by sending Jesus, His Son, to die on the cross for your sins. You have also learned that your performance did not influence God's decision. Your salvation is based solely on God's grace and through your faith in the Lord Jesus Christ.

By understanding and experiencing the above spiritual concepts, you have now a good foundational knowledge of Christianity. However, there is more to Christianity than a basic understanding of salvation. You also need to grow as a Christian so that you can attain maturity in Christ.

As a follower of Christ, you are called to be separate from the activities of darkness by pursuing holiness. While your salvation is not based on your daily performance, you have a kingdom to represent as an ambassador for Christ. For that reason, you cannot go out there acting like someone who does not know Christ.

Jesus is the light of the world. If you are in Jesus, you cannot continue to live in the darkness. You are called to live out the truth that is in you. You now know your Lord is Jesus Christ, so you must live like He would live. Be honest with yourself. You are either a follower of Christ or a follower of Satan. You cannot be both simultaneously. This is basically what Apostle John was trying to explain to the folks back there.

DECEMBER 5

"If we confess our sins, he is faithful and just and will forgive us our sins and purify us from all unrighteousness." – 1 John 1:9 NIV

*I*t does not matter if you are an experienced Christian or a novice; you are not infallible. And if you are not infallible, you are prone to sin. If you think this is not true, then you do not understand the impact of sin on the human nature.

While it is important to know that you are not immune to sin, you should know that Christians do not sin willingly. "No one who is born of God will continue to sin, because God's seed remains in them; they cannot go on sinning, because they have been born of God" (1 John 3:9 NIV).

When you sin, come to God and ask Him to forgive you through repentance. If you are sincere about what you did wrong, you will feel sorry for your act. This is what repentance means. Through Jesus Christ, God can forgive you. Keep in mind that forgiveness of sins is only possible through Jesus Christ, who died to make it possible.

It is through Christ's blood that your life can be purified of all unrighteousness. If you refuse to acknowledge Jesus Christ as your Lord and Savior, you will die in your sins.

Salvation is a necessity. You cannot enter heaven if your sins are not forgiven. It is a fact that you need Jesus because you are bound to commit sinful acts. Throughout your Christian journey, you will continue to need forgiveness. However, don't go on sinning.

With that said, you are going to heaven because your sins are forgiven, not because you are sinless.

DECEMBER 6

"Anyone who claims to be in the light but hates a brother or a sister is still in the darkness." – 1 John 2:9 NIV

When you claim to be in the light, you claim to know Jesus Christ as your Lord and Savior. It is also claiming that you are on your way to heaven. This type of claim must be supported by your lifestyle. You need to shine your light so the world can come to know your Lord and Savior just like you.

Are you still holding hatred in your heart for your brothers and sisters? If yes, go to God and confess your hatred so that you can obtain pardon. As a Christian, you are called to love people. There are neither Jews nor Greeks in Christ. In the same token, there are neither Blacks nor Whites in Christ. We are members of God's big family.

Jesus is light. As a follower of Christ, you need to ask God to help you to grow in love. As you learned earlier, you are not infallible. It might happen that you are still struggling with racial prejudices. If that is the case, ask God to forgive you and purify you of all unrighteousness.

As a Christian, you should not hate people because of their racial backgrounds. And I am not talking about just white people. If you are black and do not love white people, you are not in the light. You are still living in darkness. Allow Christ to shine through you. Hatred is not a Christian attribute; it is from the devil.

Today ask God to fill you with His love so that you can live in the light.

DECEMBER 7

"Dear friends, now we are children of God, and what we will be has not yet been made known. But we know that when Christ appears, we shall be like him, for we shall see him as he is." – 1 John 3:2 NIV

As Christ's followers, we are not aware of all the benefits we have in Christ. One thing we know for sure, based on Scripture and our personal experiences with God, is that we are now children of God. "Yet to all who did receive him, to those who believed in his name, he gave the right to become children of God – Children born not of natural descent, nor of human decision or a husband's will, but born of God" (John 1:12-13 NIV).

Being called God's children is already a huge blessing. This is a privilege that we should never take for granted. Remember we were not God's children initially. That status was reserved for the Israelites. But through the blood of Jesus, the Heavenly Father has adopted us as His children. We can now call Jesus' Father our Father in heaven. In fact, this is the way Jesus taught us to pray.

Another thing we know from this verse is that we will have a glorified body just like Jesus. In that glorified body, we will be able to see Jesus like He is. That will be an awesome experience!

In addition to these two important facts, there are other benefits to which we will have access in heaven, but they are not yet known to us. We know what we need to know for now. We know that we are saved by grace through faith.

DECEMBER 8

"If anyone acknowledges that Jesus is the Son of God, God lives in them and they live in God." – 1 John 4:15 NIV

Acknowledging that Jesus is the Son of God is key to salvation because the central theme of the Holy Bible is redemption, which is hinged completely on the sacrifice Jesus made on the cross. Without Jesus, there is no redemption; and without redemption, there is no salvation. It is of paramount importance that you recognize, without any physical and psychological constraints, that Jesus is the Son of God.

What does that mean to acknowledge Jesus is the Son of God? Acknowledging Jesus is the Son of God means that you are willing to put your faith and total trust in Him to save you. This is a voluntary act that is based on a personal experience. No one can do it for you.

When you acknowledge that Jesus is the Son of God, something supernatural takes place in the spiritual realm. Suddenly, you are united with God through His Spirit. Such a union is not possible if you do not accept the fact that God so loved you that He sent Jesus, His Son, to die on the cross for you.

Your acknowledgment is your confession of faith. This is your complete surrender to Jesus as your Lord and Savior. Without such sincere, voluntary acceptance of God's gift of salvation, you will not be able to have access to eternal life. This is what it takes for the transformational process to occur in your spirit so that you can be justified before God by grace and through faith in Jesus Christ.

DECEMBER 9

"I write these things to you who believe in the name of the Son of God so that you may know that you have eternal life." –1 John 5:13 NIV

*T*he purpose of this verse is to confirm that you are saved. As far as your salvation is concerned, you do not need to worry about anything if you believe in the name of the Son of God. In other words, if you believe with all your heart that God sent Jesus to die for your sins, and if you have put your faith in Him for your salvation, you are well on your way to spending eternity with God in the New Jerusalem. Only you know if you believe in the name of the Son of God. Now it is a good time for you to make a self-check. Be honest with yourself because this is a decision that has eternal consequences.

If you are still not sure of your salvation, simply surrender your heart to Jesus right now. Go back and read the previous devotion that addresses the idea of acknowledging Jesus is the Son of God. Examine the contextual meaning of the word acknowledgment and what it may signify for your life. If you have done those things, you have eternal life.

Once you are sure of your salvation, the next step is to continue to serve God by joining in with other Christians to make Jesus known. There are a lot of people who do not know if Jesus Christ is the key to eternal life. They too need to come to the full knowledge of Jesus. They need to have the opportunity to be certain that they will spend eternity with God.

DECEMBER 10

"Blessed is the one who reads aloud the words of this prophecy, and blessed are those who hear it and take to heart what is written in it, because the time is near." – Revelation 1:3 NIV

*R*evelation is the only book in the Bible that promises a special blessing to its readers. This is a special book indeed! Many people shy away from this last book of the Bible due to its prophetic nature. Nevertheless, you should try to read it frequently. The Holy Spirit can illuminate you so you can understand Jesus' important message about the future.

After His ascension to heaven, Jesus saw fit to reveal some key pieces of information to John, one of His beloved disciples in the form of a vision. John was on the Island of Patmos, a place off the coast of modern-day Turkey, when he received this vision from Jesus through an angel. He was in exile there because He was preaching the gospel, according to Revelation 1:9.

We know Jesus Christ is scheduled to return to the scene. This time, He will come in full glory and majesty, not like a babe in a manger. Some of the things that are revealed in this book include, but not limited, to the battle of Armageddon, the Supper of God, the wedding of the Lamb, the millennium kingdom, the judgement of Satan, the judgment of the Great White Throne, a new heaven and a new earth, the New Jerusalem, the Holy City, and the throne of God coming down from heaven. You will be blessed to read those things and take them to heart as you wait for Christ's return.

DECEMBER 11

"I am the Living One; I was dead, and now look, I am alive for ever and ever! And I hold the keys of death and Hades." – Revelation 1:18 NIV

*T*his post-ascension resurrection message to the seven churches reconfirms the death and resurrection of the Lord Jesus Christ. This is a message of reassurance for all who believe in Jesus Christ that they will live for ever and ever as well. How exciting it is to know that we are not serving a dead God! Our God is the Living One!

Our God is the greatest. "I am the Alpha and the Omega," says the Lord God, "who is, and who was, and who is to come, the Almighty" (verse 8). To be the Alpha and the Omega is to be the beginning and the end, or the first and the last, according to the Greek alphabet.

Not only has Jesus overcome death, He has full authority over death and Hell. It is a matter of time before Satan and his followers receive their just punishment. Satan will be judged by God for all his deceptive things he has done to destroy God's people. "And the devil, who deceived them, was thrown into the lake of burning sulfur, where the beast and the false prophets had been thrown. They will be tormented day and night for ever and ever" (Revelation 20:10 NIV).

Since Jesus holds the keys of death and Hades, you do not have to be afraid of death if you are willing to walk with Jesus as your Lord and Savior. Hell will not be able to attain you either, because Jesus Christ has power over Hades, which means Hell.

DECEMBER 12

"Those whom I love I rebuke and discipline. So be earnest and repent." – Revelation 3:19 NIV

Do you remember how excited you were when you said yes to Jesus as your Lord and Savior? A new relationship tends to have a sense of novelty. The euphoria you felt during your first few days, months, and years of your relationship may become somewhat lukewarm with each passing of time. That is why it is important for us to renew our minds by focusing on things that are eternal in lieu of temporary things.

In this verse, Jesus was addressing the members of the church of Laodicea whom He judged were neither cold nor hot. They became complacent in that they did not think they needed God. They were relying on their wealth.

As you become prosperous, be careful not to forget God. As far as your spirituality is concerned, your wealth cannot replace it. You will always need God, no matter how successful you may be as you journey through life.

Instead of taking God for granted because you are well off, use your material possessions to advance God's kingdom. Support your local church financially and find a few missionaries and non-profit organizations to bless on a monthly basis. In so doing, you will continue to remember God as the source of your blessing.

As you drift away from God, He will continue to woo you. Expect God to chastise you from time to time because He is not willing to give up on you. God's chastisement is proof that He really loves you. Be willing to get back to God.

DECEMBER 13

"You are worthy, our Lord God, to receive glory and honor and power, for you created all things, and by your will they were created and have their being." – Revelation 4:11 NIV

*H*ave you ever wondered why you should worship God? If you have, this verse will keep you from wondering.

One of the many reasons we should worship God is because He created all things. He created us to give glory to His Majesty. One day everyone will acknowledge that He is the Almighty. Regarding the name of Jesus, the Bible says, every knee should bow, in heaven and on earth and under the earth, and every tongue acknowledge that Jesus Christ is Lord, to the glory of God the Father" (Philippians 2:10 and 11 NIV).

The Jesus mentioned in the book of Philippians is the same Jesus who sent an angel to John to deliver His last message for us about things to come. According to Colossians 1verses 15 and 16a, "The Son is the image of the invisible God, the firstborn over all creation. For in him all things were created." Here, in Revelation 4 verse 11, Jesus Christ is being glorified because He created all things.

Do not let scientific and technological discoveries weaken your faith in the Creator. Jesus Christ created the universe and everything that is in it. From generation to generation, brilliant scientists will continue to marvel at the universe. Each new planet will bring them a sense of wonder because no one will be able to fathom the depth of the universe in all its splendor.

DECEMBER 14

"And they sang a new song, saying: "You are worthy to take the scroll and to open its seals, because you were slain, and with your blood you purchased for God persons from every tribe and language and people and nation." – Revelation 5:9 NIV

Jesus' crucifixion and resurrection have given Him tremendous power and authority over the universe. That is why He can open the scroll. There are no organized governments, rulers, or any known authorities that will be able to stop Jesus from accomplishing His mission.

Jesus is worthy to open the seals to unleash His power on earth with the purpose of putting an end to the power of darkness. In the final hours, people who are still on earth will be exposed to tremendous amount of tribulation. God's mercies will not be readily available. The Tribulation period will be a time of vengeance and great distress for those who did not have a chance to participate in the Rapture of the Church.

Now is the time for God's compassion and grace. Everyone who hears the message and accepts the gospel of Jesus Christ has a chance to be spared from God's wrath. God's wrath is reserved for Satan and those who refuse to believe in the Son of God.

Jesus was slain for the sins of humanity. He did not die just for the Jews. He died for everybody. For that reason, heaven will be a place of great diversity. People of every tribe and language will be represented in the New Jerusalem, the Holy City.

DECEMBER 15

"They called to the mountains and the rocks, "Fall on us and hide us from the face of him who sits on the throne and from the wrath of the Lamb!" – Revelation 6:16 NIV

One day, the world will have to face the King of kings and the Lord of lords. They will not be able to hide their faces from Him. Now some people pay little or no attention when they hear about Jesus Christ, the Son of God, but on that day, they will not be able to undermine Him anymore. Jesus will face all His detractors head on. He will crush the rebels and all their followers. It will be a day of reckoning indeed!

People would prefer death because of the terrible pain, but death will be rather scarce on the day of reckoning. "The kings of the earth, the princes, the generals, the rich, the mighty, and everyone else, both slave and free, hid in caves and among the rocks of the mountains" (Revelation 6:15 NIV). Jesus will be the sole dominant force on earth. Satan will not be able to overcome the power of Christ. Satan knows that. That is why he is doing everything he can to deceive God's children. He is nothing but a usurper. He knows that he does not have absolute power over the universe, and God will soon put an end to his kingdom of darkness for good.

Even during the Tribulation period, the wicked will have a chance to decide. If they refuse the gift of salvation, there will be no more sacrifice left for them. They will face the swift judgment of God and His angels when they come to destroy Babylon or the sinful system that Satan has established to perpetuate lies about God's righteousness and His wonderful plan for humanity.

DECEMBER 16

"Do not harm the land or the sea or the trees until we put a seal on the foreheads of the servants of our God." – Revelation 7:3 NIV

According to Revelation 7 verse 2, this command is from an angel who has the seal of the Living God to four other angels.

God has reserved a time for His ultimate judgment to begin, not a minute will pass. But before Jesus opens the seventh seal to give the four angels the green light to execute God's judgement upon the earth, God will choose among the descendants of Abraham 144,000 to receive the seal of His approval as His servants.

This selection will be based on God's sovereign grace. "Isaiah cries out concerning Israel: "Though the number of the Israelites be like the sand by the sea, only the remnant will be saved" (Romans 9:27 NIV). This remnant will participate in the suffering of Christ and will surely suffer death as God's servants.

The sealing of the 144,000 from all the tribes of Israel will put in motion the Great Tribulation. Keep in mind that some people will still be saved during the Tribulation period. What will change, however, will be the nature of the gospel. The 144,000 and the two witnesses will proclaim the gospel as a last warning to the inhabitants of the earth.

This is my understanding that the Church of Jesus Christ will not be present during the Great Tribulation, because Christ will have already taken His Church to heaven to wait for God's wrath to pass and participate in the wedding of the Lamb.

DECEMBER 17

"When he opened the seventh seal, there was silence in heaven for about half an hour." – Revelation 8:1 NIV

*H*ave you ever heard the expression "the calm before the storm?" This is it here. The first sixth seals will certainly cause uproar on the earth but considering what will come after the seventh seal; the first sixth seals will be warning shots.

The shock and awe will come with the opening of the seventh seal, which will introduce the seven angels with the seven trumpets. It is not unusual to hear bugle's sounds when a war is about to break out.

The first four of the seven angels will conduct a series of attacks that will tremendously impact the earth, the sea, and the atmospheric system. Those attacks will be truly devastating to every aspect of life. Imagine a situation, where trucks, ships, and aircraft are completely grounded. That will be a worldwide catastrophe.

The financial toll of those first four attacks will be enormous. The stock market will probably crash shortly after. What worse, the news media will have difficulties broadcasting those events because satellites will stop sending signals to the earth. While those four attacks are considerable, they will not be the worst.

The last three angels will hit the inhabitants of the earth where it will really hurt. It will be so bad that John in his vision heard "an angel that was flying in midair call, "Woe! Woe! Woe to the inhabitants of the earth, because of the trumpet blasts…" (Revelation 8:13b).

DECEMBER 18

"The rest of mankind who were not killed by these plagues still did not repent of the work of their hands; they did not stop worshiping demons, and idols of gold, silver, bronze, stone and wood – idols that cannot see or hear or walk. Nor did they repent of their murders, their magic arts, their sexual immorality or their thefts." – Revelation 9:20 and 21 NIV

An angel commissioned from heaven will cause the plagues to which these two verses referred. It is a "he", not a star in the field of astronomy. Most of or if not all the known stars in the universe are significantly larger than the earth, so it would not be possible for the earth to contain a star. In any case, that important angel will cause bodily sufferings by opening the abyss and releasing ferocious locusts to harm only humans, who are not marked with the seal of God on their foreheads.

After the sound of the fourth and fifth trumpets, the magnitude of destruction will surpass that of the first previous four trumpets. While the first series of attacks will cause marked environmental and material losses, the second series of attacks will be more serious in that the locusts will inflict five months of bodily sufferings and injuries, and the four angels mentioned in Revelation 7:1 will cause massive loss of lives.

Despite the cataclysmic demonstrations of God's supreme power on the earth, humans will continue to defy God's sovereignty. They will persist in their godlessness and immorality. Be sure you are sealed by the Holy Spirit.

DECEMBER 19

"So I went to the angel and asked him to give me the little scroll. He said to me, "Take it and eat it. It will turn your stomach sour, but in your mouth it will be as sweet as honey." – Revelation 10:9 NIV

During the intermission between the sixth and seventh trumpets, John had an unusual vision. He said, "I saw a mighty angel coming down from heaven" (Rev.10:1 NIV). The mighty angel had a little scroll, and John was asked to "go and take the scroll from the hand of the angel who is standing on the sea and on the land" (verse 8).

Both Jeremiah and Ezekiel talked about eating the scroll or God's words. Jeremiah said, "When your words came, I ate them; they were my joy and my heart's delight, for I bear your name, Lord God Almighty" (Jeremiah 15:16 NIV).

It is important that you eat the words so that you can have them in you in times of need. In the case of Ezekiel, "he was asked to go and speak to the people of Israel" (Ezekiel 3:1 NIV). You too are called to share the words with nonbelievers.

For you to be able to share the gospel with others, you need to become immersed in God's words. You are called to be a witness for God. Keep in mind that God's words can be both sweet and sour.

When we are headed in the wrong direction, God's words are designed to correct us and bring us back.

There are times that you may not hear what you want to hear, but you need to be willing to listen to God when He chooses to chastise you because He loves you.

DECEMBER 20

"The seventh angel sounded his trumpet, and there were loud voices in heaven, which said: "The kingdom of the world has become the kingdom of our Lord and of his Messiah, and he will reign for ever and ever." – Revelation 11:15 NIV

The seventh trumpet will follow a series of important events. By then, the two witnesses, who will be commissioned to prophesy for 1,260 days (about 3 ½ years of the last period of the Tribulation), will have completed their assignments, got killed, resurrected after three and a half days, and ascended to heaven. The seventh trumpet will announce the final series of events, which will put an end to the Tribulation period and usher in the reign of Christ, the new heaven and the new earth, and the establishment of God's kingdom in the New Jerusalem.

Finally, everything that Satan stands for will come to an end. Jesus and His angelic warriors will demolish the power of darkness once and for all. The Israelites, who were disappointed with Jesus because He did not rule the earth when He came as the sacrificial Lamb, will receive their wishes this time. The King will come in all His splendor and divine power to eliminate Satan, the accuser of the brothers and sisters.

The Almighty will move His dwelling from heaven. He will dwell among His people for ever and ever, and sin will be completely eradicated from the earth. In fact, there will be a new heaven and a new earth. People who are not sure about the origin of the current universe will see with their own eyes a brand new, sinless universe. God will have the last word.

DECEMBER 21

"Then I heard a loud voice in heaven say: Now have come the salvation and the power and the kingdom of our God, and the authority of his Messiah. For the accuser of our brothers and sisters, who accuses them before our God day and night, has been hurled down" – Revelation 12:10 NIV

The sign John saw in Revelation 12 provides us with a wonderful summary of key biblical events. This is truly an essential recap of God's plan for humanity. There are three elements mentioned in Revelation 12: the woman, the dragon, and the child, which represent past, present, and future events.

First all, it is important to know that the dragon represents Satan, an old enemy of God. Satan was hurled down from heaven because he rebelled against God. He took about a third of the angels with him. In Genesis 3:15, God announced Satan's opposition to Jesus by saying, "And I will put enmity between you and the woman, and between your offspring and hers; he will crush your head, and you will strike his heel" (NIV).

From the beginning, Satan set out to destroy the woman, who represents Israel and the Church. The child represents Christ. Even before Christ was born, Satan was planning to eliminate Him, but he failed to thwart God's plan to bring salvation through Jesus, the child (Mathew 3:1-12). Through His resurrection, Jesus Christ won the battle. And in the end, Jesus Christ will crush Satan's head once and for all and reign with authority and power as King of kings and Lord of lords forever.

DECEMBER 22

"All inhabitants of the earth will worship the beast – all whose names have not been written in the Lamb's book of life, the Lamb who was slain from the creation of the world." – Revelation 13:8 NIV

There will be no neutral ground during the Tribulation period. People will either be with God or with Satan.

In terms of the duration of Satan's dominion, he will be given power and authority to exercise his influence on the earth for forty-two months. Keep in mind with God, numbers do not mean much. He is an eternal God. Forty-two months could mean an indefinite period for God. I avoid falling into the trap of providing precise dates and numbers. This is not what the gospel of Jesus Christ is about.

The beast or Satan has fallen angels and evil spirits with him. He also has many human followers. Revelation 13 mentions a devil that has power to delegate authority. Satan does not always show up in every activity. Many of the evil things that are taking place in the world today are done by evil spirits and Satan's followers. Some people are committed to carrying out Satan's will. Sadly, they are ministers in the kingdom of darkness.

During those forty-two months, Satan will run havoc in the world. He will take advantage of that time to seduce and deceive people by performing eye-catching wonders. People who do not have solid, biblical foundations will fall in Satan's trap. That's why it is important for you to spend time in God's word so that you will be able to know when false teachers and prophets are trying to deceive you.

DECEMBER 23

"Then I saw another angel flying in midair, and he had the eternal gospel to proclaim to those who live on the earth – to every nation, tribe, language and people. He said in a loud voice, "Fear God and give him glory, because the hour of his judgement has come. Worship him who made the heavens, the earth, the sea and the springs of water." – Revelation 14:6 and 7 NIV

This passage shows how merciful Yahweh is. The Almighty is full of compassion and mercy. This is His desire that everyone comes to the full knowledge of God, even in the last hour. God will make sure that every human being can hear the gospel before the door is locked for eternity. It is a terrible fate to travel to the other side without the seal of the Holy Spirit. God has demonstrated His love toward humanity when He sent Jesus Christ, His Son, to die on the cross. God should not have to wait until the last minute for people to come to Him. Yet there will be people who will not take advantage of the angel's proclamation. They will refuse to listen to the voice of the angel. They will die without Christ.

This angelic sermon is an ultimatum from God. You still have a chance to surrender your life to God now if you have not yet done so.

For you who know God, please continue to spread the gospel of Christ so that more people will be able to have a personal encounter with God.

DECEMBER 24

"I saw in heaven another great and marvelous sign: seven angels with the seven last plagues – last, because with them God's wrath is completed." – Revelation 15:1 NIV

Seven is the number most mentioned in the book of Revelation. The use of number seven shows the Almighty is perfect. There is no imperfection in Him. We can see God's perfection in the way He executes His judgement. He is not swift to punish. He waits patiently for us to repent so we can avoid His wrath.

Throughout the Tribulation period, God will provide people with numerous opportunities to come to Him through angelic evangelism and special warnings. However, there are folks who will not make it to heaven due to their stubbornness and incredulity.

The seven angels will be given the task of completing God's judgement on the earth in the form of seven plagues. In the Old Testament, Moses had the opportunity to be used by God to execute God's judgment on Egypt because they had oppressed God's people through slavery. This time, God will use angels to pour out His wrath on the earth to finish with the wicked, who had the mark of the beast (Satan).

In terms of magnitude, God's final judgment will impact human health, land, rivers, seas, air, the weather, and the kingdom of Satan. Nothing will be spared from God's wrath. The only way people will be able to escape God's wrath is to have the seal of God. "When you believed you were marked in him with a seal, the promised Holy Spirit… (Ephesian 1:13b). If you belong to God, you are marked right now.

DECEMBER 25

"Look, I come like a thief! Blessed is the one who stays awake and remains clothed, so as not to go naked and be shamefully exposed." – Revelation 16:15 NIV

This warning emerges right in the middle of the battle of Armageddon, the mother of all battles. In this verse, Jesus is saying that His coming is sudden, but it does not have to be a complete surprise for everyone.

The people who will be caught in the battle of Armageddon, battle during the end times, are those who refuse to listen to the gospel of Jesus Christ. Those rebellious folks will miss the sudden departure of the Church, also known as the Rapture of the Church (1 Thessalonians 4:16-18). Those moments will be terrible in that God's wrath will be unleashed on the earth to put an end to rebellion and the sinful system established by demonic forces.

God has reserved a day to deal with Satan and all his followers. When you see the apparent success of the wicked, do not take it to mean that God is not paying attention. God has been in control of everything that has been taking place on earth.

The word of wisdom in this warning is to get ready. Jesus is coming in all His power and glory. The world will not be able to contain Him. He will rule over all the earth with those who have accepted the gift of salvation.

Regarding this warning, I want you to know that you have nothing to be afraid of if you have made Jesus Christ your Lord and Savior. If you have not done so, don't put Jesus on the back burner. The time is now.

DECEMBER 26

"They will wage war against the Lamb, but the Lamb will triumph over them because he is King of kings and Lord of lords – and with him will be his called, chosen and faithful followers." – Revelation 17:14 NIV

*T*here is no doubt; Satan will try his best to carry out a last battle with the Son of God. Jesus Christ's crucifixion was Satan's greatest effort to bring down the kingdom of God. Fortunately for humanity, God got the upper hand over the kingdom of darkness because Jesus Christ triumphed over death on the third day when He walked out of the tomb.

In the last battle, Jesus will show up not as a baby in a manger, but with power, might, and glory. He will defeat the power of darkness. That event will be a spectacular show of force. Satan will not be able to overcome the Lamb of God, because He will return as King of kings and Lord of lords.

Jesus Christ will not be fighting alone. He will be accompanied by those who have heard His calling to become His servants in variety of capacities. His followers and those who have been chosen by Him will be there.

If you would like to be there to witness that splendid event, embark with Jesus Christ right now. If you have made a commitment to follow Jesus as your Lord and Savior, continue to serve Him faithfully. Encourage everyone on your path to join in with you to make Him known. Jesus is coming soon, and you will never regret your choice to follow Him.

DECEMBER 27

"With a mighty voice he shouted: "Fallen! Fallen is Babylon the Great!' She has become a dwelling for demons and a haunt for every impure spirit, a haunt for every unclean bird,
a haunt for every unclean and detestable animal." –Revelation 18:2 NIV

*I*n Genesis 11 verses 1-9, the word Babel means confusion, because God came down and witnessed the construction of the tower, whose purpose was to keep the people together. This was a sign of rebellion against God's plan for humans to populate the whole earth. Given the location of Shinar, Babylon appears to be the place where the tower was being built.

This devotion is not a place to study Babylon, which has been a topic of fascinating biblical prophesies, historic events, and archeological discoveries. Both Daniel and Jeremiah have addressed Babylon. You may consider deepening your knowledge on Babylon by doing some personal research on it. With that said, what you should get out of today's devotion is that God's intent is to put an end to rebellion, whichever form it may have. Babylon represents a demonic system bent on opposing God's plan in every way.

Babylon lay in ruins fifty miles from the City of Bagdad, modern Iraq, and it is not much of a threat today. However, Babylon, the symbol it represents, will be destroyed by the Lord of lords in the end. Satan will be destroyed forever, and he will not be able to defeat God.

DECEMBER 28

"Let us rejoice and be glad and give him glory! For the wedding of the Lamb has come, and his bride has made herself ready." – Revelation 19:7 NIV

*I*n the Bible, Jesus is introduced as the Lamb of God. "The next day John was there again with two of his disciples. When he saw Jesus passing by, he said, "Look, the Lamb of God" (John 1:35 and 36 NIV)! The same Jesus who came as the sacrificial Lamb to take away our sins will someday destroy the enemies with "the sword coming out of his mouth" (Revelation 19:21).

Pre-tribulation Christians place the wedding of the Lamb during the Great Tribulation because they believe that the Church will not be on earth when the Great Tribulation is happening. Shortly after the wedding, Christ will come down riding on the white horse with His heavenly armies to put an end to the battle led by "…the beast, the kings of the earth and their armies…" (Revelation 19:19).

What a glorious day that will be when the Church will finally make it to heaven to participate in the wedding of the Lamb. This will be a special occasion for those who have put their trust in Jesus Christ as their Lord and Savior.

For you to be eligible for this exclusive event, you have to be washed by the blood of the Lamb, who is Jesus Christ, the Son of the Living God. Otherwise you will not be invited to the great Supper of God. This is my prayer that you will be there praising Yahweh, "for our Lord God Almighty reigns" (Revelation 19:6b).

DECEMBER 29

"Blessed and holy are those who share in the first resurrection. The second death has no power over them, but they will be priests of God and of Christ and will reign with him for a thousand years." – Revelation 20:6 NIV

The purpose of the gospel is to give everyone a chance to accept Jesus as Lord and Savior, thereby giving them a chance to avoid the second death. No one should face the second death, because Jesus Christ came to reconcile the world with His Father. If you have accepted Christ as your personal Lord and Savior, your name is written in the Lamb's book of life. Consequently, you will not have to face the terrible punishment that is reserved for those who have refused to acknowledge Jesus Christ as the Son of God. The Bible says, "If you declare with your mouth, "Jesus is Lord, and believe in your heart that God raised him from the dead, you will be saved" (Romans 10:9 NIV).

The opportunity to reign with Christ is one of many benefits those who have surrendered to Jesus will receive. During a thousand years, Satan will not have the power to persecute God's people. Christ will reign as King of kings and Lord of lords of all the earth. Unlike the first coming, Jesus will not be like a little baby in a manger in the second coming. We are talking about the Lion of Judah. Satan will tremble in the presence of the King!

If you want to rule over death, make Jesus your Savior while you are still in the body. If you die without Christ, you are finished. The second death will have power over you, and you will not be able to become priest of God and of Christ. Be sure you declare with your mouth that Jesus is the Supreme Savior.

DECEMBER 30

"And I heard a loud voice from the throne saying, "Look! God's dwelling place is now among the people, and he will dwell with them. They will be his people, and God himself will be with them and be their God." – Revelation 21:3 NIV

*P*raise the Lord! This is the time we all are waiting for! A time where everything will fall into place. The Almighty God will finally establish his dwelling among His people. It will be a wonderful time when God puts an end to our sufferings.

God's ultimate desire is not to keep us away from Him. He wants to bring us all together as a big family, where death and tears will be things of the past. Everything God has worked for will be encapsulated in this one final event. If you have dedicated your life to serving the Lord, be encouraged. Your life will find meaning in God's eternal plan.

When we are living with God, He will take care of us. There will be no need for sadness, because God will continuously fill our hearts with joy. We will not have to worry about temptation, because Satan, the tempter, will be no more.

God will put an end to hatred, and love will be found in the heart everyone who will live in the New Jerusalem, the Holy City. If you ever think of a dream comes true, this is it. Nothing you have experienced so far can compare with the joy of living forever with God.

DECEMBER 31

"Look, I am coming soon! My reward is with me, and I will give to each person according to what they have done." – Revelation 22:12 NIV

Jesus' death on the cross set the stage for God's eternal plan for humanity. That was the greatest demonstration of God's amazing grace and love for us. God still has more in store for us. Revelation 21 gives us some marvelous insights into what God has in mind.

Eternal life is the greatest reward those who have made Jesus their Lord will receive, and it is paid for with the precious blood of Jesus. Additionally, God will also reward us for the works we have done after salvation.

For us to receive Christ's eventual reward, we must be saved by grace. As you have learned throughout the daily devotions, there is nothing that we can do to deserve salvation. We can be saved only by grace through faith in Jesus Christ.

Jesus wants to remind us that He will eventually come back for us. He will return to finish His mission. He has done everything His Father sent Him to do by humbling Himself until death on the cross for the sins of humanity. He will come back to receive those who have honored His sacrifice and are ready for the Rapture of the Church.

He will also come back to reign after the Rapture of the Church as King of kings, which is the second coming.

This time Jesus will not be humiliated by our sins; He will rule the world in glory as King of kings and Lord of lords.

Having heard the voice of Jesus, join in with the angels and say, "Amen. Come, Lord Jesus."

ABOUT THE AUTHOR

Jean Robert Lainé earned a Doctor of Philosophy in Curriculum and Instruction from Capella University, two Master of Education degrees from the University of Central Oklahoma, a Bachelor of Science degree in Christian Ministries from Southwestern Christian University, a diploma in Theology from Transylvania Bible School, and an Associate of Arts degree in Practical Theology from Caribbean Christ for the Nations Institute.

Dr. Jean Robert Lainé lives in Oklahoma City with his wife, Cheryl Denise Lainé. He is the proud father of two sons, Joshua Robert and Josiah Andrew.

PERSONAL NOTES

Made in the USA
Coppell, TX
02 June 2020